# THURSDAY'S
# CHILD

# THURSDAY'S CHILD

## ONE WOMAN'S JOURNEY TO SEVEN CONTINENTS

### MARALYN RITTENOUR

A POST HILL PRESS BOOK
ISBN: 978-1-63758-249-7
ISBN (eBook): 978-1-63758-250-3

Thursday's Child:
One Woman's Journey to Seven Continents
© 2022 by Maralyn Rittenour
All Rights Reserved

This is a work of nonfiction. All people, locations, events, and situations are portrayed to the best of the author's memory.

Post Hill Press
New York • Nashville
posthillpress.com

Published in the United States of America
1 2 3 4 5 6 7 8 9 10

*For Ian, Moira, and Charles*

Monday's child is fair of face,
Tuesday's child is full of grace,
Wednesday's child is full of woe,
Thursday's child has far to go.
Friday's child is loving and giving,
Saturday's child works hard for its living.

# Introduction

My life has consisted of accidental twists, turns, luck, and opportunities. I have floated, mostly happily, on the full sea, grasped nettles, and usually followed Brutus's advice in *Julius Caesar*:

> There is a tide in the affairs of men
> Which taken at the flood, leads on to fortune.

In my case, it does not necessarily lead to fortune, but always to some wonderful, unexpected adventure or encounter.

The rationale for writing this book is to tell some stories from a life lived in an exceptional historical era, straddling two centuries of unprecedented change and technological advances. It is about people I have been fortunate to encounter or to be related to, and places and events that I believe are worth writing about. I also hope to interest and entertain the reader.

Actually, much of this book falls into the sub-genre of "travel memoir." I completed my bucket list with a trip to Antarctica in 2018. An article written by Isabel Carmichael in *The East Hampton Star* the following March, "A Passion for Polar Places," elicited an unexpected reaction from relatives, friends, and acquaintances asking for more. As I have also lived close to the equator, and in many countries, combining my autobiography with some history of both my families became a project.

To my family and friends in England, Ireland, France, and Hong Kong, please understand why I am writing in the language of my adopted country. Spell Check would not let me do otherwise, and I could not fight it on every page in order to write in the Queen's English of my schooldays.

I live mostly in Springs in the town of East Hampton, Long Island, close to Hog Creek at Clearwater Beach. In retirement and since the death of my husband Charles in 2010, I take care of other people's dogs as well as my own beloved ones. My stories about dogs and their owners could perhaps be a separate book, but some feature in this one.

Recently, as I was taking garbage to the East Hampton Recycling Center (the "dump"), I had a nostalgic moment as I threw an old rug from Nepal into the dumpster. In the "Rittenour Canine Ritz Carlton," rugs and upholstery do not fare well. Rugs get thrown out when stains no longer respond to scrubbing. I remember that rug factory in Kathmandu. We had trekked almost to Everest Base Camp and were returning to London via Bangladesh and Frankfurt. Trekkers are encouraged to donate unused medications and almost all their clothes to the local expedition organizers, as Nepalese people are mostly poor except for the Sherpas. My backpack was then almost empty and the rug fit into it.

What is it that is most enjoyable about travel? Is it the excitement of anticipation or the memories? On my bedside table are two small wooden carvings: a giraffe from Kenya and a lemur from Madagascar. Beside them is a diminutive onyx penguin from Ushuaia purchased en route to Antarctica, a tiny enamel box with a dog painting on its lid from a village beside the Volga on a river cruise from Moscow to St. Petersburg, and a miniature whalebone polar bear with an articulated jaw from one of my visits to Arctic Canada.

I thank my mother for giving birth to me on a Thursday.

I believe I am a typical Aries, adventurous and positive by nature. I slide into social situations effortlessly, am inclined to self-blame, am fiercely loyal but too trusting, avoid asking for help, and am generous with others but mostly stingy with myself. Survivor instincts are strong. I was also born in the Chinese year of the Tiger.

Cats supposedly have nine lives. There does not seem to be a number for humans. However, this one is on her third, or fourth if I count not being aboard the *Empress of Britain* as an infant because my mother literally missed the boat. We were still in Cape Town when she was torpedoed off the coast of South Africa early in World War II. There were no survivors. At the age of eighteen, I miraculously survived a brain hemorrhage, and on July 11, 2019, I technically died, having gone into cardiac arrest without any warning symptoms. My savior, Dr. Henry Tannous at Stony Brook University Hospital on Long Island, New York, replaced my mitral valve with a pig's one, named Petunia by a friend, and I made a complete recovery. Why am I so lucky? Being a somewhat religious person, I ask, why did God spare my life? I sometimes have survivor's guilt. Maybe one reason is to finish this story about so many well-loved friends and relatives, also in memory of those who are no longer with us.

These are my reminiscences: bear with any inaccuracies, blame my imperfect memory, but I do hope you will enjoy them.

# Chapter One

On her way to my parents' London wedding in 1935, my grandmother was crossing the street when she was knocked down by a Rolls-Royce in which the king of Siam was riding. Unfortunately, she missed the celebration, but she recovered completely and lived to be ninety-nine. I came along a few years later. Twenty-five years on, her son and my uncle, Dermot, became British Ambassador to Thailand, the former Kingdom of Siam.

My father, Wakefield Christie-Miller, was serving in the Royal Ulster Rifles in Northern Ireland at the time of my birth, and my mother claimed that she barely made it to the maternity ward in Dublin, almost delivering me on the hospital steps, determined that her child enter the world in the Irish Republic. This apocryphal myth was debunked decades later by my godmother Una, married to John Kernan and living in Connecticut, who told me that my mother stayed for three weeks with her mother in Dublin, awaiting my arrival. I have inherited my mother's keen imagination, adventurousness, and sense of the dramatic. She must have been disappointed when I acquired a British passport at the age of nine and let my Irish passport lapse. I suppose I could have renewed it later, but I tend to be politically apathetic.

My father's regiment was posted to Rawalpindi in late 1938. India was part of the British Empire until 1947. Since the Partition of India, this city is now in Pakistan. My mother and I, a babe in arms, accompanied him. In the year of my birth, in the US, Franklin Delano Roosevelt was president, a new car cost $860, an average new house $3,900, unemployment was 8 million, Howard Hughes flew around the world in record time, Spencer Tracy was Best Actor in *Boys Town*, Bette Davis was Best Actress in *Jezebel*, the New York Yankees won the World Series, a gallon of gas cost ten cents, gold was $20.67 an ounce, the Dow Jones Industrial Average was $132, and life expectancy was less than sixty years.

When war broke out in Europe, all the men returned to England to fight. It was not so easy to repatriate the families who had to wait and hope to escape before the threatened Japanese invasion of India. In fact, my mother had considered joining her brother, a rubber planter, in what was then Malaya; and had she done so, we would have certainly been sent to a concentration camp in Singapore. The Japanese overran the entire Malay Peninsula in 1942 all the way to Singapore, which they captured very easily because the guns were pointing out to sea, and the British were soundly defeated. My uncle survived four years of internment in the notorious Changi Prison camp. Luckily my mother was persuaded to return to England well before the Japanese invasion.

The last ship to leave Karachi for the UK was scheduled to depart on a Friday the thirteenth, and some superstitious eligible passengers actually declined to travel on that date. My mother, as an officer's wife, was entitled to a nanny for me. She carefully perused the many applications and finally settled on a woman who seemed the most deserving: infirm parents in Britain, no other family to help, sterling qualities, excellent references, and devoted to infants. She was hired.

A few days out to sea, my mother was aware of strange looks from fellow passengers. She often found me alone in my cabin. One day she came down to discover me sitting alone on the floor surrounded by cigarettes broken into small pieces. In those days they came in round cans of fifty and were scarce. Precocious brat that I was, apparently I said, "Look, Mummy, now more ciggies."

Shortly thereafter, one of the other passengers explained to my mother that the nanny was a notorious hooker, a high-class call girl. Now that business had dried up in India, she needed to get back to England. Meanwhile, she was busy plying her trade on the ship and had no time to look after me.

We disembarked in Cape Town. Somehow, my mother managed to miss our ship bound for England. The *Empress of Britain* sailed without us. Twenty-four hours later, she was torpedoed off the coast of Africa with no survivors. We sailed from Freetown, then Sierra Leone, now Liberia, in convoy on another ship, and landed many weeks later somewhere off the West Coast of Scotland, where we were promptly quarantined with whooping cough.

During part of the war, while my father was overseas on active duty, we were living near Bray, in County Wicklow, in a house called Hebron. We spent happy summer hours at Kilcroney Country Club. Even though Ireland remained neutral, many Irish men volunteered to fight for the Allies. The British military attaché to the Dublin embassy was overheard asking why so many young men were lounging around, enjoying the amenities of the club. It was gently pointed out to him that in fact they were on embarkation leave and imminently headed for the front lines.

In Ireland, we were spared many of the shortages suffered on the other side of the Irish Sea during the war. We never went hungry—there was no rationing in Ireland—but my first fresh orange at the age of five was a luxurious treat. I remember the unappetizing soggy biscuits that Mademoiselle, my playmates' nanny-governess, used to dole out as she sat there knitting while we played on a usually rainy, windy beach at Brittas Bay. West Coast Atlantic beaches were scenic but bleak. No wonder that later in life I have settled on the East End of Long Island, with its wonderful beaches and appropriate summer climate.

Later that year while staying at Coolavin, my mother's family estate, I begged my grandmother to let me attend the local "national" school. I went for one term until my mother took us south to County Wicklow. In the first form, five-year-old children wrote in pencil and learned Irish. At six, they graduated to pen, ink, and English. I came home in tears after my first day and begged my nanny and grandmother to let me go barefoot the next morning. I was the only child wearing shoes. Many years later, I met the famous poet Seamus Heaney in New York during one of his poetry readings. A particular poem revived this memory, and he was amused by my story. In the evenings, I sat with my grandparents listening to war news on a crackly radio.

Coolavin was a very special place for children. It had been built by my great-grandfather, Hugh Hyacinth, The MacDermot, Prince of Coolavin, a title that passes to the eldest surviving male. He served under William Ewart Gladstone as solicitor general in 1886, before being appointed privy counselor and attorney general for Ireland from 1892–95. His son, my grandfather,

Charles Edward, was chairman of the Prisons Board and brought his wife, Caroline, whom he called Girlie, children, and servants to Coolavin every summer. He was a handsome man whom I remember with a full head of white hair. He admired the patriot Lady Gregory and when she was in prison always saw to it that she received a copy of *The Times* and a red rose on her breakfast tray. He owned the first motor car in the county, which he was constantly crashing, and drove a motorboat, which likewise used to hit rocks on Lough Gara.

According to the *Almanach de Gotha*, the MacDermots are equal in rank amongst European minor royalty to the Grimaldis of Monaco, the considerable difference being their casino wealth compared with the poor, rocky farmland surrounding Coolavin.

For several centuries, before Oliver Cromwell conquered Ireland, the country consisted of thirty-two small kingdoms. These were divided into four provinces each ruled by a high king: Ulster, Leinster, Munster, and Connaught. From the twelfth to the seventeenth century, the MacDermots ruled the kingdom of Moylurg (Magh Luirg) in the province of Connaught and lived in a picturesque castle known as the Rock in Lough Key (Loch Cé). The castle's walls covered the whole of the small island. It was Diarmuid, King of Moylurg from 1124 to 1159, who gave the MacDermot clan its name. Moylurg encompassed parts of present-day Roscommon, south Sligo, Leitrim, and east Mayo. His descendant, my uncle Dermot, who wrote the comprehensive MacDermot history, originally in two volumes, reliably traced our ancestry back to Conn of the Hundred Fights in the second century. Diarmud was such a strong figure that his descendants all bore his name, MacDiarmada (MacDermot, McDermott, and other spellings in English). The MacDermot Kings of Moylurg lived on Castle Island in Lough Key until Elizabethan forces moved them off in the latter part of the sixteenth century. The last king was Rory from 1549 to 1568, after which time the chief of the name in time became known as The MacDermot, Prince of Coolavin, a title that still exists today, though not recognized by the Republic of Ireland.

County historian Terence O'Rorke described the MacDermots as "the descendants of the once powerful clan who had exercised a strong and decisive influence on the history of the Province and produced great chieftains and notable churchmen." According to Uncle Dermot, they became "penniless princelings who sat by the shores of Lough Gara reading the Latin classics." While he was writing the MacDermot history, his wife, Betty, wrote *O'Ruairc of Breifne*, tracing the history of that clan from the ninth century to our own time.

In 1981, Dermot wrote that I have an ancestor, though not a MacDermot, who was canonized as a saint. He pointed out that this was a rare distinction, because in the olden days, saints were celibate or their biographers discreet. He is King Ferdinand of León and Castile, who in the thirteenth century rescued most of Spain from the Muslims. He was not canonized until 1671, so he must have been slow off the mark in performing the necessary miracles required for canonization. His feast day is May 30. One of his daughters married Edward I of England, of the Plantagenet family, from whom my grandmother's family, the Whytes, are descended through a female line, from Robert the well-known Earl of Essex in the latter part of the reign of Elizabeth I. Dermot acknowledged that while the Whytes had many reputable ancestors, including Charlemagne and Alfred the Great, he considered them parvenus compared with our Gaelic MacDermot ancestors.

In the sixteenth century, Brian MacDermot of the Carrick, chief of the name, commissioned the *Annals of Loch Cé*, one of the most important written records of medieval Irish history. Written in Early Modern Irish and Latin, the chronicle records more than five centuries of political, ecclesiastical, and military events; succession and land disputes; even notes on the weather. It begins with the Battle of Clontarf in 1014, a contest that pitted Brian Boru, the high king of Ireland, against the king of Dublin, Sigtrygg Silkbeard; the king of Leinster, Máel Mórda; and a force of Vikings. The *Annals* end in 1590, when most of the Gaelic families were thrown off their lands by the Anglo-Normans, who ruled England after the Norman Conquest in 1066, and had invaded Ireland in 1169.

Various vicissitudes of the Rock history included attacks by Anglo-Normans, fire caused by lightning, countless clashes over succession, and the deaths of numerous MacDermot kings. The stone walls, turrets, and empty windows of the ruin visible today are probably not the remains of a MacDermot stronghold, but a product of the imagination of John Nash, the nineteenth-century Welsh architect of Buckingham Palace. When Cromwell conquered Ireland in the seventeenth century, an Anglo-Irish noble family, coincidentally called King, took possession of the Rock. They owned much of the land surrounding Loch Key and subsequently built a stately home, Rockingham, and the MacDermots were banished to an area called Clocher some miles away, later ending up on the lower Lough Gara, building Old Coolavin and finally Coolavin on the upper section of the lake, near the village of Monasterden in County Sligo. An archaeologist, Thomas Finan of Saint Louis University, has been searching for the remains of the much earlier MacDermots' castle.

The only wealthy family member at the time, Brian Hugh MacDermot, about whom I will write more, bought the Rock when the Rockingham estate was sold off at auction by the last of the Stafford-King-Harmans, descendants of the Kings, following a fire. It was prophesied that someday a redheaded MacDermot would burn it down, but arson was never proven and no doubt the culprit was an electrical fault or a careless smoker. Later, Brian Hugh gave it back to the state because insurance costs were too high, what with visitors scrambling all over the ruins.

The MacDermot coat of arms is three wild boars, symbolizing courage, strength, and determination. Our motto is "*Honor probatque virtus*" ("honor and proven courage"). The family crest is three boars' heads.

Other ancestors of particular interest were Charles MacDermot, the first to be called Prince of Coolavin, whose son Miles fathered two sons, Hugh and Andrew. Dr. Hugh married an O'Conor, and his letters to her are now in the National Library of Ireland. He was a friend of Wolfe Tone but declined to join him in the 1798 rebellion. Andrew went to Canada, where he was initially employed by the Hudson's Bay Company. He founded the Red River settlement, which became the city of Winnipeg, where many MacDermot descendants live today.

In 1993, Niall MacDermot, my first cousin, who became The MacDermot in 1989 when his father, Dermot, died, organized the first MacDermot Clan Association Gathering, assisted by his wife, Jan; son, Rory; and daughter, Siobhan. Two more gatherings took place in 1996 and 1999 in Ireland with descendants attending from all over the world. My godson, Rory, currently The MacDermot, Prince of Coolavin, is now in charge, although the planned 2020 gathering was canceled on account of the coronavirus pandemic. Easter messages in 2020 on the Clan's Facebook page came from all over the United States, including Hawaii and Canberra, Australia. Rory recently told me of newly discovered descendants in Argentina. Other MacDermots who had settled in Jamaica moved to Quebec, Canada, the most famous being the late Galt MacDermot, notable musician best known for composing the musical *Hair*.

Coolavin was completed in 1898. The architect was James Franklin Fuller, who also built Ashford Castle. Built in the Scots' Baronial style, local gray limestone with Scottish red sandstone around the windows and doors, it is situated on an artificial hill, created to afford a better view of Lough Gara. Those were the days of cheap labor and no income tax. Servants' bedrooms and the children's nursery were on the top floor. My nanny, Freda, hauled hot water up steep stairs to fill the hip bath and dry three-year-old me in front of an open fire. The dining room, drawing room, and "morning" room were very fine, and there was a large kitchen wing with pantries, larders, etc. There were eleven bedrooms and two bathrooms, only one of which had an actual bath.

There was a large entrance hall. The walls were covered with spears and African artifacts. Badly hung on the walls nearest the door to the kitchens and on the other side leading to the "gentlemen's lavatory" were framed documents, the most important being "The Title Deeds of Rockingham," signed by King James I, a good Catholic, in 1603 re-granting their original lands to the MacDermots. My godson Rory gave it to the National Library of Ireland when Coolavin was sold. A broad staircase divided halfway to the upstairs landings, covered in faded red carpeting. Bedrooms led off the landing, from which one looked down into the hall below. The most striking feature was a large, mullioned window with various coats of arms, including the MacDermots', in stained glass.

Two large bedrooms had smaller dressing rooms leading off them, which in recent times were also bedrooms. One upstairs room, however, was unique. It was the oratory, like a tiny chapel with an altar where the family used to sometimes say the Rosary. On the walls were pasted the small cards given out at funerals for deceased family members. Penciled on the walls amongst these black- or silver-rimmed cards were measurements of the various children as they grew up with their names and heights at a specific age.

There was a walled garden and farm buildings some distance from the house. The path from the house to the garden was called the Moira Walk by my grandfather, who adored his eldest daughter, my mother. There was once a grass tennis court, and family photographs were always taken on the tennis court steps. Family members became good at ping-pong because tennis parties were so often rained out and everyone played it on the dining room table. In my childhood, cattle grazed on the former tennis court and all over the artificial hill. There was a circular Bronze-Age stone fort on the estate with underground passages, which we loved to crawl through as children. A branch rail line from Kilfree to Ballaghaderreen ran through the property near the lake, and when my grandmother arrived as a bride, an engine was specially decorated in her honor.

My mother told me that W. B. Yeats came to tea once during her childhood. She loved his poetry and anticipated his visit with great excitement. Alas, she was disillusioned because he seemed to be in bad humor and made constant trips to the "gentlemen's lavatory." Another childhood memory of hers was riding in a taxi with her brother Dermot to a children's party in Dublin and diving to the floor hearing the gunshots, which began the Easter Rebellion in 1916.

Water for Coolavin was pumped from a small cement reservoir by a hydraulic ram some way from the house to a cistern in the attic. Dead cows or other livestock were sometimes found in the reservoir and the occasional bird or bat in the attic cistern, so drinking water was fetched from a historic Holy Well about half a mile away dedicated to the sixth-century Irish saint Attracta. There were several fireplaces, but stoves or electric fires were more efficient, so it was not unusual to find a dead jackdaw that had fallen down one of the unused chimneys.

It probably does not apply to our twenty-first-century "McMansions," but in those days, the definition of a mansion was that it had two staircases. The back staircase leading down to the kitchen and pantries is key to the story that follows.

The definition of a city used to be that it had a cathedral, which would have made the nearest country town, Ballaghaderreen, technically a city. The Bishop of Achonry was a good friend of my grandmother's, and when he came to tea he always brought me a book about the latest adventures of Curly Wee and Gussie Goose, the former a piglet popular in children's literature. During "the Troubles," before Ireland became a Free State and later a Republic, after the 1916 Rebellion, the British sent a motley collection of mercenary soldiers called the Black and Tans to subjugate the rebellious Irish. They got their name from their uniforms: tan trousers and black jackets.

One winter (my grandparents and their children only spent summers at Coolavin), about seventy of these rag-tag soldiers were billeted at the house. The number may be exaggerated, but there were bullet holes behind various pictures in the dining room, and they are reputed to have polished the huge mahogany table sliding up and down it in their socks. A story handed down from that time was about a young local lad who was captured and tortured in the cellar during interrogations about rebels' whereabouts. Apparently, he died and was said to haunt the house.

I heard this tale from my former nanny, Freda, during the time she was cooking for my grandmother, who was living alone at Coolavin following the death of my grandfather in 1946. I decided to revive the haunting legend while spending my Easter holidays there.

At the top and bottom of the wooden back stairs for use by the staff, lying around haphazardly was an assortment of heavy rubber boots. The noise of the thumps as I threw these downstairs were supposed to signify the soldiers dragging the hapless boy to the cellar. I found some red ink, which I stored in a china toothbrush holder in my bedroom.

Every evening, around nine o'clock, I crept out of bed with my "blood" container, some of which I spilled on the staircase, picked up a couple of boots, and hurled them down the staircase, accompanied by a blood-curdling scream.

At this time of the evening, Attracta the maid and Freda the cook, sisters in a family of eleven siblings, were relaxing in the kitchen quarters, but when they heard the noise of heavy footsteps on the staircase evidently dragging what they assumed to be the ghost of the tortured boy screaming in agony, they were absolutely terrified. During several evenings, they got on their bicycles, most likely in heavy rain, and rode five miles home to the family cottage, where they slept three or four to a bed rather than stay the night in their attic rooms at Coolavin.

In the morning, when they saw the bloodstains on the staircase, they knew the ghost had come back to haunt the house, but they were too scared to tell my grandmother, who never used the back staircase anyway.

One evening, my devoted Freda, worried that I was scared out of my wits, bravely came up to my bedroom to find me panting under the covers, so I told her I was terrified too. Of course it was the mad dash back to bed after hurling the boots (which I always retrieved the next day and took upstairs again, but no one was counting), spilling the ink, and doing my scream.

Freda and Attracta were getting ready to give in their notice, which no doubt would have devastated my grandmother, good help being hard to find, and were spreading stories about the ghost of the tortured boy, when Attracta (called after the saint I mentioned earlier, patroness of the Holy Well) was cleaning my bedroom and happened upon the container of red ink. She put two and two together, told my grandmother, who was furious, and everyone slept happily again in their own beds.

The world changed after WWII, and there was little money left. My grandfather was selling off acreage and died in debt. In 1947, his son, Charles John, called Bay, returned from Malaya (now Malaysia), to assume the title of The MacDermot, Prince of Coolavin, and ownership of the estate. The heir, his older brother Hugh, had been killed at Gallipoli, a young eighteen-year-old officer in the Irish Fusiliers, much revered by his men. Bay, being a second son and needing to earn his living, as primogeniture was still *de rigueur* in old families, went out to be a rubber planter in the thirties, working for his uncle Percy MacDermot as manager of the Jebong Estate in Perak. He was interned for four years by the Japanese at the infamous concentration camp Changi in Singapore. In spite of the terrible deprivation he suffered as a prisoner of war, he returned to rubber planting after peace was declared.

He was lonely, struggling with Coolavin and the farm. My mother decided to try to find him a bride. Ideally, she would need to be rich enough to maintain the estate, even restore it to its former glory. Although my grandfather had sold off acreage to pay bills, there was still plenty of land, farm fields, a walled garden, a nine-hole golf course, and the property, or "demesne," was surrounded by long walls and a plantation of trees—some of them quite rare in Ireland, including magnificent Californian redwoods. Sadly, over the years, Atlantic storms have destroyed many of the plantation trees. The estate stretched to the upper lake of Lough Gara where there was a boathouse, whence a canal led to the lake. My uncle Dermot jumped the canal in his late teens, quite an athletic feat. When the level of the lake was lowered many years later to create more farmland, Bronze Age crannog (lake dwellings) remains and artifacts were discovered, causing great excitement amongst archaeologists. Most of them were transferred to museums.

In those days, people put advertisements in the personal columns of *The Lady*. My mother set her sights on an American wife for Bay. No one else had any money in those post-war years, and the title Prince of Coolavin, which Cromwell allowed the family to retain as a courtesy after confiscating their lands and the castle on the island, had a certain cachet. She had heard that Americans loved titles. The term "Eurotrash" had not yet been coined.

So many poor Irish (and the West was the poorest part of the country: Cromwell in the seventeenth century banished the native Irish "to Hell or to Connaught," although the MacDermots had been there for centuries) had emigrated to America over the years. Ever since the Famine, locals used to say, "Boston, next parish." America was the Promised Land, where the streets were paved with gold. This turned out to be the fortunate outcome for one of our maids, the eldest of the eleven Regan children, who became pregnant by one of our gardeners and was sent there in disgrace. She returned to visit her family several years later, swathed in mink. The Regan children lived as adults with their parents in a tiny cottage on land close to the ruins of the former

MacDermot house, known as Old Coolavin. The girls left home when hired as our maids and nannies or got jobs in Dublin, but the boys stayed at home with their parents for their entire lives, worked the small farm, fished in the lake, and could never afford to marry without land of their own or a paying job. We loved to visit them and, poor as they were, they always produced fresh eggs and potato cakes for tea. All cooking was done on an open fire, baked in pots on coals. The beloved matriarch, Ellie, who was a character, overshadowed her silent, unobtrusive husband, Jack. There was no indoor plumbing or electricity at the time. Ellie lived until 1976 and died at the age of ninety-three. A huge treat was to be allowed to stay the night when we happily shared a bed with several members of the family.

I mentioned earlier that for many years a single-track railroad ran from Sligo to Ballaghaderreen and through part of the Coolavin estate, along the shore of Lough Gara. A favorite spot for dropping off packages from the train was by the path that led to our boathouse and short canal. Many years later, my husband, Ian, and I had the nostalgic experience of taking the very last passenger train ride. I mailed the ticket stub to my mother, who was then living in Hong Kong.

Uncle Bay had high hopes of turning Coolavin into a profitable dairy farm and even hired a bailiff, Mr. Doody, who I had a huge crush on in my early teens. Bay worked so hard driving his van to deliver milk to individual customers in Ballaghaderreen and to the creamery at Gurteen. In the old days, the cows produced milk for household consumption. Large bowls were placed in a cool pantry, and cream was spooned off the top into silver jugs. Butter was churned by hand, which also produced buttermilk.

History does not relate if Mr. Doody was dishonest or merely stupid, but he soon went through all my uncle's savings, the dairy farm failed, and he left. A few American ladies turned up in response to my mother's advertisement and were intrigued by Coolavin and the idea of the title, but no romance ever ensued. One afternoon, a third cousin, Felicity, was brought to tea by another cousin, Mary Wolfe-Flanagan, and she and Bay fell in love. In 1955, they married and lived very happily, though never had children. It was assumed that having suffered from beriberi in the concentration camp, Bay was rendered sterile. Bay and Felicity, and later Felicity as a widow, put blood, sweat, and tears into maintaining Coolavin even though there were no direct heirs because they loved the place so much. Bay took a keen interest in the Ballaghaderreen troops of Boy Scouts and Girl Guides and allowed them to camp at Coolavin.

The property entail ended with Bay's death, so Felicity could legally leave Coolavin to anyone she chose, and ultimately left it to her great-nephew, my godson, Rory, and his son, Francis. Under the laws of male primogeniture, the title went to Bay's younger brother Dermot, then to Niall, his eldest son, and is now held by his son, Rory. Bay died in 1979. His friends carried his coffin from the village of Monasteraden to St. Aidan's Catholic Church, and he was buried in the family plot alongside his father and grandfather and other male forebears. The only women buried there are the consorts of princes of Coolavin. Male chauvinism pervaded in the MacDermot family.

My mother had thirty-two first cousins. Many of them and their progeny have featured in my life. Brenda Meredith, daughter of Hal and Gladys MacDermot (she was Swedish, heiress to a match fortune), is the only other family member to emigrate to US besides myself. She and her first husband lived on Achill

Island. He drowned making a film about basking sharks, which abounded in those waters. Brenda subsequently married the local schoolmaster and they had a daughter, Diana. The Atlantic gales were so fierce that ropes with large stones at each end were thrown over roofs to stop them from being blown away. In 2020, Brenda was still living in Carversville, near New Hope, Pennsylvania at the age of 101. Diana died, but Brenda's two sons, Martin and Rowan, live respectively in Washington State and Scotland, with children and grandchildren.

Her brother, Niall, served in WWII in MI5 and was awarded an Order of the British Empire for courage during the D-Day invasions. He pursued a distinguished legal career before entering Parliament and becoming minister of state for housing and local government under Harold Wilson. If it had not been for Peter Wright and his MI5 friends who secretly wrecked the life he intended for himself and his second wife, Ludmila Benvenuto, a Russian Italian whom they wrongly suspected of being a Soviet spy, he would probably have been Lord Chancellor. He could not forgive Wilson for his apparent acceptance of his wife's espionage for the Soviets and left England, becoming secretary general of the International Commission of Jurists in Geneva where "he stood up to dictators to defend the rights and lives of the oppressed." He challenged governments around the world to respect the rule of law and criticized the Reagan Administration on aid to the Nicaraguan Contras, the "disappearances" in Argentina and Chile, and for civil rights abuses by many other countries. He died in 1996 at the age of seventy-nine.

Another first cousin, Brian MacDermot, joined the Foreign Office. He and his wife, Mary, had seven boys. He had been posted to the British embassy at the Vatican and then became consul in Porto, Portugal. Mary, a devout Catholic anxious for a daughter, prayed to Our Lady of Fatima. Happily, the next and last two babies were girls christened Lucinda and Jacintha out of gratitude to the Virgin who answered her prayers.

Brian's aunt, my grandmother, was even more devout and blessed with five male children, two of whom died in infancy. She prayed to the Virgin Mary and her favorite saints for a daughter. By way of thanks for answered prayers, she gave my mother five Christian names, Moira Madeline Sophie Geraldine Theresa. My grandmother was pregnant with my aunt Ruth when her eldest son, Hugh, was killed at Gallipoli. Apparently overcome with grief, she took to her bed and went on hunger strike. The "replacement" child, Ruth, was not loved as she should have been. Unfortunately, my grandparents favored my mother and my uncle Dermot, who were both very smart and very good looking. Tragically, both Bay and Ruth were born with the hereditary hair lip. Our family, like the Hapsburgs, had been quite inbred over many generations. In those days, operations were not very successful, although my father paid for Ruth to have one.

Frank MacDermot, a half-brother of my grandfather and youngest son of Hugh Hyacinth, Prince of Coolavin, led a very distinguished life and lived to be almost ninety. He was a barrister and a politician, having graduated from Oxford and served in WWI, where he was mentioned in dispatches four times. He became a banker in New York, where he married his American wife, Elaine Thayer (who was previously married to E. E. Cummings), and returned to Dublin in 1927. He won a seat in the Dáil (Irish parliament) in 1932 and then formed the National Center Party and became a senator. He wrote a biography of Wolfe Tone, and after his Irish political career, became the US correspondent for *The Times* and lived in Paris. He and Elaine had one son, Brian Hugh, whom I have already mentioned. I quote from a1975 obituary, "from his father, Frank inherited a romantic love of Ireland but also a cool incisive mind unsuited to the shifts and manoeuvres of Irish politics."

Over the years, the Coolavin farm limped along, cattle were fattened and sold for beef, which involved much less work than dairy cows. When Ireland joined the European Union, Bay and Felicity's fortunes improved, but they focused their time and energy on the farm at the expense of the house and garden. Local people worked part time in the house and on the farm, sometimes a Regan, never more than one or two at a time, helping Bay and Felicity, who were devoted to each other and Coolavin. They were married in London in 1954. They could not afford high wages, but most of the workers were their tenants whose rents were extremely low. We had much in common with feudal pre-Revolutionary Russia on a smaller scale. Turgenev and Tolstoy were often quoted, a favorite line being, "It's only five miles, I can easily walk," when a family member put on a martyr act.

Bay and Felicity were not very domesticated and were short of money for home maintenance. My mother and other family members deplored that animal feed was stored in the formerly lovely drawing room, and the house was generally neglected. When relatives visited, they always attempted a cleanup of enormous piles of unwashed dishes in pantry sinks, as Felicity worked her way through many sets of china, which had been given as wedding presents, until no clean ones were left. No one outside the immediate family was allowed in the disaster area of the kitchen, but surprisingly, meals were produced and consumed without any proven cases of food-poisoning. I quote from a letter from my mother during a stay at Coolavin in the sixties: "The unutterable squalor of the kitchen: gas cooker f....d up (with dirt and maltreatment), the old Aga cooker in the big kitchen is being used but gradually f….d up too, by burning any old fuel, coal, wood but not anthracite, frequently no fuel at all, no hot water in sordid sink, constant carrying of buckets of water for dishwashing for six people. Felicity's old nanny who was also visiting, tried to explain away the mess by telling us that Felicity and her sister grew up with lots of servants, but later she went around moaning, 'it's not right, it's not right!'" Dermot's response to the handwringing was to say that happiness was more important than hygiene.

Rory told me a story about a visit to Felicity at Coolavin. He and his son Francis, driving to Ballaghaderreen for some shopping, noticed a dead rabbit on the driveway near the front gates. On their return the rabbit was gone, and when they entered the house, there was a strong smell of boiling rabbit. They feared it might be lunch, but happily Felicity was cooking it for the dog, Jimbo.

Dogs featured in my childhood, not surprisingly. I remember Susan, a black Cocker Spaniel, given to me when I was about six because, like many children, I was afraid of dogs. I was heartbroken when she died, her body bloated from poison. Sheep grazed on Coolavin's nine-hole golf course, and someone must have put down poison for the dogs that were chasing them. My grandparents' Irish Terrier gave birth to puppies on their golden wedding anniversary. One pup, Mickey, lived for many years and was much loved by my uncle, Bay. For my twelfth birthday, my mother gave me a black mixed-breed puppy, Bori, who grew up to be the size of a long-haired Labrador. Once, my mother had to take him to London while I was in boarding school, but he hated city life, simply did not "get" fire hydrants or street curbs, so he was taken back to Ireland to spend the rest of his life at Coolavin. Bay and Felicity always had dogs.

Other happy childhood memories of Coolavin were when cousins visited during the summers. Being an only child, Niall and Hughie seemed like brothers. Their father, my uncle Dermot, my mother's brother, joined the Consular Service and was sent to Japan, where he became an expert linguist. On the outward journey, he met my aunt Betty Steele who had grown up mostly in China, and married her, jilting a close friend of my mother's, Monica Jervis, to whom he was engaged at the time. Niall was born in Yokohama, Japan, in 1935. They moved to Formosa (now Taiwan) where their house is now a museum. Hughie was born there in 1938, and his father as British consul signed his birth certificate. When war broke out, they were in Japan, and diplomats' families were given twenty-four hours to leave the country. Niall enjoyed early childhood in Australia. Dermot was posted to Denver, where he did propaganda broadcasts in Japanese during the war. Later, he was British consul in New Orleans, which he loved. One evening he was smoking a cigarette and walking in his neighborhood, which the police found suspicious, so they asked why he was not driving a car and who he was anyway. They did not believe him when he told them he was the British Consul, so they took him down to the station. Embarrassment all around resulted in his being awarded the Freedom of the City. Dermot loved the United States. You can read much more about his time as British ambassador to Indonesia in the fifties and Thailand in the sixties later in this book. He was always proud of being an Irishman.

During the summer holidays, Niall and Hughie came to Coolavin and regaled me with tales of life in the US, which sounded luxurious; kids were more liberated, dating and driving.

We three had great fun doing farm activities like haymaking, walking on the turf (peat) bogs, and swimming in the lakes when weather permitted, which was not often. We used to cycle all over the countryside, a favorite ride being to Kesh, a nearby mountain with interesting limestone caves. We enjoyed going to tea with the Regan family at Old Coolavin. Potato pancakes cooked over open coals on the hearth, as already mentioned, were absolutely delicious. At the age of thirteen, I fell madly in love with my first cousin Niall, sixteen at the time, having got over my crush on Mr. Doody.

# Chapter Two

**M**y first boarding school to which I was sent at the tender age of eight was Rye St. Anthony, near Oxford. It was intended as the solution to the education of children of mixed marriages, where one parent was not Catholic and did not want daughters educated by nuns. It was run by two ladies, Miss Rendall and Miss King. I was the youngest in the school by two years, so I joined a class of ten-year-olds, one of whom is a best friend to this day. Wanda Willert was my first friend, one of Eleanor Roosevelt's numerous godchildren. Hanging in the entrance hall of her house is a picture of herself aged three on the White House lawn. Her father was posted to Washington as a journalist in the late thirties. Her mother, Brenda née Pearson, was a sister of Lord Cowdray, and many years later, Wanda was married to John Rix at Cowdray Park in Sussex.

Miss Rendall decided when I was nine that I was destined to read classics at Oxford. I started Latin and Greek the following year. There was a lengthy correspondence between Miss

Rendall and my father about my present and future studies, but after four years, I wanted to go to St. Mary's Ascot and was allowed to leave.

It was then, and still is, England's premier Catholic boarding school for girls, which was run by Institute of the Blessed Virgin Mary nuns, founded by Mary Ward. The nuns were inclined to be snobs, and so parents of daughters who were peers of the realm or came from "old families" or whose fathers were extremely successful businessmen were placed in front rows of the auditorium at school plays. In the fifties, there were no lady tycoons amongst the parents, but Reverend Mother herself was the heiress to a fortune generated by the London department store Marshall & Snelgrove; and as a bride of Christ, she brought her considerable dowry to the convent. Those were the austere post-war years in Britain, but the convent was well heated at a time when few private houses or apartments had central heating, and we were well fed from the convent's farm.

Our teachers were all nuns who had degrees from Oxford or Cambridge and who taught superbly. The class system was alive and well in the convent. The lay sisters who were dowry-less and degree-less did the cooking, cleaning, and gardening.

We were extremely fortunate to benefit from so much talent and received a first-class education. The nuns had none of the distractions of lay teachers such as money worries, sick children, or difficult marriages, and they were dedicated to their vocations as educators, instilling in me a lasting love of English literature, history, and geography. The fees in my day were a ludicrous fifty pounds a term: now they are in the thousands, and all the teaching is done by lay men and women.

Long before Vatican II, the nuns were rigid in their interpretation of Catholic doctrine. Predictably, they were appalled by divorce, still relatively rare in the 1950s. Another girl in my class and I were singled out because our parents were divorced, so we were likely to "go to the bad" because of our parents' mortal sins. For the record, I was happily married twice and widowed twice, and before my first marriage was rather a prude because those were the days before the pill, and the fear of pregnancy was strong.

Sixth-form girls were allowed to subscribe to the *Times*, but sometimes it was not delivered at breakfast, usually during a particularly lurid sex scandal. One day—I was thirteen at the time—the headmistress, Mother Mercedes, called me in to her office and asked if I had noticed the absence of the newspaper earlier in the week. Then she showed me the announcement of my mother and stepfather's marriage. Heaven forfend that the sixth formers might have seen this tiny notice under "Hatches, Matches and Dispatches," as the births, marriages, and deaths section was informally called.

In those days, large Catholic families were admired by the nuns, examples being a Dutch family and English expatriate, one living in Portugal, both families consisting of ten children. If four sisters attended the convent at the same time, we were given a day's holiday, which happened when the fourth daughter of the famous author Evelyn Waugh arrived. Teresa Waugh, the eldest, who was in our class, used to tell us that her father was an enthusiastic convert to Catholicism, as well as a friend of Graham Greene, another convert. However, she admitted that he was a grouch at home, they hardly ever saw him, and he treated his wife in a cavalierly male-chauvinist manner. The seventh child was called Septimus. Their brother, Alec Waugh, followed in his father's footsteps and also became a famous writer.

I dearly loved my stepfather, Robert Niven. The following biographic notes were written in the official magazine of the Royal Army Medical Corps in the late 1960s when he was commandant there at Mytchett:

Robert John Niven, MC, MRCS, LRCP. MB, BS, DPH, was born in Turiff, Aberdeenshire. Educated at Dulwich College, London University and St Thomas's Hospital, he was commissioned into the Corps on 23rd October, 1935.

He served in India from 1937 to 1940 and in the Middle East and Central Mediterranean Forces during the War. He won the Military Cross in 1942 for gallant and distinguished services in the Middle East. His war record was one of unusual distinction. He was mentioned in dispatches in 1941 and again in 1945.

As a postgraduate in 1947 he was awarded the Katherine Webb prize in Tropical Medicine and Entomology. Since the War, he has seen service in Korea, Norway, Germany, Singapore, Hong Kong and home stations as Professor of Public Health, and was Professor of Public Health on loan to the Government of Iraq in Baghdad. He was made an officer of the Most Venerable Order of the Hospital of St John of Jerusalem in March 1967.

During Brigadier Niven's term as Commandant the Corps celebrated its seventieth anniversary, and the Training Centre had the honor of a visit by the Colonel-in Chief, HM Queen Elizabeth, the Queen Mother.

I still have his first Christmas present to me, a copy of the complete works of Shakespeare. At the time, he and my mother rented a charming flat in Chelsea Studios on Fulham Road. When they were ready to move, the actor Peter Ustinov came to see it and rented it for his mother. Robert was a Scot from Aberdeen, son of a doctor, a grammarian, with a wonderful sense of humor and an appreciation of Georgian furniture and nineteenth-century English prints. He was extremely modest. He adored my mother, whom he met in India when he was a young bachelor medical officer in Rawalpindi. He waited more than eleven years to marry her.

As stated above, early in WWII he received the Military Cross, a very distinguished decoration, for his bravery in a field ambulance in Eritrea. The MC was not "given out with the rations." The other day, I found a postcard he sent me from South Africa in the '70s of giant baobabs in the Transvaal, which reminded him of "trebelde" trees he had seen in during the war in Sudan and Eritrea. Sadly, he has been dead for many years, so I could not send him photos of giant baobabs we saw in Madagascar. After his death, his sister, Mary Niven, and I sorted all his military documents, including the letter of congratulations signed by King George VI, and gave them to the Royal Army Medical Corps Museum at Mytchett.

After my father disinherited me, my stepfather offered to pay for me to attend Trinity College Dublin when I finished my year at the University of Fribourg. I thanked him profusely but refused his generous offer. In resumes for job applications, I probably "stretched" my year at the University of Fribourg and New York University night courses, but in those days, and with my proverbial good luck, lack of a degree was no setback to my career—often the contrary. Also, I could not have accepted such largesse from Robert when my father could have easily afforded to send me to university.

Mary Niven, Robert's sister, was a wonderful woman who lived to be ninety-nine and died in her beloved Edinburgh. She graduated from St. Andrews and was a trailblazer career woman ahead of her time in what is now human resources for Phillips Electric. She wrote a definitive history of personnel management. A strong, independent woman, she never married. After my mother's death and my move to New York, she lived with my stepfather in her London flat and the seventeenth-century thatched house that Ian and I had found for my mother and Robert when they returned from Hong Kong in the '60s. They had loved their garden with its old, velvety lawn and beautiful roses. He scattered my mother's ashes amongst the roses, and five years later, Mary did the same with his.

However, she was anxious to sell the house as quickly as possible after Robert's death. We had inherited it jointly in 1976. At that time, I was working for the British government in New York in their trade section. A UK-based colleague with whom I shared an office warned me against the hazards of being an absentee landlord, because his tenants in England had reneged on the rent and, under a Socialist government, it was almost impossible to evict them. Although Charles wanted me to buy out Mary's share of the house, I listened to Brian's advice, but we sold at the bottom of the market.

My father was posted to the British Zone of Austria in 1947. We were assigned a house in Millstatt on the shores of the very scenic Millstätter See. The military paid for officers' children to join their parents serving in Germany and Austria, traveling to and from boarding schools for the holidays, in this case Christmas vacations. We left by ship from Harwich and disembarked in Holland, where we boarded trains. I have a vivid memory of very stodgy food and traveling through Germany, throwing our half-eaten buns, puddings, and cakes out of the train windows, where they were seized by groups of starving children as we steamed slowly through stations.

A sensitive child, I was not happy with our situation as conquering occupiers. The family who owned the house was relegated to living in the basement, cooking and serving our meals and cleaning the house. I had a crush on the seventeen-year-old daughter who would invite me to visit the family in the evenings. I remember being offered black bread. I hope they supplemented their diets with our leftover food. Other memories were of deep snow and learning to ski, also lines of DPs, or displaced persons, slogging along the main roads—refugees, mostly concentration camp survivors.

That was the last time my parents were together. However, being at boarding school and going somewhere different for most school holidays, I did not question spending time with one or the other but not both together. My father was still serving overseas in the British Army. My mother, when not at Coolavin, was usually in some temporary country house in Ireland or England, or in a London flat. That they were separated did not occur to me until my dear friend Wanda Willert came to stay at Coolavin and told me about her parents' divorce, which seemed shocking and unreal, during our time at Rye St. Anthony. We stayed with each other during school holidays, riding ponies at Coolavin or being together in Phillimore Gardens, Kensington, where her new stepfather, Hugh Carter, was more than a little controlling. I can remember him hurling an orange across the kitchen at Wanda because he believed she had paid a penny more than she should have when he made her responsible for buying groceries. He was a professional ballroom dancer who married Brenda, Wanda's mother, after she and Arthur Willert divorced.

I must have subconsciously been thinking about Wanda's parents' divorce, because one night at Coolavin, I had a very vivid dream. My mother told me she was getting a divorce from my father, and I asked if she was going to marry Robert Niven, one among many social adult visitors who came and went frequently and to whom a small child paid scant attention, and vice versa. We children had our nannies and our own friends, and found other grown-ups incomprehensible and boring.

In the morning, I woke up in tears and described the dream to my mother. She was speechless but after a few minutes, said, "Well, I suppose, this is the time to tell you, darling. I'm afraid it's true. We are separated and going to be divorced."

"Are you going to marry a man called Robert Niven?" She made some vague reply. She never mentioned him again to me, but about four years later, they were married.

I often wonder why I remained a Catholic, because during my long life, there have been many times when I have questioned extreme interpretations of the Church's dogma. My mother was separated from my father but had not yet married Robert Niven, so she came to Coolavin to keep house for her brother Bay. Freda, my former nanny, and grandmother Caroline were old-fashioned Catholics. I can remember running down to the garden in the dark crying my heart out because they told me that my mother would go to Hell for all eternity for divorcing my father. In later years, ironically, when my grandmother was in Our Lady's Manor, a retirement home in Dalkey near Dublin, it was my stepfather who paid the bills, even though she could not bring herself to acknowledge him as her son-in-law. She was overheard saying, "Moira [my mother] is so good; what a pity it doesn't count."

To quote a deceased sister of Brian MacDermot and one of great-uncle Percy's children, Patricia MacDermot, "The Catholic Church towered over our lives as Croagh Patrick towers over Clew Bay. Moral codes were implicitly related to God, judgment, Heaven and Hell and not to the sanctions of 'nice people,' least of all to the State. This attitude was bred from centuries of Catholicism and we were as unconscious of the legacy passed down to us as we were of the air we breathed." Of course, this does not apply to all MacDermot descendants, especially younger ones. My grandfather said to Patricia, "Never, my dear child, let your religion be a burden to you. Remember that everything the Church teaches can be scribbled in a few lines on the back of an old envelope." My mother evidently took this advice; my grandmother and others, myself included, did not. She once said giving up Catholicism was like shedding a heavy overcoat on a hot day.

Patricia also wrote about family Freudian complexes, inhibitions, repression, and depression: "But through it all, humour ran like a rod of gold, unbreakable and undimmed." I have found this to be true of all my MacDermot relatives.

During two summer holidays, I went to Germany to spend time with my father, now stationed in Kiel, Schleswig-Holstein, the first time on a cargo ship headed to Danzig via the Kiel Canal. The second time, I flew to Hamburg. Driving north through the city, I remember how shocked I was in 1952 to see smartly dressed men and women appearing on the street carrying briefcases, climbing up from the cellars where they were still living. In Kiel, I saw and heard the shipyards working all day and all night, this being the regeneration of Germany and the "German miracle," while victorious Britain lagged hopelessly behind in their economic recovery.

The small British garrison in Kiel was part of B.A.O.R. (British Army on the Rhine) while Germany was still occupied by the four powers: US, Britain, France, and the Soviet Union. The cadre of British officers had a good life, unpressured by an excess of work. They spent much time enjoying what had formerly been the Kaiser's Royal Yacht Club in Kiel. They and their families sailed in a variety of boats from large hundred-square-meter and fifty-square-meter cruising yachts to dragons, stars, and sharpies. Smaller boats used to race from Kiel in the direction of Lubeck, which was in the Russian zone. Sometimes a storm blew up. The sailors were rescued, but some boats never returned.

My father became an enthusiastic sailor, and I accompanied him on some weekend cruises to Denmark. I remember tacking into a port, which took forever against the wind. When the Danish customs officer came aboard and looked at our chart, he roared with laughter, telling us that we could have sailed in on a broad reach. The charts were printed to fool the Germans during the war.

Visits to my father in Kiel took place when I was twelve and then fourteen. He lived as a bachelor in the officer's mess, so I stayed with a brother officer, his wife, and their boxer dog. I enjoyed the Baltic beaches, but that first summer learning to sail I used to get seasick when we were drifting on heavy swells waiting for wind.

Life changed in 1952. My father was an eligible divorcé. My mother used to say I was a real-life version of the obnoxious child in Nancy Mitford's novel *The Blessing*, in which women make a fuss over the child of a sought-after available man in the hopes of landing him as a husband. Of my father's aspiring lady friends, I only met two: a "sensible" English woman, and a glamorous but hysterical Greek who stalled the car going uphill in the middle of a busy London street when my father was teaching her to drive. I knew nothing about other girlfriends, but either of these two would have been infinitely preferable to the lady who landed him.

Hilda Fix was Austrian. She had a son by her Danish husband and another by his successor, a Nazi officer. When she met my father in Kiel, she had come there from the Russian zone of Vienna where she claimed her fur coat was taken off her back by a Soviet soldier. Maybe worse things had happened to her, or maybe she was always tough and ruthless going after what she wanted.

At first she could not do enough for me. She encouraged me to take her sons to Mass on Sundays. I liked them, one older, one younger, and fantasized about having stepbrothers because I hated being an only child. Actually, I had had a stillborn older sister who was strangled by her umbilical cord. Tragically, my mother had a premonition and begged for a Cesarean section, but the doctors ignored her requests. When I was on the way, my mother, fearing another tragedy and being superstitious, refused to buy any baby clothes and had to borrow from the hospital when I emerged intact and unscathed.

We all went sailing together. After Hilda appeared on the scene, I heard no more of my father's plans with a Polish officer friend and his wife that we would sail around the world when their daughter and I finished school. She and I were very excited at the time, but we should have taken into account the heavy drinking that went on in the yacht club waiting for a wind to rise or a gale to subside before taking to the water, and been more skeptical.

Before the sailing era ended, my father and fellow crew members won the Copenhagen to Kiel race in 1953. Buoyed (bad pun) by their success, the following year they entered the Fastnet Race, one of the toughest ocean races, from Cowes in the Isle of Wight around the Fastnet lightship off the South Coast of Ireland and back. They were dismasted and lost a man overboard. I never heard if he was rescued.

In 1954, I left St. Mary's Ascot with three A-levels and several O-levels as they were called then, enough to enter a top university. Our class was considered precocious, younger than the class behind us. However, only a few chose higher education and a college degree over finishing school, secretarial college, and "coming out" as debutantes. I was hoping to go to Trinity College, Dublin, but being only sixteen, it was decided that I would spend a year at Villa Beata, a finishing school run by Holy Child nuns in Fribourg with the intention of attending classes at the University of Fribourg.

Hilda and my father were married in 1954. He had left the army and taken up farming. The previous year, he rented a flat in Narrow Water Castle, near Newry in County Down, an area in Northern Ireland where I had some Whyte relatives and he had regimental friends. By contrast, after their marriage, their house was nondescript, and I immediately felt unwelcome. Hilda claimed that I made her feel ill and accused me of petty lies. I went to stay with some army friends for a few days. This embarrassed my father, who put me on a ship to England and his parents in Cheshire. My grandparents were appalled but assured me that it had to be a temporary situation. Being the kind of people they were, very conscious of their social position and with strong ideas about proper behavior, they did not want me to talk about it, nor could they comprehend such behavior in their eldest son.

So far I have not written much about the Christie-Millers. Uncle John Christie-Miller ran the family firm, Christy's Hats, in Stockport after my grandfather retired. A treat during childhood was to visit the factory to watch the hats being made, as machines forced large circular masses of felt made from rabbit fur into tighter and tighter circles, which became men's headwear, top hats, bowler hats, and so on. My father was the oldest son, but he wanted nothing to do with the business, so my grandfather bought him a commission in the Royal Ulster Rifles after Sandhurst. I was extremely fond of John and his wife, Bridget, and I am very close to their three daughters, my first cousins, Caroline, Lydia, and Charlotte. After my father's desertion, John used to call me his fourth daughter. John was also a justice of the peace, chairman of the Stockport County Bench, high sheriff of Cheshire—which involved much entertaining of the assize judges—and like his father, he was active in the Territorial Association (the British equivalent of the National Guard, more or less). Between them, they did about fifty years as chairman. He served on several boards, and for his dedicated public service, he was awarded Commander of the Most Excellent Order of the British Empire. Caroline became an art historian and married Peter Cannon-Brookes. Lydia married a naval officer, Ian Mclure, and Charlotte became a barrister and married Jack Beatson. I will write more about them later on.

I also loved my aunt Mary, the only daughter of my grandparents, who was married to Dick Freston. They had two daughters and a son, Jill, Patricia, and Martin. The eldest, my cousin

Jill, is closest to me in age, and one of the bravest people I have ever known. In 2016, she was crossing a street in Oxford when a bus hit her (I will never again use the cliché "If I get run over by a bus, then you inherit my Landseer oil painting," or some other coveted possession). She has coped with the loss of her leg with fortitude and good humor.

Uncle David Christie-Miller was a distant, glamorous figure, living in Kenya as a district commissioner, part of the dissolute "Black Mischief" crowd. His first wife, Jane, was nearly twice his age and known as Silver Liz, who, like Beryl Markham, had flown solo around Africa. When they returned to England on leave, they went their separate ways, saying it was embarrassing to be mistaken for one another's son or mother, but threw a party in London for all their friends before embarking for Kenya once more. After Jane died, David married Joan, and they raised a son and daughter, Stephen and Diana. When Kenya became independent, David returned to England and enjoyed being a salesman for Guinness and giving tours of Eton and Windsor Castle.

The youngest uncle, Stephen, close to David in age and affections, served in the Queen's Bays and was killed at the Battle of El Alamein on October 25, 1942. The day before the battle, he encountered his older brother John, an aide to Field Marshall Montgomery, and told him they were headed for the front and would never see each other again. My grandfather created a scholarship in his memory at Trinity College, Oxford, for which he, Sir Geoffry Christie-Miller, was made an honorary fellow.

My grandparents lived at Stapeley House in Nantwich, Cheshire. During both World Wars, it became a Red Cross Convalescent Home. After WWII, I remember staying with them as a small child in a converted staff cottage. Stapeley House was sold to Nantwich Rural District Council. It is now a computer center.

My mother recounted her first visit to Stapeley House when she and my father got engaged. She and my godmother, the Honorable Blanche Hanbury Tracy, daughter of Lord Arundel, ran a fashionable little sportswear boutique in Soho at a time when "ladies" did not work. They were both beautiful, with a wide range of aristocratic but often penniless admirers, who occasionally helped themselves to the contents of the shop's till, with or without permission. They led glamorous and rather promiscuous lives, postponing matrimony, which was unusual in those days, because they were having too much fun. *Sex and the City*, circa 1933? Lack of money did not seem to matter. Their giddy London lives were preferable to the conventions of the times, where impoverished aristocratic daughters were expected to languish in their crumbling ancestral homes until suitable suitors came along. Brave, too, since the pill had not yet been invented. So, when my mother went to stay at Stapeley, Sharratt unpacked her suitcase, as servants did in those days. (As in *Upstairs, Downstairs* or *Downton Abbey*, ladies' maids were called by their surnames and cooks were always missus.) My mother was ashamed of her threadbare underwear and meager wardrobe, no doubt a topic of discussion in the servants' hall that weekend.

One of the admirers of Blanche and my mother described the latter as "a girl with good legs and the face of a fallen angel." I adored her, and I can still remember as a child not minding too much when a passenger on a Dublin bus commented in a broad Dublin accent that my mother was so beautiful and what a pity I did not look more like her. She found my generation rather dull as we grew up in post-war Britain. Life was relatively easy for us, and she once remarked that unlike herself, I had never had to choose between a meal and a pair of stockings.

The Christie-Miller history has been well documented by family members, so I will only add a truncated version of the complicated story, which started in the seventeenth century in Scotland. Our earliest recorded ancestor was William Miller, born in 1655, a Quaker. In 1689, he was appointed master gardener at the Abbey of Holyroodhouse in Edinburgh. He and his wife, Margaret, had seven sons and four daughters. His third son, William, joined his father as a gardener at the Palace and built up a lucrative seedsman and nurseryman's business. With his profits he bought up land, which became the Miller Estate at Craigentinny. William married Ann Adam, and they had nine children. In 1734, their eldest daughter, Mary, married John Christy. The Christy family came from Aberdeen and in the seventeenth century had settled in Moyallon, County Down, Northern Ireland, as linen bleachers and was a prominent Quaker family. John Christy introduced linen bleaching to Ormiston, County Haddington, seventeen miles east of Edinburgh. The fifth and youngest son of this marriage was Miller Christy, who broke his apprenticeship to come to London in 1773 and, with fellow Quaker Joseph Storrs, opened a hat shop on Gracechurch Street next to the Quaker Meeting House. The following year the partnership was dissolved, and Miller Christy founded Christy & Co. Hat Manufacturers.

The third son of William and Ann was William Miller, who served as his father's heir, carrying on the seedsmen's business and becoming the most prominent member of the Society of Friends in Edinburgh. After his first two wives died in childbirth, he was disowned when it was learned that he intended to marry Martha Rawson, contrary to the rules of the Society. They moved to London where their son William Henry Miller was born and who, after his father's death, lived with his mother. Both were painted by Sir Thomas Lawrence, and William also by Raeburn. He became the Member of Parliament for Newcastle-under-Lyme for five terms, and in 1830, he bought Britwell House in Burnham, Buckinghamshire, which had room for his extensive library of Elizabethan literature and Shakespeare's First and Third Folio manuscripts. He made the first purchases for the Britwell Library in 1824.

Samuel Christy, born in 1810, a grandson of Miller Christy and partner in Christy & Co., inherited the Miller Estate. He assumed by Royal License for himself and his descendants the name of Christie-Miller, quartering the arms of Miller of Craigentinny with those of Christy. He was extremely wealthy and restored the house at Craigentinny, oversaw the building of the family mausoleum, and owned 21 St. James's Place in London. Samuel died in 1889 and left his entire estate to his nephew Wakefield Christy who assumed by deed poll the name Christie-Miller. Wakefield's father, Thomas Christy, was the grandson of Miller Christy. His mother, Jane Sandwith Wakefield, was descended from John Christy's younger brother, Thomas Christy of Moyallon. In 1872, Wakefield married Mary Elizabeth Richardson of Kircassock, and he rebuilt Britwell House, which became Britwell Court. Their first two children were born in Bramhall Hall, Stockport. My grandfather and two more brothers were born in London. In 1889, his uncle Samuel died, leaving his entire estate to Wakefield, consisting of the Britwell Estate and Library, 21 St. James's Place, and Craigentinny, Midlothian. Wakefield died in 1898, leaving all his property in trust to his wife until his eldest son, Sydney, reached the age of thirty. In a codicil, he left the

Craigentinny Estate to his four sons and the library to Sydney and Charles.

Britwell was sold in 1920 and the contents removed to Clarendon Park, Salisbury. Sotheby's sold the library, taking sixty-seven days and totaling six hundred thousand pounds, many millions in today's currency. It was unrivalled among private collections for its numbers, rarity, and condition of its manuscripts, comprising the finest examples of early English and Scottish literature, especially Shakespeare.

Mrs. Wakefield Christie-Miller lived at 21 St. James's Place until her death in 1929. It was destroyed by bombing during WWII.

My grandparents spent their honeymoon at Craigentinny in 1908. By 1937, the house had been completely rebuilt, surrounded by multistory apartments on land compulsorily purchased by Edinburgh City Council for slum clearance. One wing was destroyed by bombing, but the house remains a social center, having sold for a paltry thousand pounds.

Some members of each generation retain a talent for and pleasure in gardening, no doubt inherited from our early Miller ancestors. There is a beautiful pink hybrid rose at Kew Gardens that was bred by Samuel McGreedy in 1909. It was introduced into Australia in 1910 as "Mrs. Wakefield Christie-Miller." My cousin, Caroline Cannon-Brookes, is a keen gardener as is her daughter Emma, with her husband, Andrew Coker.

When my grandfather was at Eton and hunted with the Eton beagles, he often ran home for tea at Britwell Court, where his parents lived. After Eton, he went to Trinity College, Oxford, and took a second-class honors degree. He was an amazing athlete, rode his horses to hounds, and rowed his boats well into old age. He and my grandmother, Olive, were happily married for fifty-six years until she died in 1965. For many years, they lived in a large, attractive house, Acton Grange, near Nantwich in Cheshire. Of all the Stapeley servants before the war, only Sharratt and Mrs. Rees, their maid and superb cook, remained with them into relatively old age. As a child, I adored Mrs. Rees's cooking, especially gooseberry and raspberry fool made from their homegrown berries with lashings of whipped cream.

My grandmother's nephew, my father's first cousin, Jeremy Thorpe, born in 1929, was probably our most famous—or infamous—family member, having recently been the subject of a popular TV movie in which he was played by Hugh Grant, *A Very English Scandal*. His father had died young, leaving his widow, Great-Aunt Ursula, née Norton Griffiths, in what used to be called "straightened circumstances." My grandfather came to the rescue, paying for Jeremy to attend Eton and Oxford. He was an excellent student, a brilliant debater, and became president of the Oxford Union. When he asked how he could repay such generosity, which included reading for the Bar after Trinity College, my grandfather suggested he always wear a hat.

His political ambitions started early. He was elected Liberal Member of Parliament for North Devon in 1959 when he was only thirty and retained the seat until 1979, leading the party from 1967 until 1976. His mother was always at his side campaigning for him.

At the height of his success in the '70s, there was talk of a coalition government with the Conservatives led by Edward Heath and Jeremy, leader of the Liberal party. I was working in the British Trade Development Office in New York at the time, and I once saw a margin note in a memo from a senior member of the staff never intended for my eyes: "Be nice to her; her cousin may be the next prime minister."

In 1968, he married Caroline Alpass, who died tragically in a car accident in 1970. They had one son, Rupert, who now lives in California. In 1973, Jeremy married Marion Stein, a classical pianist and ex-wife of George Lascelles, 7th Earl of Harewood, eleventh in line to the throne, and technically a member of the royal family. Mana Donata Nanetta Paulina Gustava Wilhelmina, always called Marion, was born in 1927 in Vienna, daughter of Erwin Stein, an eminent musicologist, pupil of Arnold Schoenberg, and friend of Benjamin Britten.

I went to their lavish wedding reception at Burlington House, attended by prime ministers past and present, plus other political dignitaries. Marion stuck by him through the trial, and after his fall from grace and his lingering illness suffering from Parkinson's disease. She died in 2014, nine months before Jeremy.

Much has been written about his affair with Norman Scott, a.k.a. Norman Josiffe, which was revived in recent years by the Hugh Grant movie. Jeremy was almost certainly bisexual, and his affair and the cover-up by the Thatcher government was fodder for the press. Uncle John believed that he owed much of his popularity to the media, given his charismatic personality, but ultimately they helped to destroy his reputation. As a brilliant, ambitious politician with no money of his own, he was manipulated by wealthy friends and supporters.

The trial took place in 1979. Andrew "Gino" Newton was the hitman hired in 1975 to murder Scott, who threatened to go public about his 1960s affair with Jeremy. He shot Scott's Great Dane Rinka; the gun jammed before he could shoot Scott. He was jailed for two years for killing the dog. At the 1979 trial, Jeremy was acquitted, but his career was over.

I believe he was capable of great kindness and cared very much for his family. Caroline Christie-Miller, while studying at the Courtauld, spent weekends with Jeremy and Ursula. He used to play the violin before breakfast. He made a speech at Caroline's twenty-first birthday party at Quaglino's, and she often acted as his hostess at Liberal party dinners at the Café Royal before his marriage. She attested to his wit and kindness. He asked me to tea in the House of Commons when I returned to England after the death of my first husband.

Caroline attended his funeral service on December 20, 2014, at St. Margaret's, Westminster, with her husband, Peter, and sister, Charlotte. As the coffin was carried out, Jeremy's brown hat was on top of it. Our grandfather would have been proud and happy.

Geoffry, who was knighted and became Sir Geoffry later in his life, lost his right eye as a result of contracting smallpox when he was six weeks old. It was replaced with a glass eye. He managed to pass the army eye test by memorizing the alphabet panel. He fought in WWI with the Oxfordshire and Buckinghamshire Light Infantry. He was awarded the Distinguished Service Order and Military Cross, and he was mentioned in dispatches in France in the 1914–8 war. He fought at the Battle of Fromelles. Four volumes of his typed diaries are in the Imperial War Museum.

He was appointed a deputy lieutenant of Cheshire in 1939. He was chairman of Cheshire Territorial Association from 1945 to 1950, and was honorary colonel of the 81st AA Regiment, Royal Artillery, TA, from 1937 to 1948. He was a director of Christy & Co., first chairman of Stockport and Buxton Hospital Management Committee, and had been president of Stockport Savings Banks. He opened an account for each grandchild with five pounds. He was also chairman of Stockport Grammar School.

He died on a Caribbean cruise in 1969, peacefully in a chair on deck after lunch, and was buried at sea next morning. He went at eighty-eight, as he always meant to go, without any concessions to old age or ill health, without medical aid and with his clothes on.

I was instructed by Uncle John to meet the ship in Southampton, because he did not trust his older brother, my father, who had accompanied our grandfather on the cruise, to handle the formalities following his death and burial at sea, believing that I would do better with the paperwork and any other requirements. I protested that my mother was dying and I should not leave her, even for a few hours. In fact, she died three days later. John prevailed. It was an awkward, stiff, brief meeting with my father. We probably discussed the weather.

An ironic footnote: Did I have a penchant for being disinherited without being a prodigal daughter or granddaughter? Before she died, my mother felt guilty that her life had been so much more comfortable than her sister Ruth's and asked if it was alright by me to leave Ruth the interest on her modest capital in her will, assuming that my grandfather would provide for me knowing that his son would not. Of course, I concurred. My grandfather never accepted his son's behavior, believing that he would come to his senses and provide for his only child after his death, so he left his money—except for hefty estate duty to the British government—to his four surviving children, including my father.

Edward Christie-Miller, my youngest great-uncle, outlived his brothers. He had a glamorous wife, Beatrice, and no children. He used to run the General Trading Company, a very upscale store in London. After a falling out with a brother-in-law, he started the Gift Department of Fortnum and Mason, and he was commissioned to buy gifts for Queen Mary to give away. Edward and Beatrice lived lavishly in a beautiful London townhouse on Hyde Park Street and traveled extensively. On one of their cruises, they visited us in Hong Kong. Beatrice outlived Edward by many years with a happy disregard to her less affluent status as his widow, maintaining her lifestyle. I was told by Uncle John that she even bought her toilet paper at Fortnum and Mason. Years later, I met some of Beatrice's relatives and heirs in New York.

# Chapter Three

After my four years at St. Mary's Convent, my father agreed that I should go to Villa Beata, a finishing school in Fribourg, Switzerland run by Holy Child nuns, attending classes in French language and literature at Fribourg University.

When he married Hilda, she wanted everything for her two sons, and she exerted her all-powerful influence to detach my father from his family and his regimental friends, starting with his only child. She believed, wrongly, that having been on the other side during the war, she would not be accepted by his family. He sent a letter, which I received just as I was leaving for Switzerland and my mother and stepfather for Singapore. He wrote that he never wanted to see me again, that I preferred my mother and was only interested in his money. He had already paid for the year in Switzerland but would not give me another penny. Under English law at the time, it was perfectly legal to abandon a child of sixteen unless he or she was physically or mentally disabled. Everyone, including his family, assumed this was a temporary aberration, being infatuated with his new wife, and he would come to his senses before long.

I have happy memories of my year at Villa Beata. When not attending classes, we were engaged in finishing school activities, like cooking, dressmaking, drawing, and painting. During the winter months, we skied on the weekends in different parts of Switzerland; and for Christmas vacation, those of us who did not go home went skiing at St. Anton in Austria.

The other girls came from different countries: the US, France, Spain, Italy, Germany, Holland, and Mexico. The French girls were innately chic. Although they had limited wardrobes, the way they wore their scarves, sweaters, blouses, and skirts had a flair that the rest of us could never imitate. Two American girls, both called Pat, had large wardrobes, as did one English girl, whom the rest of us envied. A Dutch and a German girl constantly argued with each other. For them, the war had not really ended, and the German occupation of the Netherlands had not been forgotten or forgiven. One of the two American Pats married Chuck Thorne and they had nine children. We kept in touch and I visited them later in California. I have remained in contact all these years with Deidre Humphreys, née Flanagan, who still lives in Dublin, and Valerie Hayman, who still lives in Yorkshire. Both had children and grandchildren. Deidre is a widow and Valerie divorced many years ago.

The University of Fribourg was half French and half German. The faculties of medicine and law were situated in the German part; arts, humanities, and languages in the French section. We ate, slept, and studied in two buildings at Villa Beata, and we were supposed to speak French at all times.

Two rather trivial memories of the university have stuck with me. During breaks between lectures, we used to buy "têtes-de-nègre" from a street vendor, a delicious Swiss chocolate-covered nougat over a cookie base. These days, if they still exist, they surely have a more politically correct name. The other recollection was of a professor who taught us advanced French. Every time in the ensuing decades when I look at the new moon, I remember him saying it was a liar. The new moon is shaped like a D for "decroissant" while the waning moon a C, "croissant." Of course, the truth is the exact opposite.

I shared a room with Margaret de Salis. Her delightful brother was a count of the Holy Roman Empire who ran a laundry in Dover and came to Switzerland to take us out, which was enormous fun.

Halfway through the academic year, two second cousins of mine, the Cobbold twins, arrived at Villa Beata. Because they argued a lot, it was decided to split them up, so Anne shared a room with me and Clare with Margaret in the other building. Every morning, Anne or Clare would hold at the window whatever outfit they planned to wear that day. They always dressed identically.

In April that year during spring break, a group of us went to Italy and visited Venice, Florence, Fiesole, Sienna, and Assisi before spending the final week in Rome. In those days, the Uffizi and other important museums and cathedrals were not as crowded as they are today—or were, pre-pandemic. It was very hot in Rome and serious sightseeing was exhausting. No sitting around in cafes for us students. Probably the most fun we girls had was being whistled at by young Italians whizzing by on Vespas. For my seventeenth birthday, a cousin of my mother's, Christopher Lamb, a Jesuit priest, said Mass in the catacombs for our group.

At that time, Brian MacDermot (one of my mother's first cousins, mentioned earlier) was the number two British diplomat to the Vatican (no Catholic can be the ambassador). He and his wife, Mary, loved living in Rome and kindly entertained us during our stay. A few years later, he became British ambassador to Paraguay. I almost went there in 1959 to stay with them instead of going to New York, but more of that later. Over the years we saw them in London with their various children, all grown up. Mary lived to be ninety-six and died in October 2020 in their Hampshire home surrounded by family. I am in touch with their oldest son, Alan.

We saw the Holy Father several times during Holy Week in procession and stood in St. Peter's Square for his Easter address.

To my great disappointment, an invitation to travel around the opera circuit of Italy teaching English to the daughter of wealthy Italians later that spring and summer was vetoed by Reverend Mother, as well as mine in Singapore, who insisted that I finish my studies.

The Reverend Mother did not like me and found several occasions to reprimand me. We were very innocent compared with today's adolescents. Someone gave me a sachet of bubble bath, sufficient for only one bath. I invited my cousin Clare to share it. Word reached Reverend Mother and we were practically expelled. It never occurred to either of us that we would be suspected of being lesbians. Those were the bad old days before LGBTQ rights and awareness. My mother told me a story about another Holy Child convent school for girls, Mount Anvil, outside Dublin. An aunt of hers who was a boarder asked the nuns why they were obliged to wear two-piece costumes in their baths. The answer was: "Your guardian angel might be a man."

In the summer of 1955, after Switzerland, I stayed with my grandparents at Acton Grange where Aunt Jane, David Christie-Miller's much older wife, was slowly dying of heart disease. She wore a huge diamond ring and feared it would be stolen when she was in the hospital. She had a marvelous sense of humor. She and my grandmother, who were about the same age, constantly joked amongst themselves and teased me as they helped me prepare for my journey to Singapore to live with my mother and stepfather.

In September, I boarded a troopship, HMS *Devonshire*, which carried an entire regiment, the King's Own Scottish Borderers, plus other assorted military personnel and their families. I was chaperoned by a charming couple, the Kohanes, Irish colleagues of my stepfather's in the Royal Army Medical Corps.

On certain evenings, the haggis would be piped into the (first-class) officers' dining room, in true Scottish fashion, by kilted bagpipers. There was dancing most evenings after dinner. Some officers were accompanied by their wives, but many were young and single, and there were hardly any single women on board. I fell for a handsome, fair-haired young Royal Artillery officer named Peter Waring. It was an innocent romance for the journey and during my first few weeks in Singapore. When my mother and I went to Hong Kong and Japan later that year, he abandoned me for one of my friends, which for a short while felt like the end of the world. A young Scotsman serving with the King's Own Scottish Borderers, Jock Foulis, whom I met on the ship, pursued me, but I was not particularly attracted to him and treated him badly. He kept in touch for many years, a kind and faithful friend even after I turned down his proposal of marriage. Ever the realist, I accepted the fact that so much male attention was due to the scarcity of single females on board the ship and in the Colonies, not to my exceptional beauty and charms.

Mike Kohane had a drinking problem, which drove his poor wife to distraction. After a while, she asked me to chaperone him and to steer him to their cabin while he was still vertical, because she preferred to go to bed early. Usually I succeeded in this role reversal with the help of one or two young officers.

We docked for the day in Colombo when Sri Lanka was still the British colony of Ceylon with a huge naval base. We went ashore for lunch at the beautiful old hotel at Mount Lavinia and spent the rest of the day and evening sightseeing and enjoying being on dry land. Previously we had stopped in Port Said before entering the Suez Canal but had not gone ashore. Gully-gully men surrounded the ship and were allowed on board to sell Egyptian trinkets and souvenirs and perform magic tricks, which involved chickens emerging from their voluminous robes. As we steamed out of the canal and into the Red Sea, it became very hot. We went ashore at Aden, a large British military base at the southern tip of what is now Yemen, a place of no great scenic or historical value, referred to by a poet as "the barren rocks of Aden." Although officers' quarters on troop ships were very comfortable, the food was mediocre and a swimming pool nonexistent. We welcomed an excursion to an air force club for a cooling dip in the Arabian Sea. We might not have plunged in so enthusiastically had we been told beforehand that there had been a hole in the shark net and the previous week an air force wife had been grabbed while swimming and never seen again.

Returning to the ship from our day in Colombo, exhausted and hot—cabins had fans but no air conditioning in those days—I stripped and went to sleep under a sheet. Hours later, the door was flung open, and one of the senior naval officers accompanied by a couple of drunken friends, including Mike Kohane, tore the sheet off my naked, sweating body saying,

"Get up and get dressed and go entertain the young officers." I declined and suggested they go to bed like good chaps and leave a girl to her beauty sleep. I noticed that one of them had managed to smuggle aboard an enormous stalk of bananas, which must have been against regulations.

My stepfather and I both loved Singapore and our army quarters on Russell Road near the military hospital. Once again I was a spoiled young girl surrounded by young men where we were very much in the minority. There were endless parties, evening tennis games despite being so close to the equator, swimming, and flirting at the Tanglin Club. It was still very much a British colony, with a large government staff, a major military presence, army, navy, and air force, plus the usual commercial enterprises, banks, trading companies, shipping lines, all of which hired young single men from Britain. As "army brats," my friends and I socialized mostly with the young navy and air force officers, but because of the scarcity of young single females, we went to all the parties.

Favorite cousins were stationed at Changi (site of the WWII Japanese concentration camp where my uncle Bay was interned): Bunty, née Whyte, and Toby Simonds and their three young children, Jacquie, Michael, and Clodagh. Bunty used to ask me to take the wheel of their ancient Jaguar while she lit a cigarette. I did not have a driver's license, but fortunately, we were never stopped. Now, so many years later, I am very close to their children and became godmother to the youngest, Veronica, who was born four years later. Toby had served with the Royal Irish Fusiliers through the Burma Campaign fighting the Japanese. The family lived in Ireland after his retirement in a beautiful house, Clonlost, on a hillside in Dalkey with sweeping lawns, a tennis court, and a view of the Irish Sea. Bunty bred prize

Dalmatians and Jacquie, the eldest daughter, became a model and was often photographed with these handsome black-and-white dogs. Michael and Clodagh have always lived in Ireland, Clodagh becoming a musician and composer, Michael owning and running a bookstore until he sold it recently. Veronica lives in Connemara and has three children, Max, Molly, and Kate, mother of the first grandchild, Rui.

One other cousin, Lydia Christie-Miller, who was working for the Red Cross, visited my mother and stepfather during their time in Singapore before I joined them in September.

In November, my mother and I took what used to be called an "indulgence trip" to Japan on another troopship en route to Japan and Korea, which, having unloaded military personnel in Singapore and Hong Kong, had plenty of room for extra passengers. American military officers and their wives were also included. The latter were fascinated by the food, which we considered stodgy, overcooked, and unappetizing. The menus intrigued them. Their favorite was spotted dick.

We took trains from Osaka to Kyoto and Nara, admired the temples and beautiful scenery, stayed in Japanese inns, and were taken under the wing of a charming Japanese film producer and his entourage as was a tall, young New Zealander. There were very few foreign tourists in Japan at that time. A visit to Hiroshima was depressing. Smiling Japanese touts tried to sell us tourist paraphernalia including small replicas of the skeleton frame of the famous domed building. We could not bring ourselves to enter the museum.

Back in Singapore, my mother and I took Chinese cooking classes given by a very distinguished lady, the wife of the future prime minister, Lee Kwan Yew. Amongst many succulent dishes she taught us, alas long forgotten, one tip remained with me. In order to cook perfect rice, she insisted that it needs to be washed at least ten times beforehand. All too often when my rice is soggy, lumpy, and less than perfect, I think of Mrs. Lee and tell myself a little laziness is allowed as I stir a little oil or butter into the pan.

There was one family tragedy while we were living in Singapore. My stepfather Robert's cousin, James Cruickshank, was also serving in the Royal Army Medical Corps, so we saw quite a lot of James and Isabel and their four children. One Sunday they came for lunch, and then the two couples went to the yacht club for an afternoon sail while I looked after the children at our house. The phone rang a couple of hours later, and I heard the shattering news that James had suffered a fatal heart attack while swimming out to a mooring where his boat was anchored. Trying to entertain those little children and stay cheerful till their mother returned was probably the worst afternoon of my young life. Isabel was a plucky woman who, like her husband, was a doctor and raised her children as a single mother when they returned to England. All of them turned out exceptionally well, and I remember a son visiting us years later when he came to New York to run in the marathon.

During our last few months in Singapore, I took a job with a publishing company, which was a useful experience for my future.

We returned to Britain earlier than expected because of my stepfather's career. Robert had been promoted to colonel. He and I both hated leaving Singapore, though my mother was delighted. She was a dutiful army wife but missed family and friends in England and Ireland. We sailed home on a rather horrible troopship, the HMS *Asturias*.

That spring, I attended St. James' Secretarial School (the best and snobbiest in London). As mentioned earlier, Robert kindly offered to send me to Trinity College, Dublin, since there was no change in my father's attitude and he did not answer letters, but I told him I would always be extremely grateful for his paying for St. James. His sister, Mary Niven, asked me years later if I regretted not going to the university and I replied that I did not. My mother said that if I had been brilliant rather than merely intelligent, she would have insisted on my accepting Robert's offer, but she figured, and I agreed with her, that those three years were better and more interestingly spent traveling and working overseas. At that time, most of my female contemporaries were not interested in university degrees, but of course this has changed in recent times. Most of us settled happily for finishing schools, secretarial jobs—which often led to travel all over the world—some debutante parties, and sooner or later marriage and children. I did not "do the season" because we could not have afforded it, but I attended the coming-out dances of my friends. Anne and Clare Cobbold, whom I had not seen since Villa Beata, had a party in the cellars of Justerini & Brooks, famous wine merchants.

Relations with my father's family were always excellent. In those days, mothers usually presented their daughters to the queen. However, as my mother was divorced, and divorced women were banned from Court, my aunt Bridget Christie-Miller was happy to do the honors. Her own daughters had no interest in the London social season or in being "presented." For the occasion, I wore a pale aqua silk cocktail dress, matching hat, silk high-heeled shoes also dyed to match, and long white leather gloves above the elbow. We paid three guineas (quaint, now-obsolete British currency, a guinea being a pound and a shilling) for a curtseying lesson with an eccentric elderly lady, Madame Vacari. We learned how to curtsey: one, two, three, bob, left leg behind right, and repeat twice, to music.

March 22 was a beautiful day and we did not mind sitting in a long row of black London taxis waiting to drop us off at the entrance to Buckingham Palace. After we made our curtseys to Her Majesty Queen Elizabeth, Her Royal Highness Princess Margaret, and Her Royal Highness Elizabeth the Queen Mother, tea was served. We were assigned colored cards. Mine was purple, and with my hands sweating nervously, the purple ink bled inside my gloves, which I probably would never have worn again. The chocolate cake was particularly delicious.

Before one debutante dance, I was at a dinner party attended by the Duke of Kent, who seemed to be suffering from a dearth of sleep or an excess of alcohol, or both, because he kept nodding off. Later in the evening he revived, and I observed him disappearing up a staircase with a debutante he was supposed to be dating. Regaling the slightly older man who took me home in a taxi with these anecdotes, I thought no more of it until my version appeared in *The Evening Standard* next day (luckily unattributed). My escort had been the paper's reporter.

My mother and stepfather were living near Farnham in Surrey after we returned from Singapore, in Binton Barn Cottage, which they owned since my boarding school days and where I spent many holidays. I remember on more than one occasion while shopping at a gourmet grocery store in Farnham, the door was held open for us by a very distinguished elderly gentleman, Field Marshall Bernard Montgomery (retired).

That summer, we splurged on renting a house in Ballsbridge for a week for the Dublin Horse Show. There were lots of parties and family gatherings. We enjoyed watching the horse show events, but one day I saw my wicked stepmother in the distance. My father had bought her a couple of show horses. At that point, I was technically penniless although living comfortably with my mother and stepfather. My Christie-Miller grandmother generously paid for midweek lodgings in London.

Just before the end of the week, helping my aunt Betty make beds in a house nearby, which they were renting temporarily between diplomatic postings, she asked me if I would like to come to Indonesia as my eleven-year-old cousin Conor's nanny. My uncle Dermot had just been appointed British ambassador, and he was entitled to salary and first-class transportation for a live-in nanny. Betty abhorred the idea of a stranger living with them in Asia, where she would neither be part of the family nor of the Asian servants at the residence. Pausing my courses at St. James, I accepted enthusiastically.

# Chapter Four

Whcn car after car and sack after sack of mail, clearly marked "Airmail," was hoisted into the fore and aft holds of the Dutch liner *Willem Ruys*, I realized we were really on our way to Indonesia. In that bygone era, visitors were allowed aboard. In fact, my mother, Moira; Robert, my stepfather; Granny MacDermot; and Niall, Dermot and Betty's oldest son, had lunch on board with us. It was served by grinning Javanese stewards, no doubt happy to be homeward bound, and the food was excellent. I shocked Granny by ordering tongue, forgetting it was Friday. The system of ordering by numbers was by no means foolproof; Niall and I had difficulty acquiring stewed blackberries and pineapple.

Robert was the first to leave, because he needed to walk Dougal, their Scottie dog waiting in the car, quayside. We spent the afternoon on deck with Tipsy, Dermot and Betty's black Cocker Spaniel, until she was whisked away to the kennels on the top deck (visiting hours 9 to 11 a.m. and 4 to 5 p.m.), fed and cared for by crew members, exercised by me. No twenty-first-century cruise ship offers such amenities for pets, as far as I know.

It has always seemed to me that the British government was extraordinarily generous about transportation for family members. Children of government and military officials, in addition to accompanying their parents to overseas postings up to the age of eighteen, were also flown from their boarding schools for the long summer holidays and back for the autumn term. I mentioned my mother and Dermot's cousins, Brian and Mary MacDermot, in an earlier chapter. The British taxpayer covered the cost of all nine children flying to and from their boarding schools to whichever foreign country Brian was serving in as Her Majesty's diplomatic representative.

Serving one's country abroad did not necessarily mean leaving the family dog behind. Thus, Tipsy was en route to Indonesia with us. Four years later, my mother and stepfather's golden Cocker Spaniel Sober was flown to Hong Kong. There was just one major drawback. In those days, dogs returning to the United Kingdom after their owners' overseas posting was completed had to spend six months in quarantine kennels at their owners' expense. Neither Tipsy's nor Sober's "people" demurred, and they lived out their lives in England.

We finally sailed at 5 p.m. and watched the English coast, the familiar docks, the fluttering handkerchiefs, and my mother's yellow coat disappear from view. A glimpse of the Isle of Wight and the Needles, and then it was time for dinner. The ship was grander than the *Devonshire* or the *Asturias*, which transported us to and from Singapore, with luxurious lounges, beautiful paneling, and excellent service from the mostly Javanese staff. I shared a cabin with a Mrs. Middleton, whom I described in my diary as "a charming elderly lady, rather deaf, on her first trip to

Malacca, and so far we have not fought over the lights, the closet space, or anything else."

Next morning I exercised Tipsy and met her kennel companions, two Alsatians, a Boxer belonging to a Japanese gentlemen, an adorable terrier with a German owner, and another spaniel that seemed unhappy. We attended obligatory lifeboat drills, sat in the sun until it was time to escort Conor to the children's tea, after which we played all sorts of games and I beat a charming young Dutch officer at ping-pong. On Sunday, we attended a badly sung Mass with many priests and nuns, and a long sermon in Dutch, so we nearly missed breakfast.

Having reached the Bay of Biscay, according to my diary, "a storm continued through the night which was extremely noisy with the sound of breaking crockery. Mrs. Middleton's flower vase fell down and the water drenched my clothes. Spray was lashing over the bow and we had to hold on tight as we staggered around the upper deck. Soft music continued to play in the background, occasionally strains of Bach were audible above the waves and creaking boards. Many a sufferer from mal de mer lay 'cribb'd, cabined, and confined,' having parted with dinner, consisting of partridge, coupe Jacques, and Galantine Garibaldi."

While typing this, I was accosted by an elderly Dutchman who wrote books on aviation. We discussed Françoise Sagan and the novel in general. We agreed to compare notes on our literary efforts between here and Colombo.

The captain's cocktail party was a fairly subdued affair. Dry and sweet martinis soon ran out. Dermot and Betty were not the only "excellencies." We sat with the recently appointed British ambassador to Cambodia and his wife, Mr. and Mrs. Brain, and their son Quentin. There was complimentary red wine with dinner, and a three-piece band seemed to play on every possible occasion.

During dinner, compliments of the shipping line, which was excellent, the captain made a sudden surprise announcement that we would proceed via the Cape of Good Hope. This was during the beginning of the Suez Crisis, and there could be disruptions going through the canal. In fact, Egypt's President Nasser threatened to close it. Most passengers seemed to welcome the lengthy detour around Africa. Dancing after dinner with one of the ship's officers, he told me he was disappointed about the detour, because he would not be home for Christmas in Holland, after nine years of organizing Christmas parties for passengers.

Fellow first-class passengers were an interesting mix: diplomats, military officers and their families, businessmen, young German men and girls, and one Dane en route to Bandung. A German girl told me she was going to dance in second class, which would be more fun than our first class, with thirty-five unattached males. I used the word "elderly" quite often in my diary. From my eighteen-year-old perspective, I doubt that a couple thus described bound for India, Singapore, and South Africa on business were more than middle aged. We were somewhat shocked that the bishop of Singapore and his wife were not traveling first class. As we sailed past the coast of Morocco, the weather heated up, and by the time we had crossed the Tropic of Cancer, the swimming pool was in constant use. Betty, Conor, and I took Indonesian lessons every morning for an hour. Food on board the *Willem Ruys* was copious. Every day at lunch, the menu was headed Dutch Luncheon, which was really breakfast with ham, eggs, cheese, bread, and butter marmalade. This preceded an entire lunch, soup, entrée, and dessert eaten regularly by our Dutch passengers.

Bingo was popular with the adults, as was horse racing. Dermot always enjoyed gambling, and on one occasion bought a horse for several guilders and christened it Tipsy. Unfortunately, it did not do well. There were many games for children, and also two clowns, Kiki and Koko. During a singing contest I heard a young Indian boy, Ranjit, give a perfect rendering of "Danny Boy."

It seems I spent many hours swimming but also did my daily exercising of Tipsy. Conversing with a young Chinese woman who had been studying music in England, she helped me with my Indonesian pronunciation and told me that Tipsy's kennelmate, the Boxer, was expected to give birth before we reached Djakarta.

By September 11, we were inside the Tropic of Cancer, passing the Canary Islands. Our first sighting of Africa was off Dakar, French West Africa, now Senegal. (Fast forward to the millennium year when we attended the wedding in New York of our dear friend Jack McGrath's daughter, Paula, to Pape, son of the former president of Senegal, Abdou Diouf.)

We had a tour of the bridge and all its latest instruments. Two radar screens had been installed since the *Willem Ruys*'s collision with her sister ship, the *Oranje*. We studied the course plotted for Cape Town.

Next day, we crossed the line. Sixty-two years later, on a Hurtigruten cruise through the fjords of Norway where there was much splashing and hilarity as ice cubes were put down the back of our necks by Neptune as we crossed the Arctic Circle, I was reminded of this first time crossing the equator. We assembled by the swimming pool to greet Neptune and his court, his wife with flaxen rope pigtails, wearing a bedraggled flowered dress. His cohorts sported beards made of string and wore rope skirts. They carried fishes in buckets, shells around their necks. Neptune waved his pitchfork and "baptisms" duly began. Everyone was made to drink sea water and had pink and white shaving soap sloshed all over their faces and clothes, and then some were thrown into the swimming pool, with shoes, watches, and whatever they were wearing.

After we crossed the equator, several people rushed to their cabins to test the bathwater theory, to check whether the water flowed down the drain counterclockwise. Dermot's other theory was that the moon was upside-down east of Suez.

Dermot walked miles around the deck every day, forty-two circuits being five miles. On September 17, there was another gale, the ship pitching like a mad thing. It gave me and Conor a huge appetite, although Betty suffered from seasickness. We were nearly blown away visiting Tipsy in her kennels on the top deck. Often we would be covered in smoky dust after exercising the dogs because the kennels were close to the ship's funnels.

Quoting from my diary, "This morning Dermot and I visited the captain. He told us lots of interesting things: it cost six thousand pounds to go through the Suez Canal. Fuel costs a thousand pounds a day. The ship carries enough food for six months. She has no stabilizers. Atlantic liners are more expensive because they need them but they take up valuable cargo space. The Far East run is considered calm, except for this one time circumnavigation of Africa avoiding the Suez Canal. The Egyptian passengers will be flown from Cape Town at government expense. He has many interesting paintings and books in his suite. He told us stories about petulant princelings, once the Sultan of Johore and the Sultan of Perak sailed on the same voyage but did not speak to each other."

Then there was an announcement for all passengers that Cairo radio had broadcast the news that the *Willem Ruys* had been stranded off the west coast of Africa and all nine hundred passengers and crew had to be rescued by helicopters. Nasser was apparently getting even for our unpaid canal fees. We were told we could send telegrams to loved ones at home that we were safe and well. There was a stampede to the radio room. Later my mother told us she was mystified by the "all's well" telegram. She never doubted for a moment that we were cruising luxuriously toward Indonesia. The term "fake news" had not yet been coined.

On September 19, we saw South Africa about ten miles away. By teatime, we were in Table Bay and could see Cape Town nestling under Table Mountain. There were several peaks and strange trees that looked like men marching up the slopes. The harbor being quite small, we paused outside it to take on the pilot. It was refreshing to see green grass, houses, cars, and roads again. We spent a few hours ashore. I bought a woolly doll, a flag for my new collection, and postcards. We walked and drove around the city, climbing through pine treelined roads, past Kloof Nek to a lookout with a splendid view of the city, with the sea beyond, the rotating beam of a lighthouse and the gray bulk of Table Mountain behind us. We spotted *Willem Ruys* far down below, gaily illuminated. We explored farther along the sea front, drove through Seapoint with its hotels, shops, and homes of rich whites. Hot dog bars seemed to be to Cape Town what coffee bars were to London. There were notices all over that proclaimed, "Europeans Only," this still being the apartheid era.

From Cape Town, we sailed up the east coast of Africa into the Tropic of Capricorn, sighting Mauritius. Ship life continued with fun and games, lots of deck quoits competitions, as well as ping-pong, dances, musical evenings, and harmless flirtations with ship's officers and a few young single male passengers as we sailed toward Colombo and Singapore. I had not expected to revisit Colombo exactly a year later and wrote ecstatically about the spell of the East. We entered the harbor, flying the Dutch, Singalese, pilot's, and doctor's flags, with ships of every size from many nations, a beautiful sunset, local color provided by catamarans. (Visiting Colombo decades later, Ceylon having been Sri Lanka for quite a while, the much larger harbor was filled with giant container ships, which were also colorful, with their multi-colored cargo transporters.)

Having skipped many accounts in my diary of gargantuan meals, it is perhaps worth mentioning the Diner d'Adieu for passengers disembarking in Singapore. We started with lobster mayonnaise in cognac, consommé accompanied by little rolls tied with red ribbon and paillettes dorées. Salmon came next and then goat. Dessert was green ice cream with petits fours in decorated baskets like sheep pens, and white swan meringues. Much champagne was drunk, and in those days, dinner ended with coffee and liqueurs.

The captain made a farewell speech in Dutch and English, and said we could tell our friends we traveled via the Cape because the weather was so bad the Suez Canal froze. Mr. Viruly, my writing critic friend, responded in both languages, saying a speech should be like a woman's skirt, long enough to cover the subject but short enough to be interesting. Sixty-four years later, I realize he was quoting Winston Churchill. Dermot made a good diplomatic speech and told us about Raffles's journey around the Cape and commented on the many albatrosses we saw. An important Indonesian gentleman who had been military attaché in their London embassy made a speech. The Dahlan Djambeks who hailed from Sumatra were known on the ship as the Darling Jumbos. I described Mrs. Djambeks as being like a baby elephant with masses of hair piled on top of her head. She would hardly have been flattered, though I thought she was lovely.

I am amused and appalled by my youthful pomposity and censoriousness. The party continued after dinner with gay abandon and much dancing and drinking. "I left about three a.m. because I did not want to put a damper on the enjoyment of the ambassadors and their wives, and I don't approve of the generations keeping an eye on each other, so after I had seen Mrs. Gordon fall flat on her back while dancing with the captain, I went downstairs and went to bed."

Being back in Singapore briefly was wonderful. I had been so happy there. I saw lots of old friends, and Dermot and Betty were entertained by the Governor Sir Robert and Lady Scott. For the last lap of the journey to Djakarta, the ship was practically empty. It had been rather smoky on the upper deck near the funnels, so Tipsy was given a bath before we disembarked.

There was a yellowish haze over the water, and since early morning, we passed small, wooded islands, several sampans, and small junks called prahus.

We took the pilot on board and steamed slowly through the harbor entrance to the port of Tanjung Priok. It took a long time to tie up and there was a horde of people on the dock, including many members of the press. Our reception committee met us in the library where, now that we were in a Muslim country, only iced water was served. We met Dermot's head of chancery, Mr. Saner, and his wife; the military attaché, Colonel Dunn; the air attaché Wing Commander Roache; and also the Canadian and Australian ambassadors.

We were then driven to the Residence at Number One, Jalan Imam Bonjol. We arrived to find the flag flying. My first impression was of space and coolness. A lovely tree, supposed to be very lucky, spread its tangled roots over the front lawn. The house was white, oblong, with blue shutters and a high roof. There appeared to be six front doors open to a large room used as a dining room. There were two large polished tables, chairs, sideboards, small tables, lamps, and the usual picture of Her Majesty Queen Elizabeth II, another hung in the drawing room.

We found the house full of roses, gladioli, orchids, and other lush tropical flowers arranged in baskets and sent by the American and Canadian ambassadresses. Then we met the servants: Silim, the head boy or bapu; the cook Ali, babu koki; a second boy, Mammud. There were also a jagar, or night watchman; a babu tjutji (wash amah); a babu rumah (housemaid); and two kebons (gardeners), Awi and Djalan.

The garden, though small, was lovely, with lawns back and front; flowering shrubs; white and colored frangipani, called cumbodia here; pink Honolulu creeper; a jacaranda tree with blue flowers; a yellow flowering cassia tree; tree orchids; deep mauve bougainvillea; hibiscus; papaya and banana trees; gardenia; and flame of the forest. Fauna consisted of many birds and butterflies, the latter ranging from small blue to large black with brilliant blue spots on their wings. There were bats at night and ubiquitous mosquitoes, tokehs (geckos), spiders, and centipedes.

The Saudi Arabian legation was next door. Occasionally, we saw beautiful women on the upstairs balcony wearing the latest Paris fashions, but they were never seen out in public. The Canadian ambassador's residence was two doors away and the American's just opposite. On our other side was an attractive Dutch church and manse.

We gradually explored this city of contrasts. Its vast urban sprawl ranged from spacious Dutch colonial buildings on wide, treelined streets, to the dilapidated wharves and ramshackle kampongs (villages), which were really shantytowns along "canals" (euphemism for open sewers). Betty liked to think of it as old Batavia of the Dutch East Indies. Gaily colored betjaks (trishaws) were everywhere, and the roads were always full of street vendors. We enjoyed the balloon man who passed by at teatime squeaking a balloon loudly. There were reputed to be more than fifteen thousand betjaks in Djakarta. The wooden sides depicted garishly colored pictures, ranging from leaping horses and buffaloes to picture-postcard pretty scenery. Until he went back to England before the end of his posting, I had made friends with a young third secretary, Patrick Laver. We often used to ride in a betjak together to Sunday Mass. Mass was usually at the chapel next to the papal nuncio's residence.

Tropical fruit and vegetables were delicious and varied: papaya, sweet potatoes, a bittersweet puree consistency fruit called sirsak (soursop), many kinds of banana, little green limes, eggplant, a fruit that looked like a scaly anteater, mangoes, mangostines, guava pears, and another pear that tasted like toffee. Our first lunch out was at Mr. Wardle-Smith's, a member of the embassy staff. A dish of prawns and mushrooms was followed by venison. Dessert was the natural puree of sirsak, which we grew fond of. Over coffee, we met his parakeet who ate coffee sugar, dead matches, and cigarette ash. We expressed the desire to own a similar bird and to acquire sarongs or batiks, which are worn, like Scottish tartans, to denote a particular family or clan.

We drove around in a Humber, registration plate CD2, known as the hearse. Dermot sat on the right-hand side, and when he was with us, the flag was flying. Plates were changed to CD14, Dermot being the most recent ambassador, whereas his predecessor, Oscar Morland, had been the second-most senior member of the corps diplomatique. When Dermot was not with us, the flag was rolled up. During the following months, this official car broke down several times and seemed to be falling apart. As Dermot said, it was more suited to being driven from Grosvenor Square to Buckingham Palace than on Javanese mountain roads.

Shortly after our arrival, we had the first of many servant panics. Mammud failed to show up, saying his little brother had died, and the new cook disappeared, supposedly sick. Embassy staff members were full of depressing tales of servants trying to murder each other and robbing their employers. We suspected the trouble was that they were all scared of the Number One boy, so they stayed away. Dermot's third secretary, Patrick Laver's boy, was actually knifed, and Dermot and Betty's predecessors, the Morlands, were apparently robbed of thousands of pounds worth of jewelry.

For our first weekend away from the city, we drove through the suburbs of Djakarta, neat beds of spider lily giving way to hibiscus, rice paddies, and rubber plantations. Rambutans grew on trees like tropical mulberries. We passed many deep canals, relics of Dutch colonial days, but as we drove further into the country, these became fast-flowing and occasionally rocky torrents. Alongside the road were attap houses nestled among banana and nipa palms, neatly cultivated groves of tapioca, sago, and pineapple. We saw several "walking walla," men carrying attap for the walls of their houses over their shoulders so that only their feet showed. Village names flashed by, Tjisalag, Tjibinong, and others. Soon we reached the picturesque old town Bogor, up in the hills. It appeared peaceful and slightly dilapidated.

We drove past the residence of the former governors general. We were told an amusing anecdote about former Dutch governors, who sat drinking gin on the verandah staring at the flagpole. When they saw two, it was time to go inside for lunch. At this time, it was a vacation home for President Sukarno and one of his wives lived there more or less permanently, situated in a wooded park filled with deer, including majestic stags.

Bogor was colorful, with fruit vendors and women wearing bright sarongs, some carrying babies wrapped in batiks on their hips. The Botanical Gardens were exotic in their tropical splendor. I was fascinated by the pitcher plants, the handkerchief plants, a pandanus tree with roots sticking out of its trunk, a jade tree with snapdragon-like hanging flowers, chemical green and quite unreal. A lizard darted about, with a breathing hole in the side of its face. We stopped to buy Escort cigarettes for the police when they came to call socially.

After almost two hours of driving into the mountains where attap houses gave way to sturdier, brightly painted stone ones, we arrived at our Villa Soulaes, situated among other embassy- and bank-owned bungalows. Our bungalow belonged to the ambassador, but he shared it with his staff. We were greeted by Jussuf, with a large floppy umbrella, who led us to a comfortable, simply furnished room where a rather smoky fire was burning, before supper of canned salmon, but we were too famished to complain. The smoky fire reminded Dermot of his youth at Coolavin, and he expected a dead rook or two to fall down the chimney. The beds, plain wooden boards covered with light mattresses, were surprisingly comfortable. It was cool enough for blankets and closed windows.

The secluded garden was delightful. A tiny mountain stream ran through a terraced lawn: rose bushes grew under banana palms. Begonias grew wild and were also cultivated. Dark-leaved cannas grew beside michaelmas daisies, lantana, lilies, and red salvia. Bougainvillea grows everywhere in the tropics, but we were surprised to find bright blue morning glories. We discovered a small, thin snake about two feet long in the grass early in the morning.

We had drinks with the American ambassador, his wife, and various guests at their bungalow. The décor consisted of Chinese masks, batik cloths, and fish kites on the walls. There were three American bungalows; a Mr. Palmer owned the one with the swimming pool, and he hired a gamelan orchestra to play every Sunday.

Next day, we breakfasted early and went for a two-and-a-half-hour walk through tea plantations. Shiny green shoulder-high bushes covered the hillsides as far as one could see. Passing through the factory where tea leaves were being dried by fans on huge conveyor belts, we visited a nearby kampong, or village, where sarong-clad women sat in front of their houses, some feeding their babies, as cheerful children swarmed round us. We took a winding path hugging the side of a hill and were rewarded with a magnificent view of the surrounding mountains and villages; a large volcano loomed in front of us, another behind.

On our way back to Djakarta, we visited the Canadian ambassador and Mrs. Heasman in the village of Megamendung. We had a refreshing swim in their pool and admired their house and garden, especially the gold, blue, and gray carp in their fishpond. They grew bananas, oranges, grapefruit, limes, lemons, pineapples, coconuts, mangoes, avocadoes, and many other fruits. The countryside looked almost artificial as the sun set between rainstorms, producing a technicolor rainbow against a backdrop of improbable brown and purple clouds. The palm trees appeared to be floodlit, the whole sky a kaleidoscope, one moment bright orange, scarlet, or silver-bordered clouds, the next a shimmering cloth of gold.

October 18: pomp and circumstance. Three senior staff and the military attaché, resplendent in King's Own Scottish Borderers ceremonial dress with lots of braids and tassels, accompanied Dermot, who looked very distinguished wearing his white hat and sword. He rode in a limousine, registration Indonesia 1, with the president's aide-de-camp. The following news bulletin appeared in Pers Biro, Indonesia:

> Newly appointed British Ambassador to Indonesia, Dermot Francis MacDermot presented his credentials to Vice President Mohammed Hatta at the Merdeka Palace on Wednesday afternoon.
>
> The British Ambassador in his address said that since the beginning of the exchange of diplomatic relations between the British Kingdom (!) and the Republic of Indonesia six years ago, the relationship and friendship between the British and Indonesian people have always been cordial and full of mutual understanding.
>
> In his reply Vice President Hatta said that "since the beginning of the exchange of diplomatic relations between both countries Indonesia feels that Britain has the fullest understanding of and adjusted itself to the developments which have taken place at a quick rate in all fields in all Asia in general and in South East Asia in particular since the end of the last World War.

"This policy is one of the reasons that no principal difficulties have been encountered by the British diplomatic representation in Indonesia in maintaining good relations with the Government.

"On this ground," he concluded, "I am therefore convinced that you will always get support from the Indonesian Government in performing your noble task as British Ambassador."

Things turned out somewhat differently, although the government considerately gave due warning about what was to happen and, in doing so, probably saved lives.

# Chapter Five

Djakarta has come a long way since the thirteenth century, when it was a large garden owned by the sultan of Bantam. In the sixteenth century, the Dutch landed there to set up the Commercial Company of the Dutch East Indies. The sultan was alarmed and called in the British. However, they were not strong enough to overcome the Dutch, who set fire to their commercial outpost, razed the town to the ground, and eventually built the city of Batavia. The Dutch colonists survived the malaria epidemic of 1725 but massacred the Chinese in 1740. Only 150 survived out of nine thousand. Indonesia declared independence on August 17, 1945, but it took four years of diplomacy and armed struggle till it was formally granted by Queen Juliana of the Netherlands. When we arrived, President Sukarno and Vice President Hatta were still in charge of the Republic of Indonesia, and Batavia had been renamed Djakarta.

An anonymous writer in 1830 described the inhabitants as follows: "The Javanese are remarkable for their unsuspecting credulity. Hospitality is universal. It is enjoined by the most ancient institutions, and practiced with readiness and zeal. They are extremely sensible to praise or shame." Loss of face is humiliating, which explains why, when Betty asked Silim for Horlicks, he brought Bovril, hot chocolate, and finally the correct article for my inspection rather than admit ignorance. "They are ambitious of power and distinction, but they are more remarkable for passive fortitude than active courage and endure privations with patience, rather than make exertions.... The home of a Malay [Javanese people are Malays] is not a fortress against the elements, but a cool retreat where sheltered from the sun, in the hours of his ease he may chew the betel of happiness in somnolent content."

A Javanese saying goes, "Fire is hot, and the sun hotter still, but neither is to be compared to the heat of a man's heart."

The Indonesian archipelago has the largest Muslim population in the world. Small numbers of Buddhists, Hindus, and Christians coexist peacefully.

We settled into a routine. Unfortunately, Betty sometimes did not feel well, so Dermot asked me to take on many of her duties, learning enough of the Bahasa language to deal with the servants, and unlock necessary supplies each morning. If there was a diplomatic dinner at our residency, I was often responsible for the seating plan, according to the protocol book. Seniority depended on length of time in the post of ambassador, not the importance of the country. Unfortunately, amebic dysentery was endemic throughout the international diplomatic community, and guests were inclined to cancel at short notice. This meant reassigning places at the table for up to as many as twenty guests. I was often the de facto acting ambassadress at eighteen, too young to be sufficiently scared by the responsibility.

During daytime office hours, after dealing with the residence staff and allocating food requirements for the day's meals, sometimes involving a diplomatic lunch or more likely dinner, I worked in the consulate for Peter Lake, the consul. The biggest challenge was trying to locate all British subjects residing in Indonesia in case of an emergency evacuation. We managed to research and prepare a remarkably comprehensive list, quite an achievement in that pre-internet, pre-Google era.

It was daunting at first, but I learned Foreign Office procedure. Notes to other embassies and to the Ministry of Foreign Affairs usually began, "Her Majesty's Embassy for Great Britain and Northern Ireland present their compliments to the Ministry of Foreign Affairs for the Republic of Indonesia and have the honor to request . . ." They usually included something fairly trivial like, "Why did you not tell us so-and-so was in prison?" I was required to type "unclassified" and "confidential" reports, stamp visas, and do the filing. Peter Lake dictated letters to me about many subjects: Poppy Day, seamen attempting to desert, requesting a birth certificate for a British subject from a seminary in Bangalore, detaining someone from Aden, refusing visas and passports, and so on.

As time went on, I became fascinated by life in Djakarta and its people. There were the tukangs, itinerant workmen or vendors, who balanced bamboo poles on their shoulders, carrying their wares or tools of their trade. The glass tukang struck a musical note on his frame of glasses, and I've already mentioned the balloon tukang who squeezed a balloon squeakily.

Indonesians were superstitious by nature. They would never kill a tokeh, or gecko, the ubiquitous nocturnal lizard. These little creatures are supposed to protect people in their houses, but desert them if death hovers over the dwelling. Apparently people bet on the number of times one chirps "tokeh" as the Chinese bet on the "doc doc" birds. With the latter, five times means happiness, seven times wealth, and generally, uneven numbers are deemed lucky.

Social events often included attending evenings of Balinese dancing to gamelan orchestras. (Sixty years later, I still cherish a set of tiny musicians with their instruments carved out of wood in my East Hampton bedroom.) Musicians sat cross-legged on the ground, never needing a score sheet. Percussion instruments are called genders and sarons. These were large xylophones fastened onto sound boxes of carved and painted wood. More primitive xylophones, composed of a dozen or more pieces of bamboo of varying lengths, called gambangs, were less shrill than the genders. Behind them sat cymbal and flute players, also kettle drum players, bonangs, and kedangs, the latter covered in buffalo hide.

Besides the traditional Balinese and Javanese male and female dancers with which readers are probably familiar, I was fascinated by a monster known as the Barong, manipulated by two men inside its huge body covered with human hair and quantities of sparkling mirrors and gilt baubles. It reminded me of a gargantuan Pekingese dog, its tail soaring skyward, adorned with tiny gold bells, the tip sprouting a bunch of cock feathers. Its head was a wooden mask, with huge protruding blood red eyes and jaws that opened and shut incessantly. It sported a magnificent beard of human hair, strewn with flowers, trailing to the ground. The Barong was often accompanied by the Rangda, more human and female, embodying evil, illness, and death. She had eyes like billiard balls, huge chalk-white fangs, and hair falling to the ground. Her nails were about ten inches long and, according to legend, she used them to disinter freshly buried bodies. Around her neck dangled the entrails of the corpses she had devoured. Her breasts hung to her waist, and her tongue reached to her knees. She waved a white rag with evil properties, supposedly bringing death to anyone who touched it.

One weekend, bandits in the Puntjak made various rioting sorties, and several bungalows were attacked. One British businessman who was robbed at gunpoint said his greatest sorrow was losing all his whiskey. One guard, when reprimanded, replied, "Well, I was asleep at the front, so how could I be expected to know what was going on at the back of the house!" It was suggested that owing to the absence of Mr. Palmer's Saturday night film show, which the bandits liked to watch from the other side of the hedge, they returned to banditry for want of anything better to do.

On October 23, Field Marshall Sir William Slim, governor general of Australia, passed through Djakarta on his way to Australia. Dermot complained that the only drink offered during the reception was orange squash. The following day, he hosted a lunch for the New Zealand ambassador. One lady turned up unexpectedly and, upon requesting the bathroom, was ushered to the men's room, which was full of badminton equipment and no soap.

In the evenings when not on duty at our dinners or when Dermot needed me to take Betty's place, I went out on dates, often for Scottish dancing. Sometimes in the late afternoons, I played field hockey in mixed teams with large Dutch, British, and Australian young men. There was also tennis on the American ambassador's court or at the Box Club. Living almost on the equator, we must have been quite mad, but we were young and considered ourselves immortal and indefatigable.

It was obvious soon after we arrived that Conor did not need much nannying. He and his mother were always very close.

Betty, with her lifelong love of birds and flowers, her collections of butterflies and shells, instilled in Conor an appreciation of nature, which in all likelihood led to his later career in geology.

One evening, Dermot and Betty went to dine with the local head of Royal Dutch Shell. When it was time to leave, the car would not start. It had run out of gas, which was ironic, considering who their hosts were.

We had been in Djakarta a month before the threat of war caught up with us. Our weekend at the bungalow was canceled because Dermot needed to be in the city, and because of the bandits, it probably would not have been safe anyway. British and Israeli planes were bombing Suez, Cairo, and Ismailia after issuing an order to cease fighting, which the Egyptians ignored. The French and the British lacked supporters. The Australians abstained from voting, the Americans and the Russians were against us. The French ambassador asked for police protection. Most governments expressed disapproval of British action except for M. Potier, the Portuguese minister, who telephoned Dermot to congratulate him. British ships were boycotted, as were British businesses.

A state of emergency did not yet exist, but we were on high alert, senior staff on around-the-clock duty. Although I had not yet officially received security clearance, Peter Lake gave me confidential letters to type and asked me to prepare envelopes for all the British residents in readiness to mail warnings in case of evacuation. Miss Martin in the consular office wondered if she would be able to leave for Holland after all. Her previous unsuccessful attempt was at the beginning of World War II.

On November 5, Britain, France, and Israel invaded Egypt. Dermot had a friendly visit to the Ministry of Foreign Affairs that morning. A demonstration was threatened for Wednesday, so he canceled his lunch at the Chamber of Commerce.

Our residency being next door to the legation for Saudi Arabia, we considered seeking refuge there because no Indonesian Muslim would attack the premises of another Middle Eastern Muslim state.

Meanwhile, Betty continued with diplomatic visits, calling on the wife of the Belgian chargé d'affaires, the Japanese ambassador's wife, American and Canadian embassy wives, also Madame Potier of the Portuguese legation and Madame Amin, wife of the Iraqi minister. Dermot declined a reception at the embassy of the USSR because he did not approve of the Russian invasion of Hungary.

On November 7, the residency was a hive of activity starting at 6:30 a.m., with the servants shutting doors and locking cupboards. We were driven to the Saners' house, and as we crossed the railway bridge, we saw truckloads of demonstrators waving banners and shouting pro-Egypt slogans. From the safety of the Saners' house, we could hear shouts and the occasional gunshot. It transpired that an offshoot group from the rally stormed the Box Club, breaking windows, raiding the bar, throwing stones, and smashing the back window of our Humber car, which had been left there. Oddly enough, the rioters who tore down the queen's picture did not damage the light above it, nor the radio on which they stood to remove it.

Mrs. Dunn came around before lunch, having held her English class despite the riots, and surprisingly, all her Indonesian students turned up. The staff guarding the chancery described a scary fifteen minutes during the morning with only seven police officers to protect them until reinforcements turned up.

During the crisis, embassy staff had to cope with a dearth of telephone lines. It was necessary to keep in touch with the prime minister's office in London, the Indonesian Ministry of Foreign Affairs, government and military headquarters in Singapore, the police, and distraught British subjects. At the height of the emergency, the secretary to the head of the Standard Chartered Bank phoned to accept a black-tie dinner invitation at the residence.

The hero of the hour was a relatively lowly local employee, Joseph, who rushed to put out the fire in the British Information Services building with his bare hands.

The English-language daily reported as follows:

> Tens of thousands of demonstrators stormed the British Information Service offices here, burned books and magazines, destroyed furniture and other equipment, protesting the armed aggression launched by Britain, France and Israel against Egypt.

> At the same time, another group of demonstrators attempted to force their way into the home of the French Ambassador Jean Brionval, but failed as the house was strongly guarded by security forces.

> At the British Embassy, demonstrators hauled down the British Union Jack and in its place hoisted the Indonesian red and white flag. Many Europeans riding in their cars were booed and pelted with stones by the demonstrators. Three who were pursued by an angry mob took shelter

in the Seventh Infantry Regiment headquarters. It was learned that Abdulkadir, believed to be the instigator of the assault on the British Information Services was arrested by the police.

Earlier this morning the demonstrators attended a mass rally organized by the Support Egypt Committee with the Egyptian Ambassador presiding. The feelings of the crowd were aroused by the speeches delivered by representatives of youth, workers, students and women who all condemned the Anglo French attacks. The wrath of the Indonesian people against this wanton action was expressed by the burning of Prime Minister Anthony Eden in effigy.

In fact, we were subsequently told that most of the demonstrators formed part of a rent-a-crowd who were paid a pittance of five rupiahs for the day. So much for militant anti-imperialism.

We returned to the residence later in the afternoon to discover that all the servants with the exception of Ali and one babu, Anna, had run away in terror. The house was being guarded by seven or eight policemen.

His Excellency (Dermot) called on the prime minister and Mr. Subandrio to register a strong protest, demanding assurance of organized police protection. Apparently they were very contrite and claimed it was all an unfortunate mistake.

At 6:30 p.m., the rest of the servants returned, grinning from ear to ear.

From then on, guards were provided at the residence, and it was my job to provide them with cigarettes. During dinner that evening, the Portuguese minister, M. Potier, a rather portly gentleman, came striding up the drive and into the house, announcing that he wanted to congratulate Dermot in person, saying England was Portugal's oldest ally, and at this moment, probably its only supporter. After dinner, Dermot dictated a telegram addressed to the prime minister, Sir Anthony Eden, which I typed and gave to the appropriate telegraph operator for encryption and transmission to London, describing the day's events, a heady experience for an eighteen-year-old.

Three weeks later, Peter Lake dictated a letter addressed to the Right Honorable Selwyn Lloyd, C.B.E., M.P., Her Majesty's Secretary of State, about Mr. Joseph's bravery putting out the fire in the information building during the riots, his subsequent threats of reprisals, and requesting for him the protection of a British passport in spite of his birth certificate being untraceable in Rangoon and all other records at the Batavia consulate general having been destroyed by enemy action during the Japanese occupation. Later, he dictated a long letter to Admiral Scott-Moncrieff about accommodating a wartime naval control of shipping at all Indonesian ports. This did not happen, although there had been a brief boycott on shipping arriving from or destined for Britain. Airlines QANTAS and BOAC (predecessor of British Airways) refused to fly into Djakarta for a short while.

It seemed strange to hear about our dramas on Radio Australia and the BBC next day, and that Lord Reading had protested to the Indonesian Embassy in London. Otherwise, life was peaceful, and the police continued to lounge about on the premises, consuming large quantities of coffee, sugar, beer, biscuits, soda, tonic, and cigarettes.

Later, we inspected the wreck of the information services building. Conor salvaged a film about aircraft, and we all helped ourselves to souvenir cartridge cases. It looked a mess with papers and glass all over the place, lots of broken furniture, and, incongruously, the leg of a chair stuck in a wall eight feet above the ground. Otherwise, except for no flag (the Indonesians had taken measurements and patterns for a new one), life was back to normal.

I was personally disappointed during this period of British unpopularity that for several weeks we were not allowed to play tennis on the American embassy's court.

The consul, Peter Lake, was cool, stern, disapproving, and as disobliging as possible without actually being rude, and he insisted on seeing personally any Indonesian who wanted a visa. When the wife of Indonesia's most famous painter arrived, she was subjected to the same treatment.

Life in Djakarta during the rainy season continued. Her Majesty's government paid me a salary as a local employee in Indonesian rupiahs plus rice money for working at the consulate for Peter Lake. I asked Dermot to reduce my pay as Conor's nanny/governess since he was at school all day. In the late afternoon, we continued to play field hockey in steamy downpours, with the field under water up to one's ankles, against mostly large Dutch men, often followed by Scottish dancing after dinner. Weather permitting, we played tennis and went sailing. Ken, who worked for the US Secret Service, took me to the Indonesian Yacht Club at Tanjong Priok, which is called Pulau Seribu, meaning a thousand islands. We sailed a small gaff-rigged Dutch boat up and down the harbor twice; tricky winds but most enjoyable.

A weekend off from minding Conor was pleasantly spent at a villa in Megamendung with a young embassy staff member, Kim, eating, drinking, and winning at blackjack at another bungalow with Australians who worked for QANTAS, their national airline. The next day, Kim and I took photos of little boys wearing large coolie hats and riding water buffaloes, played tennis, and swam in the Royal Dutch Shell pool.

One day, Peter Lake was not feeling well, so he left the office early, asking me to cancel their dinner party for that evening. I suspected the real reason might have been that their principal servant had just walked off the job, leaving his wife for another woman. He also asked me to continue delving into the files of British subjects in Indonesia for accounts of their brave exploits during the Japanese occupation. For instance, a Mr. Plaschek had been decorated with the King's Medal for Courage "for displaying a man's courage at the age of sixteen."

My natural curiosity and girlish sense of adventure, with talk of revolution brewing in Sumatra, I longed to meet a real, live guerilla leader. At a party just before Christmas, I met an intriguing Dutchman, Mr. Burgher. His wife was writing books and spent most of the evening talking to John Stirling of *The Observer*. Mr. Burgher teased me that at my age I could not possibly find ambassadors interesting, despite my protests. He allowed, however, that my job was great experience for one so young and obviously ambitious. To make my life more exciting, he offered to introduce me to Colonel Lubis, leader of the Sumatran rebels, and claimed to be among a small minority who knew where the rebel leader was hiding, and that the Indonesian government was too frightened to arrest him. He further boasted that he would be among the few to obtain a permit to visit the Achinese, who were also trying to claim their independence (and still are, sixty-four years later) as he was an intimate friend of the chief princeling. He described Djakarta as "the pot that simmered but never boiled."

That evening's news, December 22, announced that revolution was spreading throughout northern and central Sumatra, the army in place was refusing to acknowledge the government in Djakarta, and Mr. Abdulgany was being arrested for corruption. Dermot was supposed to meet him at an Indonesian Foreign Ministry party that evening. Mr. Subandrio, the secretary general, Indonesia's counterpart to our Foreign Secretary, Sir Ivone Kirkpatrick, had been friendly recently, having apparently forgiven the Brits for the Middle East crisis.

Setting the simmering rebellion in Sumatra aside, the independence movement having subsided though travel to the area was restricted due to occasional guerilla uprisings, duty called me to oversee Christmas preparations and forego sailing with Ken, my Secret Service friend.

# Chapter Six

Expatriates the world over share a nostalgia for home, especially at times of national festivals. Aspiring to lead the third world, Indonesia struggled with corruption and chaos in the late fifties, the last years of President Sukarno's power. Living and working in an overpopulated Asian country known for its active volcanoes, batiks, wood carvings, puppets, and ineffectual government, foreign diplomats and businesspeople did their determined best to produce a traditional Christmas—in our case, an English one.

Odd little things reminded me of the festive season, such as the sight of millions of stars in a clear sky, the silhouette of the Dutch church across the street, colored lights winking from the street below, Christmas hymns issuing from the church, and shoppers on the Pasar Baru busy with last-minute purchases.

The residence was festooned with many Christmas cards to Dermot and Betty from all over the world. Ali, aided by the other servants, including Ali Koki, the number one cook, spent three days jumping enthusiastically on ladders to put up decorations as instructed by those peculiar ferengi (foreigners). There were crepe paper bows and friezes everywhere, garlands hanging from the walls and the chandeliers, blue and pink candles on the sideboard, and small artificial Christmas trees adorned with tinsel. There was an excess of crepe paper around the chandeliers, but we did not interfere, not wanting to hurt any feelings. There was a willowy local conifer, a casuarina, in the middle of the little drawing room, gaily adorned with colored tinsel balls. Ali cut out little silvery stars from the lids of cookie tins, which glittered on the trees or formed part of the wall decorations. In addition to the Christmas decorations, we enjoyed typical English fare: crystallized dates, figs, walnuts, candy, cookies, and oranges, and looked forward to Christmas pudding and mince pies.

On Christmas Eve, with other embassy staff and their wives, we drove to Bogor and the Puntjak. While waiting to collect Leonard Forman—the botanist from Kew, currently with the Bogor Botanical Gardens and our guest for Christmas—as dusk fell, we spotted flying foxes as well as the Raja of Perlis entering his presidential palace. The Puntjak, shrouded in its usual mist and cloud cover, was seasonably alpine with its chalet-like houses and people out buying Christmas trees. Hard to believe we were in the tropics and so close to the equator. On the way back, we bought masses of flowers, large daisies, orchids, and also white chrysanthemums and gladioli for the chapel's midnight Mass. Leonard bought flowers to be delivered tomorrow, red and white chrysanthemums, Indonesia's national colors, and also bulrushes.

That evening, we wrapped presents before going to midnight Mass, offered by the papal nuncio, including gifts for all the servants of assorted sweets and nuts and two weeks' extra pay. We must have been exhausted by the time we all went to bed.

Conor got us all up at seven thirty to open the presents under the tree. Several Balinese wooden carvings were exchanged (I received two water buffaloes), along with paintings, jewelry, sandalwood fans, etc. Conor was given construction sets, a student's microscope, and books. Leonard gave me a lovely batik, the kind Indonesian women use to carry their babies on their hips. I gave Dermot a cigarette box. He smoked three packs of Chesterfields a day until he died well into his eighties. He gave Betty a gold watch, ostensibly from Tipsy, the spaniel. Some gifts of books and cosmetics ordered from England were delivered by diplomatic bag.

Traditional Christmas lunch was a great success, despite the stifling equatorial temperature and 100 percent humidity. We tucked into our customary turkey, bread sauce, chestnut dressing, and hot vegetables; washed down with heavy claret; followed by Christmas pudding, brandy butter, mince pies, and assorted tropical fruits; accompanied by champagne and liqueurs, all perfectly prepared and served by our Indonesian household staff. Conor found most of the coins concealed in the plum pudding. The old-style punka swayed gently back and forth above the dining room table, providing the lightest of breezes. A small, wizened Sundanese woman seated behind an ornamental screen controlled the fan by a cord tied to her big toe.

In the evening, Dermot hosted a black-tie party for the embassy staff. Guests arrived looking tanned and rested after the Christmas holidays. At the end of dinner, Mr. Saner toasted Dermot, Betty, and Conor, and Dermot responded. Then we all moved next door for the queen's speech. She stressed the importance of Christmas as a family feast and the need to welcome refugees to Britain. After that, the dancing commenced. The festive season continued the next day with a children's party for

Conor, attended by the children from other embassies and the international community.

We went to the bungalow on New Year's Day. We thought we had bought steak for lunch, but after it had been neatly wrapped in a banana leaf and tied with raffia, we saw the severed head of a water buffalo in a corner of the shop and made the obvious connection. Indeed, it was tough and tasteless.

Sapri, the chauffeur, left us with four months' salary to go to the hospital for tuberculosis treatment and was now pestering us to pay for treatment for his number-two wife. It later transpired that in several cases, Dermot paid servants' medical expenses out of his own pocket, a gesture of incredible generosity.

In post-colonial Indonesia, the Dutch were still running most commercial enterprises. Soon after Christmas, Dermot, Conor, and I left Djakarta (Betty elected to stay at the residence), driving through rice paddies and swampy forests, with a backdrop of the Gede, Salak, and Pangrango mountain ranges silhouetted against the morning sky, watching people bathing themselves and their clothes in the river, children riding water buffaloes and bullocks, crossing the river on rickety bridges, observing that in one place where a bridge was being constructed, they actually were diverting the river to flow under it.

When we reached Tjekampek, Dermot, Conor, and I accompanied Mr. Van Der Struys, the Dutch manager of the sisal factory at the Sukamandi estate, along with Mr. Mackay, a director of Anglo-Indonesian plantations visiting from London. We drove in jeeps to the sisal factory and the tapioca processing plant, which was being reconstructed after being damaged by the Japanese during World War II. At the sisal factory, fiber is extracted from the porcupine-like plant by machine, then goes through several washings and drying until it achieves a deceptively silky-looking appearance, and is compressed into two-hundred-kilogram bales for shipment to England, America, Germany, and Australia. Ninety-six percent of the sisal harvested is recycled as malodorous manure.

During the war, many planters were interned, and their Japanese captors were unable to keep the factories and plantations going, but worse damage was done by the Indonesians during their struggle for independence in 1949.

We stayed at the Big House in Subang, which boasted fourteen bedrooms and had a lovely garden. There were giant hibiscuses, yellow, orange, pink, and white bougainvillea, and several heavy-scented frangipani. There was a grass tennis court and a swimming pool in a hollow, reached through rubber trees, where gibbon apes hung out, but we did not see any that day. Teak trees grew alongside Cinchona trees, from which quinine was extracted. At that time, 90 percent of the world's consumption of quinine came from Java, but it was a dying industry due to manufacture from synthetics.

On the Monday morning, we visited the Tambaram Prahu volcano, the fourth largest in the world. We looked down into the smoking and hissing crater from which sulfurous fumes emanated. We inspected the Kawah Ratu, or Queen's Crater. "ASIA AFRICA CONFERENCE 1956" was written in stones on the crater floor. After buying postcards and lava ashtrays, we left when it got cold and cloudy.

On the way down, we called on the Cheriexs, a handsome Dutch couple who treated us to coffee with fresh milk and meringues. Mr. Cheriex was the manager of the Tjiater tea estate and factory. A rather gruesome discussion took place over coffee. Many inhabitants apparently were undergoing an unpleasant series of injections to counteract bites by rabid animals. A man drove over a kampong pi-dog that bit him, and apparently he died "the most horrible death imaginable" within six months. We were also told that estate managers and assistants were rotated at regular intervals to prevent breakdowns resulting from isolation from other Europeans. This reminded me of a Dutch short story set in a remote Indonesian island. A government inspector was sent from Amsterdam to investigate a feud between a postmaster and a customs officer, which had been going on for years by mail. It turned out that the same lonely civil servant occupied both positions and was writing letters to himself.

We watched the tea pickers, who were all women, wearing brightly colored sarongs and working rapidly and methodically in rows. Then we were shown the factory where the green leaves were unloaded from trucks then taken by elevators to lofts where they were dried for twelve hours, after which they were brought down, rolled in high humidity, sorted into rough or fine leaves, fermented for an hour and a half, then passed on trays through drying furnaces for eighteen minutes at two hundred degrees. They were sorted again by women who used the same graceful and rhythmic movements employed for sorting rice. The tea was then packed into chests lined with tinsel from Germany and compressed into wooden boxes from Sweden. These were weighed, sealed, and stenciled to be sold on the Djakarta market, where much speculation was engaged in by Chinese brokers. The tea was mostly exported to Ireland, and Lipton's was reputed to buy large quantities of Java tea.

There were further visits to factories, plantations, and staff dinner parties before returning to Djakarta. Our last visit was to the local hospital—small, modern, cool, and clean, with just over a hundred beds. Indonesian trainee nurses were supervised by a European matron. In the maternity ward, the doctor wanted to present me with a newborn triplet. Twins and triplets were considered unlucky here. The custom still existed that if the twins were a mixed pair, they must marry one another.

Fast forward to 2020 during the coronavirus pandemic. This morning's news reported that in order to enforce social distancing in Indonesia, the authorities, preying on national superstitiousness, sent people dressed as ghosts into the streets to scare people into going home. Apparently, the policy was not successful. Twenty-first-century Indonesians are unfazed by the fake ghosts.

The duck herders of Subang were usually young boys or old men unfit for other work. They drove their ducks from village to village, and at night constructed a miniature padang, or pen, wherever they happened to stop. In the morning, the eggs lain during the night were sold, and the herders moved on through the rice fields where the ducks foraged for food.

After our return from Subang, Tipsy gave birth. My journal did not mention her pregnancy or who the father might have been. Having taken Conor to the children's movie at the Box Club, we came back to the residence to find that Tipsy had delivered a little black puppy on my bedroom floor but was shrinking away from it in horror and trying to hide under the bed. Conor and I installed a whelping area and attended the accouchements of the rest of the puppies, born without apparent difficulty. The second, a rather repulsive pink creature, was born just before Dermot and Betty left for dinner at the American ambassador's residence next door. Dermot came home briefly for the arrival of number three, almost pink with two black ears and a black tail. The fourth was born just before they came home, a piebald puppy, and the fifth and last just before midnight. Gradually, Tipsy became a good mother. The vet called a couple of weeks later to have a look at mother and puppies, and prescribed some postnatal care, notably pills to counteract a vitamin deficiency. Four days after their birth, it was the ambassador himself who took the puppies to have their tails docked, as was the custom for Cocker Spaniels. According to my diary, it seems I had grown attached to the one that was born a hairless pink and was now golden.

Sometime in February, I wrote the following letter to my mother.

> I've been burning the candle at both ends and in the middle. I had to give up my bedroom to Sir Harold and Lady Nicholson (remember when you and I and Robert saw Lady N, digging in her garden at Sissinghurst Castle?) which I did not mind doing because they were the most wonderful guests and we all loved having them. I was thrilled to be in the company of two famous authors, one also being a well-known politician. We toasted their son at dinner to celebrate his election to Parliament. Sir Harold is an absolutely adorable old man with lots of curly hair and bald in the middle. He told us he refused to shed his woolly underwear even in the tropics. She is exactly how I imagined Vita Sackville-West would be, very keen about gardening, wore rather old-fashioned straw hats and bought lots of pottery and baskets. [A historical note: Sir Harold Nicholson had rented his house, Long Barn, to Charles and Anne Lindbergh in the 1930s when the Lindberghs left America after

the murder of their son, which they attributed to being hounded by the media, a situation that had made their lives unbearable. Anne Morrow claimed these were the two happiest years of her life. Sir Harold encouraged her to write novels, which were successful.]

On Friday morning we took them to a factory and watched the fascinating process of creating batik. An artist outlined a pattern onto the cotton fabric, usually geometric patterns drawn from memory. Using a jantung or special pen containing hot wax, the artist then went over every line of the original drawing. The process of putting on the wax, dyeing the cloth, re-waxing and re-dyeing continued till every bit of fabric was covered with color. The pattern was then imprinted with a heavy copper stamp (which would make a fine doorstop or teapot stand), as well as being very ornamental. Twice a day the batik is hung out to dry in the sun and takes up to twenty days to complete. Tens of thousands work in the batik industry in South Java.

In honor of our distinguished visitors, the orchid house was open. Being in Bogor's famous botanical gardens, Lady Nicholson thought she had died and gone to heaven. Every visit was special, and this time we saw every imaginable orchid: scorpions, lady's slippers, moon orchids, those antler-like ones whose name I have forgotten, and many others. We were each presented with sprays and I was able to wear a different corsage for the next three evenings. There were many weird cacti and other succulents. We walked beside the large pond covered with Victoria Regina lilies, whose giant floating lily pads with vertical sides reminded Lady Nicholson of Japanese lacquered serving dishes. We showed the Nicholsons the lipstick palm so called because of its bright red stems, known in Singapore as the Sealing Wax Palm, also the giant Jade tree and the Liver Sausage tree. We visited a hot house with more exotic plants and tanks of tropical fish. Happily, a picnic lunch which I had organized was a great success. That evening we took them down to old Batavia and the fish market which intrigued them; they looked at lots of shells, stuffed fish and baskets.

Dermot, Conor and I after our return to Djakarta attended a reception at the airport celebrating a Twin Pioneer plane from Scottish Aviation. We were taken up for a trial flight. It was a splendid little plane, but quite alarming as it took off and landed almost vertically, stalled on purpose in mid-air and flew on one engine.

I was in charge of the planning for an Anglo Portuguese dinner to celebrate the Queen's visit to Portugal. Dermot and the Minister from the Portuguese Legation made speeches. [At that time, in addition to embassies and consulates, there were legations, headed by a minister who outranked a consul but was in turn outranked by an ambassador.]

You will be amused by the "affaire chicblind." Our new awnings (chicblinds) finally arrived from the docks for the drawing room windows. When we questioned the delay, we were told the port authorities wanted to know why we were importing blind chickens, and where were the vet certificates!

On February 21, I was running a fever and did not go to work, nor did I play squash the next day. According to my diary written much later, I remember nothing further for several days. When Dermot checked my room on the 23rd to tell me the car was ready to take me to the hospital for a dysentery checkup, he found me red hot, eyes rolling, and completely delirious. An ambulance took me to the KPM (Royal Dutch Shell) Hospital at Petamburan, where I had to be tied to my bed by my wrists and ankles. Dr. Schaafsma did a lumbar puncture and discovered I had a subarachnoid hemorrhage and was in a coma for three days. This was my first miraculous escape from death (not counting not being torpedoed)—the next one did not happen until 2019. Most brain aneurysms are fatal.

Treatment required complete rest and immobility. Much later, while I was still in the hospital, Dr. Schaafsma, who treated most of the embassy personnel in Djakarta, told me that he had a premonition while having supper with his wife that I needed to go to the hospital a day earlier than scheduled, so he rang Dermot that evening and said I should be ready to go next morning. There had been plans to go to the bungalow that weekend. The drive to the mountain would have certainly killed me.

There is a curious twist to the story of Dr. Schaafsma, loved and respected by all his patients in the embassies and legations. It transpired that he had never actually completed his medical training to become a doctor. He was interned during the war and treated his fellow internees, who were so grateful that afterward he became accredited to the embassies. To this day, I believe I owe him my life.

My mother told me that when she left London on March 1 for the long flight to Djakarta via Amsterdam, Geneva, Rome, Beirut, Karachi, and Colombo, she feared she might never see her only child again. The Foreign Office in London had persuaded the Indonesian embassy to give her a compassionate visa "in a matter of minutes," and a colleague of my stepfather's fudged the dates of inoculations, which were required in those days.

I regained consciousness on Tuesday, the 26th, and three days later, Dermot told me that my mother was on her way. Visitors came, including Betty and Conor, who had both had the flu, bearing lovely flowers, mostly orchids. I missed the puppies, which were getting large and frisky, able to play in the garden but keeping the family awake at night, and were not exactly housebroken.

My mother explained what had happened to me and that we would fly home together where I would need to go to London's most famous neurological hospital at Queen's Square after about seven weeks of rest in the hospital. I was typically distressed and guilty about letting Dermot, Betty, and Conor down, as well as Peter Lake in the consulate, and missing planned trips to Jogjakarta, Bali, and Bandung. I had no pain and was told no long-term effects were likely. A congenital weakness caused it, and it either healed itself completely or it did not.

I received many visitors and wonderful bouquets during my hospital stay as well as letters from back home in England and Ireland from friends and relatives. Embassy people came in droves, including the papal nuncio. The wife of the Burmese ambassador visited several times. Mrs. Boonwatt was a beautiful young woman, always impeccably dressed in the national costume of Myanmar (then Burma). Some years later, we read of her death under suspicious circumstances when her husband was ambassador to Sri Lanka. It was suspected that he murdered her, but it was never proven because he had diplomatic immunity.

Madame Potier, wife of the Portuguese minister, came, annoyed that she was not with her husband in Bangkok. The queen of Siam (Thailand) was having a baby, and His Majesty did not receive women in her absence. Madame Potier had a special long dress with long sleeves made as required by court etiquette. She told me of a strange Javanese taboo: when you go swimming on the west coast, as we had planned to do some day, you must never wear a green bathing suit, because it incurs the anger of the sea goddess.

All the puppies got adopted. My mother was well entertained at the various embassies and went to Bogor and the bungalow. A new American ambassador arrived who was an old friend of Dermot's. He attended Vatican National Day (anniversary of the pope's coronation), "Te Deum," at the cathedral, followed by a reception for men only. The volcano, Gede, erupted, and mushroom clouds like an atom-bomb explosion were visible for many miles.

One of the nurses explained to me the fine art of banditry in this country. Perpetrators greased their arms so they could not be caught and scattered datura, a strong soporific, so the occupants whom they were robbing did not wake up. By some extraordinary coincidence, the following night, a burglar got into Dermot and Betty's room where Conor and a puppy were also sleeping and stole Dermot's wallet and Betty's color camera. A night nurse told me that the minister of Saudi Arabia was the previous occupant of my hospital bed, a week before I came. During Ramadan, the nurses went off duty at 6:30 p.m. to eat, having fasted all day. They ate again at 3:30 a.m. and returned to the hospital at 7 a.m. I could hear the kampong drums beating all night in honor of Ramadan. The nurses said they would be sad when I left because there would be no more "ketawan" (laughing). I remember how they used to giggle while bathing me, saying, "so big, so white," which of course I was compared with their small, lissome, brown selves. We grew attached to each other in a girly sort of way. I helped them with their English and they taught me more Bahasa. Many came from Sumatra. Senior nurses were mostly Dutch or Eurasian. Doctors were Dutch, and although owned by Royal Dutch Shell, the hospital with approximately 250 beds also served European and local staff of KLM, the Dutch airline; and Garuda, the Indonesian airline; as well as KPM, the inter-island shipping company. Nurses back then wore masks because of the many cases of tuberculosis, a practice that strikes a familiar chord these days. I had one of the three "first-class" single rooms.

On March 28, I wrote in my diary that ten visitors came that day, and I had been given eighteen presents of flowers to date. It was not about me. It was about the ambassador's niece, who was recovering from a near-death experience against considerable odds.

Visitors regaled me with goings-on in the outside world. The local news agency, Antara, wrote a vitriolic article about Sunday's lunch guest at the embassy, a certain Dr. Keenlyside, who on a previous visit to Indonesia at a party given in his honor had refused to shake hands with Dr. Schwartz, an ex-Nazi. Antara reminded him of this incident and pointed out that there were three air routes out of Djakarta.

Mr. Currie, head of the Chartered Bank, had been put in prison because he declared an unlicensed ancient firearm in their vault. There was also something about some foreign currency business according to Radio Malaya. Dermot paid an official call on President Sukarno and put in a strong word for Mr. Currie's release.

There was no TV in those days but rather a plethora of radio. In the evenings, I could listen to all the Indonesian stations: Djakarta, Bandung, Jogjakarta, Surakarta, and Palembang, Radio Malaya, Australia, Ceylon (now Sri Lanka), Pakistan, and Pnom Penh, Cambodia, still a French Colony. There were Thai and Chinese stations, and sometimes the Voice of America, and broadcasts from as far away as Lisbon and Zurich. Plied with many magazines, I commented on the American ones as seeming "to consist entirely of articles about statistics, dollars, mortality rates, depressing diseases, Russia phobia, and Presley mania." Such a patronizing dismissal of my future adopted country!

Returning to the Residence at No. 1, Imam Bonjol, was a thrill. The house seemed larger and cleaner, the servants all smiling. The puppy, Spotty, was enormous and slept on Dermot's bed. The garden looked glorious: a new herbaceous border, two moon orchids blooming, and the African tulip tree about to blossom. The frangipani was as fragrant as ever, and the ixora were a mass of reddish and yellowy pink flowers, the hibiscus a riot of red and pink, a wax plant and purple bougainvillea flowering. The bride's tears, or Honolulu creeper, had spread. I discovered a huge spider in the bathroom, my mother heard her first tokeh, and Conor pointed out a giant grasshopper.

Mr. Currie had been sprung from prison, but Mr. Watson, his second-in-command, had taken his place. I returned to my old job of preparing the seating plan for a diplomatic dinner but had to redo it when the Thai ambassador's wife dropped out because of a sick child. I was told that Admiral Sir Charles Lamb, Second Sea Lord, had sent me get-well messages, but I had no recollection of him. I suffered mildly from amnesia for a few months. For example, when I opened my closet, I did not recognize my clothes. Actually, they were much too big for me since I had lost about fifteen pounds in the hospital. I met the new Indian ambassador and the Dutch high commissioner. There were several other guests and a boringly repetitive menu, but I reveled in my final diplomatic dinner party, seeing the "slinky black cars" lined up outside to take everyone home.

The next day, several people came to say goodbye. There was a big party given by the foreign minister's wife for all the ladies of the diplomatic corps, of course including Betty. The Canadian ambassador's wife told me that she met the daughter-in-law of the Saudi Arabian ambassador, our next-door neighbors. She was a beautiful young woman of twenty-three but very sad because her mother-in-law had taken her children back to Saudi Arabia. Although she never appeared in public, she owned twelve Dior dresses. On the subject of clothes, the American ambassador had sixteen shirts stolen, this being the season for burglaries, a popular topic of conversation, be they armed holdups, cat burglaries, or inside jobs. My mother bought a copy of *Macbeth* in Bahasa (Indonesian), causing amusement all round. Conor gave a firework display, and Dr. Schaafsma remarked in a farewell speech that I had been a good patient, if disobedient at times.

As I ended this exciting chapter of my life, I wrote: "I hope I have learned much, gained in wisdom, grace, patience, sophistication and understanding. I have learned more about human nature and to be more considerate of others. By observing Dermot I ought to have become somewhat diplomatic. Throughout these seven months my admiration for him has never waned. I am leaving many good friends. Living in the Embassy has been a wonderful experience, meeting such a wide circle of international diplomats, being in Java and working in the Consulate was wonderful. Although I never completely mastered looking after Conor or the housekeeping, I did my best and have so many memories to treasure and be grateful for."

We were ready to leave. The Saners presented us with pink and spider orchids, which we later presented to our hosts in Singapore. Captain Solly of Quantas rang my uncle to ask if we would mind flying tourist class as far as Singapore. Dermot was miffed that members of his family were asked to give up their first-class seats for two Australian members of parliament. Not like him to pull rank for, although he was always dignified, he was never pompous. In fact, we kept our seats, and the Greek ambassador and his wife were demoted to tourist class.

Ali, our wonderful head servant, insisted on coming to the airport to see his friends, as he had been a former customs man, but also to see us off, as did many friends from the embassies bearing farewell gifts. I wonder whatever happened to the heart-shaped box of Balinese coins, which I planned to dip in gold and wear as a bracelet.

# Chapter Seven

We boarded the Bristol Britannia and took off at 1:15 a.m.
leaving Djakarta prettily lit up, then dozed in our slum-
berettes. Singapore was a blaze of lights as we descended,
but instead of a gentle landing, the plane hit the runway with a
bone-shaking thump. My mother said it felt like her teeth came
out through the top of her head and dared not look at me to see
if I was still alive. I reckoned that if I survived a brain hemorrhage on February 23, I could survive a crash landing on April
23. My mother suspected every nut and bolt on that plane must
have been loosened and guessed correctly, as it turned out that
we would not take off again anytime soon.

Indeed, there was a three-day layover in Singapore, where
we stayed with old friends who now occupied our former house.
It was Easter weekend, and my mother and I visited many old
friends, including our favorite cousins, Bunty and Toby Simonds,
who came with George de Stacpoole, who told us he planned to

retire from the Irish Guards; take over from his father, the duke; grow orchids; and corner the market.

We were lucky to get back on the Britannia since BOAC failed to notify us of the new departure time, but luckily Bunty had phoned the airport and was told the flight left at nine. We scrambled into our clothes and off to the airport just in time.

Flying up the coast of Malaya (now Malaysia) trying to spot Malacca, thinking of happy weekend memories during our life in Singapore, Port Dixon, and Port Swettenham, we were served sandwiches, biscuits, and coffee, followed by pre-lunch cocktails and champagne, and then a delicious lunch over the Indian Ocean. We seemed to eat and drink nonstop except for brief sleeps between Karachi and Bahrain, and Bahrain and Istanbul. Other first-class passengers were mostly Australian and scruffy looking (especially in the middle of the night); mostly elderly; an amusing, obviously wealthy couple (he was the plane's funny man); and a good-looking younger couple with two children, one of whom threw up every time the plane landed. The ladies (there were segregated bathrooms on planes back then) had Elizabeth Arden samples. There were fourteen stewardesses (politically correct terminology at the time, as was "air hostesses") on the Britannia. They told me they worked for three weeks straight then had three weeks off. With my active imagination, I presumed they probably had a boyfriend in every layover country. We changed crews in Karachi and Istanbul. The Britannia was flown for a brief period; a combination prop and jet plane, it was soon succeeded by jets.

Calcutta was an oven, exceeding 110 degrees Fahrenheit. We disembarked long enough for a cold drink in the airport lounge, waited on by handsome Indians in white suits with embroidered sashes and turbans. A boring stretch ensued across brown India except for the pilot pointing out Mount Everest in the distance. Of course, I did not know then that some forty years later I would trek in Nepal along the Everest trail, almost to base camp.

We skipped a curry dinner in Karachi in order to reach Bahrain ahead of a storm. Our flight took us over Indonesia, Malaya, the Indian Ocean, India, Pakistan, the Persian Gulf, Oman, Saudi Arabia, Oman, Turkey, the Dardanelles, Greece, Italy, and Switzerland before landing in England. We took off from Istanbul at dawn, a glorious sunrise above the clouds, along the coast of Italy, the Alps, exquisite snowy rugged peaks, Lake Como, and Lucerne. We ate chocolate at Zurich Airport after a huge breakfast on the plane and, before a "light" lunch of veal and rum babas, saw our first landmark, Eton College Chapel, before arriving at the London airport.

We had flown nine thousand miles to have an angiogram, though the equipment at Westminster Hospital failed and I had to have two further sessions at Queen's Square, both eminent London hospitals. The first one was given without an anesthetic. Nurses and aides forcibly held me down while I screamed in agony. Afterward, the famous surgeon said, "Oh dear, did that hurt a lot? Sorry, I've never done one before."

During this time, I stayed in the female officers' ward of the Royal Army Medical Corps Hospital at Millbank. The famous Roger Bannister was doing his national service in the hospital at the time, revered by staff and patients, having just won the four-minute mile.

The neurosurgeon who pronounced me totally recovered recommended a lazy summer, and to avoid underwater swimming and diving forever, no hunting (on horseback) or violent exercise. I was never a keen rider, and scuba diving had no appeal. During my subsequent long life, my most strenuous exercise has probably been some hiking at high altitudes and regular tennis. He surmised that I could never purchase life insurance, except at a very costly premium.

There were many cocktail parties, dances, and weddings that summer. My uncle, John Christie-Miller, who was Master of the Feltmakers, invited me to the Lord Mayor's Banquet, a ceremonial affair held annually in the magnificent Egyptian Hall of the Mansion House in London. John was still running Christy's Hats in Stockport. All the rabbit fur came from Belgium, so my date was a young Belgian, scion of the fur-selling family, Robert Flechet. The food and wine were excellent. The Loving Cup was passed to all the guests, and speeches were made by the lord mayor, the high commissioner for New Zealand, the recorder of Manchester, and other dignitaries.

I went to a May Ball in Cambridge with my cousin Hughie MacDermot. He was already dating his future wife, Jean. They married after Hughie had completed his national service, which was obligatory for two years at the time. They became the parents of Hal and Fergus. Fergus is my godson.

Olivia Rogers and John Barratt had a very smart wedding at St. Margaret's, Westminster (which dates back to the thirteenth century), followed by a reception at 45 Park Lane. I went with Aunt Bridget and her three daughters, my first cousins, Caroline, Lydia, and Charlotte. Uncle Edward and Aunt Beatrice Christie-Miller were also there. According to my diary, "The bridegroom's mother and her two poodles were dressed in diamante and gold."

Another smart London wedding was Susannah Begg's, the first of my classmates at St. Mary's Ascot to get married. I mentioned her father in Chapter One, the British military attaché in Ireland who during the war undiplomatically accused young men of lounging around the country club pool when they were on embarkation leave before heading to the front. I hope I never told his daughter. By the time we were school friends, the war was a vague memory of our early childhoods. However, I owe Susannah a debt of gratitude for introducing me to Michael and Tessa Till in Cambridge, about whom I will write later.

Somehow in the middle of all these parties and attending my secretarial courses, I managed to win a two-guinea book token for creating a literary crossword for "Books and Bookmen," which made me inordinately proud.

Watching polo at Cowdray Park with Wanda Willert, her sister Pauline, and their mother got a passing mention in my diary, whereas Henley Regatta with my grandfather rated three paragraphs.

England looking her best on a warm summer day that became a sweltering one. The grounds are beautifully laid out with striped tents, flowers, comprising leafy Leander Gardens, and Phyllis Court.

The races, many of which were fine sport, were supported enthusiastically but not rowdily. The overly ornate trophies on show in a tent with early Henley prints, were won throughout the day. Princeton won the Challenge Cup against the National Provincial Bank for the tenth time in eleven years. The scarlet clad Russians beat the London Rowing Club. Pembroke College had a double victory over Christchurch in the Ladies Challenge Cup. Russians also distinguished themselves winning the Double Sculls, but their Ivanov was beaten by the Australian Olympic rower, Mackenzie. One of the few home wins was Leander against the Austrians.

In the refreshment tent we were served fresh salmon, followed by strawberries and cream. At one point while watching the racing, Princess Anne almost fell over my feet, exiting our row of seats. Men looked good in their traditional blazers and flannels, women wore summer dresses and hats.

During the summer, I had a romance with a fascinating young man, Richard Raphael, whom I described as having a "nice voice, nice hair, adorable face, greeny brown eyes." He had been acting and producing in repertory for four years and was looking for a job in television. He was living with his grandmother in Alton because his parents were "lost" in America, mother a dancer, father a stockbroker. He went to Harrow, liked me to wear high heels, and told me not to put the knife handles in hot water while doing the dishes, which endeared him to my mother. He was a very fine pianist.

On the dark side, he told me about a company he managed that was about to be sued or go bankrupt, and that he once killed someone riding his motorbike, but it was not his fault. I was falling passionately in love with him and agreed to marry him at St. James's Spanish Place. We discussed how many children we would like to have, whether we could afford a car, and whether we would go to America. He took me to the Test Match at Lords, where no doubt I asked silly questions about cricket.

Alas, the romance foundered and ended because of religious differences. Richard was half Jewish and would never countenance Catholic children. I quoted St. Thomas More in my diary: "There can be no compromise where principles are concerned." My mother had an acute attack of the guilties, which I assured her was unnecessary, because it was my choice to remain a Catholic. I knew she gave up Catholicism when she left her convent boarding school run by the Sacred Heart nuns at Roehampton. However, to spare her mother, she went through the motions of being a Catholic, marrying my father in a Catholic church and having me baptized in one.

The parties went on. At a dinner with two Royal Fusilier officers, I was justifiably reprimanded for using my plate as an ashtray. Everyone smoked in those bad old days. Shortly afterward, I noticed one of the young officers, Maurice French, flicking ash into his trouser turn-ups. When I chided him, he explained that he needed to make sure his batman (officers had a personal manservant) was cleaning them properly. Although they were stationed at the Tower of London, they never made good on their promise to take us to see the famous keys ceremony.

There was a wonderful Ball at Greenwich in the Painted Hall. The supper table included whole boars, not just their heads. Remembering it was Friday and being a strict Catholic, I ate lobster but then consumed meat during the second supper after midnight. The flowers were by Constance Spry, London's premier florist.

I went to my first Hunt Ball that winter while staying with my grandparents in Cheshire. Our escorts were officers of the Royal Welch Fusiliers and young men who worked for ICI (Imperial Chemical Industries) or for Rolls-Royce. The North Staffordshire Hunt Ball was a splendid party. We dined first in a very grand mansion, where there were two pianos and a clavichord in the drawing room. We were driven by Raymond Salisbury Jones to the ball in the latest Rolls-Royce, the Silver Cloud, by now a venerable vintage car. We danced till four-thirty in the morning but somehow managed to go beagling the next day. Raymond was charming and attractive, the son of a diplomat, former household cavalry, who held some chef-du-protocol function, because his parents lived in a grace-and-favor residence in St. James's Palace.

On the following Sunday, it was Raymond's job to drive the first model of the Silver Cloud to the London showroom of Rolls-Royce, and he offered me a lift. I believe it was an American who once said a Rolls-Royce was not a car but a way of life. We barely noticed when we reached ninety miles an hour on the straight motorway, and luckily no police were around. It was sleek, silent, fast, and luxurious. I was in heaven. When we reached Oxford, we needed a pit stop and refreshment. Those were the days before credit cards and ATMs, and it being Sunday, we could only rustle up a few shillings between us, enough for tea and buns at a cheap cafe. You can imagine the stunned expressions on bystanders' faces at the sight of England's newest Rolls-Royce, and a slightly scruffy, very young couple exiting it outside the cafe.

A new man in my life, Henry Rogers, escorted me to the Royal Engineers Ball. He drove a Daimler, frequently exceeding the speed limit and endangering our lives. Most young men drove too fast in those days, especially when they had too much to drink. This was one of the reasons my mother insisted I always remain sober enough to take over the driving if I had to.

To reciprocate, I invited Henry to the Twelfth Night Ball at the Mayfair Hotel, organized by Lord and Lady Birdwood in aid of refugees. In the tombola (which is like a raffle), Henry won a rug, which he reluctantly gave me; some too-large slippers;

and a length of yellow silk, which I gave to Monica Kempton, one of my mother's best friends, upon her return from Tenerife to thank her for making me a beautiful evening dress, which also happened to be yellow. Henry and I had a rather turbulent relationship, though he invited me to one more ball, the Old Berkeley Hunt Ball. We went to his sister's flat, where in bad humor I ironed her evening dress while she took a bath. After a few more social dates, Henry, serving in the Royal Engineers, was posted to the Trucial Oman Scouts. British forces at that time kept the peace in the Trucial States, which included Oman and parts of the United Arab Emirates. It was considered a hardship posting situated in the desert. (In Colonial times, Washington, DC had also been one for the British military and its diplomats because of its damp, swampy climate.)

At this time, I had a crush on Monica Kempton's nephew, a cavalry officer, who later was lucratively employed by the sultan of Kuwait. Christopher Johnson-Ferguson was extremely amusing, but I realized that he found my mother much more entertaining than me. Four years later, my husband, Ian, told me that one of the reasons he married me was that he hoped I would turn out to be like my mother as I grew older. Did I want to murder her in a jealous rage? No, I loved her more than ever.

Saturday afternoons in the country were often spent beagling, a healthy sport. We followed a pack of hounds on foot instead of on horseback. They flushed hares, not foxes. Usually there was a hearty tea in a pub afterward. My diary at the time mentioned the Great British Animal Loving Public's condemnation of the Russians sending a dog into space, and I wrote sanctimoniously that I hoped they were not the same people who left their dogs in cars to suffocate on hot summer afternoons.

After I finished my secretarial course at St. James, I boarded luxuriously with Great-Aunt Dorothy Whyte (née Hibbert) in Cadogan Square, widow of my grandmother's brother, William Whyte. She was an exceptional woman from Plainfield, New Jersey. By the time I knew her, she was a widow settled in London, with grown-up children John and Ursula. A woman named Celia, whose full name I forget, her daughter, and another girl, Fiona Douglas-Nugent, were all lodgers in the large two-story flat consisting of the street floor and the basement. Dorothy, well-traveled and a close friend of the late Queen Marie of Romania, admitted to having double-dated with the prince of Wales and Mrs. Simpson before the marriage and abdication. Her accomplishments included translating Greek into braille, being a crossword puzzle and chess expert, and a fine cook. We paid the princely sum of two pounds a week for bed and board, the latter often included lobster for dinner. Her only requests were that one of us walk her elderly Labrador, Dandy, around Cadogan Square and help with washing the dishes. I usually walked Dandy because of my lifelong love of dogs. On the telephone, it was assumed Dorothy was a man. She had the deepest woman's voice I ever heard.

Ursula and I shared a bedroom. She had sung on Vatican Radio when she and her mother lived in Rome for a while. Ursula aspired to be an opera singer. We often went to Covent Garden and sat in the "gods," the uppermost, cheapest seats in the balcony. Cash was short, and Ursula used to use black shoe polish for mascara and loo paper instead of Kleenex tissues.

Patrick Laver invited me to dinner at his parents' house. He very charmingly and diplomatically told the Ford family who were present that I ran the embassy in Djakarta! His father was James Laver, head of the Victoria and Albert Museum at the time, and his mother was the actress Veronica Turley. The conversation was mostly about Russian art and music. There was a spectacular four-poster bed in their bedroom. Later, Patrick married Marianne Ford.

She and I were at St. Mary's Ascot together, and I used to visit her at her parents' house in Bryanston Square during school holidays. A beautiful young German princess, Mariga von Urach (Marie Gabrielle von Uragh-Wurttemberg, daughter of Prince Albert of Wurttemberg-Urach), often stayed there too, and we had schoolgirl crushes on her, being six years older. We used to play a game called "loonybins" until grownups stopped it because Mariga's mother spent many years in a private mental institution until her death. Mariga married Desmond Guinness in 1954, and together they founded the Irish Georgian Society and lived in Leixlip Castle, which they restored along with many Georgian buildings in Ireland.

Marianne's mother, Joan, and my mother were old friends. My mother was mortified when one of her many cousins, Christopher Lamb, jilted Joan after they were engaged in order to become a Jesuit priest, the same cousin who said Mass in the catacombs of Rome for me and fellow students on my seventeenth birthday. Nevertheless, Joan remained a devout Catholic and tried unsuccessfully to bring my mother back to the Church on her deathbed. Joan married Brinsley Ford, head of the National Arts Council, and a serious collector himself. I was too young and ignorant at the time to appreciate the many fine works of art in the huge, chilly house, cared for by a series of Irish maids who were terrible cooks.

The marriage of Patrick and Marianne lasted all of a week, but a child was born of the union and raised by her mother. In fact, Patrick was gay. After travels with his father, and a losing battle with alcohol, he died quite young.

I shared my twentieth birthday with Monica Kempton's father, Colonel Jervis, who turned eighty on the same day, so my mother gave a Centenary Party to which many guests were invited. Dorothy and Ursula came from London, as well as Ursula's distinguished brother, John Whyte. He was born in Malaya when Dorothy and Willy were living there, went to Ampleforth and Oxford, and spent his career as an academic in politics. His first university post was Makerere College in Uganda, where he gained a lifelong interest in African politics. However, he was best known for the books he wrote, *Church and State in Modern Ireland* and *Catholics in Western Democracies*, and the time he spent at Queen's University, Belfast, and University College, Dublin. He was also a research fellow at Harvard's Center for International Affairs, and at the Netherlands Institute for Advanced Study in Humanities and Social Science. He did much to bring political scientists from the Republic and the north together.

A young man arrived in the summer of 1958 with an introduction to Dorothy from Jamaica, where he lived with his widowed mother. The family fortune came from Brand's Essence. Lachlan Macneal knew no one in London, and Ursula was expected to show him the sights. She was anti-men at the time and found him boring on the few occasions they met. Dorothy begged me to step up to the plate, and I was happy to oblige.

This was the London of coffee bars where Ursula and I would meet friends. They were cheap and the coffee was good. For hard liquor there were bottle parties, crowded, late-night affairs in scruffy flats attended by young men and women from different social backgrounds. Fashion was not very important. Men wore "brothel-creepers," rubber-soled shoes, jeans or slacks, and sweaters. Women sported too much makeup, high heels, and sweaters, usually V-necked and on the large side. Girls went to pubs and bars with dates but not with each other.

Music, pre-Beatles, tended to be imported from the US in the late fifties: The Kingston Trio; Harry Belafonte; Peter, Paul and Mary; Joan Baez; et al. We went to the theater and concerts, good seats if taken by parents or rich boyfriends, otherwise we bought the cheapest ones.

My first meeting with Lachy was at a dinner party with Dorothy and friends of hers, where I replaced Ursula. The Belfry restaurant, an unconsecrated church, was famous because the Duke of Edinburgh gave stag parties there. Lachy invited me to *My Fair Lady*, followed by the Chelsea Flower Show. We dated all that summer, and he apparently fell for me. He was a kind man, if somewhat naïve, actually telling me that his mother thought I might be after his money. There was no spark on my side, but I loved being spoiled and taken to so many theaters and restaurants, which other friends and I could never have afforded to set foot in. Despite a few tiffs, he appeared to have honorable intentions, and he agreed to come to the Dublin Horse Show with us. Fiona Douglas-Nugent said I would probably marry him because "one drifts into these things." I replied that I wished she, being some years older than me, would do more drifting in that direction herself, but she was very choosy, and no man had yet come up to snuff for her. Some years later, she married happily.

There were several weddings that summer, but the one that meant the most to me was Wanda Willert's marriage to John Rix at Cowdray Park. Her uncle, Lord Cowdray, appeared briefly wearing his polo clothes. Wanda had been working at the

*Financial Times*, which was owned at the time by the Pearson family, so many guests at the wedding were her colleagues.

Earlier that year, Aunt Dorothy, going through the *Times* one afternoon, read a job ad to me: "West End publisher seeks secretary for executive for Far East; graduate, mid-twenties preferred." She encouraged me to apply. I suspect that my scanty knowledge of Bahasa and kitchen Malay, learned in order to give instructions to the embassy household staff in Djakarta, got me the job. No one asked about any degrees, and I spent two very happy years in the textbook department of Longmans, Green on Bond Street, an illustrious firm that had published many distinguished authors, including Graham Greene.

While working there, I made two American friends who became important in my future. Sallie McKee and Susan Stanwood had graduated from Vassar, and their first jobs were at Longmans, Green.

I was by then sharing a flat in Emperor's Gate with a friend from St. James's who worked for an art gallery on Bond Street. We had little money, less furniture, and a fun life. We went home to our parents on weekends to eat, sleep, and do our laundry, usually returning with some home-cooked food for the weeknights. Sue Davies was going steady with the man she subsequently married, David Lloyd Evans. I am godmother to their son, Simon, now married with children, and Sue and I still keep in touch.

While working for Ben Gingell in the Far East Department of Longmans, Green, I celebrated my twenty-first birthday. My stepfather, now a colonel, and my mother gave a wonderful party in the headquarters mess of the Royal Army Medical Corps at Millbank in London. Among the guests was my mother's old friend Maureen O'Sullivan, of *Tarzan* movies fame. Ben and I announced our engagement during the evening. In those days, a female planning to marry her boss was obliged to resign from her job. So, I went to work for the London office of a New York real estate company, Previews International, run by the charismatic John Tysen. He offered me a job in the New York office, which I accepted when Ben and I first broke off our engagement that summer.

My mother and stepfather did not think Ben was good husband material. Our engagement was on again, off again all that summer. Their solution was to give me a one-way ticket to New York, cabin class, on the French Line's *Liberté*, to stay with my godmother, Una Kernan, and her husband, John, a Wall Street lawyer at the time, in Englewood, New Jersey, another move "taken at the flood," and clearly a good one, as things turned out. Perhaps I was heartless, because Ben pursued me by mail, and at some point, I finally broke things off. However, to this day, whatever his shortcomings may have been, only one other man in my life ever made me laugh so much.

My stepfather had just been seconded to the University of Bagdad with no loss of military seniority, and they were looking forward to living in Iraq for two years just after they saw me off at Southampton aboard the *Liberté*.

The sea journey was wonderful, but my best memories are of accompanying the famous guitarist Julian Bream to the first-class lounge in the evenings to listen to his magnificent playing. He was about to embark on his first US tour with Sol Hurok.

# Chapter Eight

Life in Englewood with the Kernans and their daughter Brigid, who was twelve at the time, was very pleasant for a few months.

I commuted to Previews International in midtown Manhattan where I had a sort of floating job thanks to the president, John Tysen, who kept his promise about giving me employment. In those days, green cards were obtainable within about three weeks of application by British citizens. Mine took longer because the US embassy in London was suspicious of people who had previously lived in Switzerland and Indonesia. One of my oldest surviving friends in the world became John Tysen's secretary, because John could not wait any longer for me to be granted my visa and cross the Atlantic. A few years older, Valerie de Lagatinerie seemed to me the epitome of glamor. Divorced from a French baron, she always attracted men and had many affairs. Sometimes the men were married, but she always had a big heart and a wonderful sense of humor. Later, she married

Don Kaempf, who worked for IBM. They lived on 57th Street in New York and also had a beautiful house and garden in St. James, Long Island, which they tended to lovingly. They had a daughter, Alexandra, of whom I am very fond, but the marriage ended in divorce.

Peter Chance, who headed Christie's in London, came over to open a New York office. John Tysen introduced him to Robert Leylan, who was appointed to the position of US representative. He was eminently qualified to run Christie's US operations. Although his expertise was Impressionist art, he had ample knowledge of paintings, silver, furniture, and jewelry, which enabled him to procure high-end treasures for auction in London. He was also well connected socially and excelled at finding collections through his wealthy friends. Divorced, handsome, and very bright, he was sought after by many ladies, including Margaret, the Duchess of Argyll, who was going through a scandalous divorce. I remember typing a document saying he had bid her farewell on the sidewalk. Those were the days of needing to prove adultery in order to obtain a divorce.

Sotheby's followed Christie's example shortly afterward, sending Peregrine Pollen from London to run their New York office. By this time, Bob Leylan had hired me, and my counterpart at Sotheby's was Virginia Battye, another English girl in New York. English secretaries were highly sought after, and I was often asked if any of my friends were looking for work. Most of our American contemporaries would have still been in college and perhaps had higher career aspirations than secretary, though marriage was generally the goal. Although most of us came from privileged backgrounds, private schools, finishing schools, and "coming out," we were well trained, but the appeal was pure snobbery. Our English accents were the main attraction.

Shortly after going to work at 21 East 57th Street, I moved into an apartment on East 82nd Street with two other English girls and one American. Jenny, who had been to university, was sexually adventurous, which Rosemary and I were not. Rosemary Tigar worked at the UN and later married the famous Nicaraguan artist Armando Morales. She put up with years of financial struggles and bore him two children, but they were divorced before he became famous. Barbara, the only American, worked at the Metropolitan Museum of Art and did not waste her time on unsuitable men. We were not thinking of marriage, but simply having a very good time enjoying New York City. Barbara had set her sights on my very eligible cousin, Brian Hugh MacDermot, whom she had met in London; but as mentioned earlier, he did not marry until he was fifty and was not particularly interested in Barbara. Many years later, she and I reconnected. She was married to an important Republican in the Nixon administration. I remember going to a very boring party where only sangria was served, which Charles swore he would never drink again. And he was a Republican too.

Those were the Camelot days. We all had crushes on President Kennedy. All the men we knew had good jobs and fine career prospects. They took us out in groups for dinner and nightclubs. We reciprocated by cooking for them in our scruffy apartments. There was little pairing off and no living together. This was pre-pill and long before AIDS, so the fear of unwanted pregnancy kept most of us technically virginal. No one earned enormous salaries, some friends had private money, but we managed to pay our rent, buy clothes, have fun, and travel. I moved in with June Hare, later Dickinson, to a small apartment on Central Park West before Lincoln Center was built. I do not remember our very modest rent, although in those days, it was usually one week's take-home pay per month. My salary was $5,000 a year, and I lived well on it.

Aunt Dorothy had provided me with wonderful contacts amongst her old friends on the East Coast, and I was well entertained. I remember a scion of the Reynolds aluminum family. I dated him more seriously on my return ten years later, and he took me to New Mexico, where he was a serious buyer of artifacts in Santa Fe and Taos. Traveling with him was the only time in my entire life I have missed a plane. The Christie-Millers make a fetish of being on time or early for every event and every flight.

My two friends from Longmans, Green days, Sallie McKee and Susan Stanwood, both invited me for weekends. I spent my first Thanksgiving with Sallie's family in Pittsburgh, and went sailing in New England with Susan's father. Sallie's mother had died giving birth to her and her twin sister, Susan, which she described to me as the ultimate guilt trip. After her father died, they were adopted by a wonderful couple. Sallie became engaged to James B. (Jimmy) Warden, but I missed their 1961 wedding, as I was living and working in Hong Kong at the time. Susan worked for *The Saturday Evening Post*, and I attended her wedding to Howard Kaminsky in January 1970.

Lachlan Macneil came back into my life briefly. A dear friend, Tessa Greig, was recuperating from tuberculosis, so he invited us both to stay with him in Ocho Rios. He lived in considerable luxury in Jamaica, which was similar in many ways to the louche life of the Kenya of Black Mischief days, a lot of parties and drinking, although Lachy was always a perfect gentleman. We three had a very pleasant time together. We swam in his mother's pool with her and her Labradors, and I loved Lachy's yellow lab, Honey, though it would be another thirty-five years before I owned one of the breed. I no longer presented a threat as a gold digger, because he had met his future wife, who was much nicer to him than I would ever have been, and gave him lovely children too.

I loved my job. Bob Leylan was my Svengali. I had a huge crush on him, and we had a perfectly happy platonic relationship. I did a good job, was quick to learn, and made a positive difference in his work life. The biggest responsibilities were transmitting bids to London by telephone or telex (God help me if I omitted or added a zero) and running the office on my own when he traveled. I rose to the challenges, contacting lawyers when an important collector died, dealing with the aftermath of a burglary in his apartment, and handling clients who were buyers or sellers at auction. He introduced me to senior staff at the museums, galleries, and art dealers in New York and other cities. A highlight was visiting the Barnes Collection when it was very difficult for the public to obtain admission.

In a letter to my mother, I wrote:

> I'm almost tempted to put in for a commission on the Robinson deal to which I devoted a whole week of attending legal conferences and being the liaison between London and New York.

> My present life requires dressing well every day. I never know when some lawyer, broker, dealer, collector, museum curator or boyfriend is going to ask me out to lunch. Days of slopping to the office in a shirt and skirt with laddered nylons are over. Also I often have to leap into a little black number after work, seize a taxi and attend two or three cocktail parties at different ends of

Manhattan. You wouldn't know me now, but perhaps from all this, you wouldn't want to. [Admittedly, going through letters and diaries sixty years later, I find my twenty-two-year-old self rather tiresomely naïve, so I hope I have acquired some wisdom and mellowed over the years.]

I was very daring this morning and went to see a dealer who has a fabulous suite in a Fifth Avenue hotel, and while comparing London, Berlin and Moscow prices, was shown important paintings by Boudin, Tiepolo, Lautrec, Fantin Latour, Vuillard, Degas and others.

We had the big Impressionist sale in London on Friday, which kept me frantically transmitting results to bidders, buyers and sellers. I have now made friends with one of the most famous artists and collectors in America, resulting from my acting like a little girl lost when she became abusive over the way we handled the sale of her Renoir.

Our party was a huge success. Rosemary and I did all the work while Barbara and Jenny sat at their hairdressers. We turned my bedroom into "the ballroom," and liquor flowed like water till 5 a.m. The next week was utterly exhausting with parties every night. My friends Tessa and Lisa gave an excellent one, attended by Charles

Addams, among other distinguished guests. On Friday there was a huge party in a penthouse. Sandy Davis came up from Washington for it and afterwards took me to an Italian place where we danced till 4 a.m. We had a wonderful weekend, taxis everywhere, countless bloody marys which we both go for in a big way, dinner and dancing at El Chico's, our favorite haunt in the Village, bed at 5 a.m. Next day was cold and wet so he came to lunch and we sat around reading the papers till it was time for him to fly back to DC. Barbara perked up when she discovered his father is a prominent portrait painter who shares a studio in Florence with Annigoni [the internationally prominent portrait painter who painted Queen Elizabeth, also one of my Christie-Miller second cousins], and his mother's ancestral home in South Carolina appeared on the front page of *The New York Times*.

In another letter I wrote:

I was invited to visit the Nation's Capital by Sandy Davis, who worked there for *The National Geographic*. He asked my friend Donna and me for Memorial Day weekend to stay in his house in Georgetown, which I described as the most beautiful town within a town—Georgian houses, cobbled streets, lots of trees and walled gardens. Sightseeing began with the Archives Building, the Declaration of Independence and the Bill of Rights, and moved on the National Gallery which was extra special for me. However beautiful pictures are, I wilt after a couple of hours so Sandy took us to the Occidental for lunch where senators and presidents eat.

We drove down Massachusetts Avenue to leave a message at the British Embassy for my uncle Dermot who was visiting Washington. We had tea with the illustrious Katharine Graham of *The Washington Post*, friend of Bob Leylan's, in her Georgetown house, a patroness of the arts, who fosters young artists, nurses lap dogs, and can talk knowledgably about any subject under the sun. I just sat back and listened to her and Sandy.

Sunday was another blissful day. Visited some more galleries and museums, the Capitol, the Senate, the Jefferson Memorial, and the Lincoln Memorial. On Monday, Memorial Day, we drove out to see Lee's mansion, Arlington Cemetery and Mount Vernon. We drove back to our hotel to meet Dermot. He had flown out on the Britannia but halfway across the Atlantic they had to return to London with engine trouble. As you may know, he is here as Selwyn Lloyd's representative to the SEATO (South East Asia Treaty Organization) conference.

Then came my once-in-a-lifetime visit to Hollywood. I wrote to my mother from the Beverly Hills Hotel in September 1960:

It's a Cinderella story and the clock will strike twelve and the pumpkin will waft me back to dirty old New York and our grubby little flat . . .

I've been living in a sort of Paradise. Went to a dinner party given by the MacDonald Careys and met film people, Iris Tree, Lorraine Sherwood, David McLean, Caesar Romero, Jack Kennedy, Ida Lupino, Hugh O'Brien, Ronald Lee and his wife.

I had the most fascinating evening listening to Maureen (O'Sullivan) and Mrs. Charles Boyer (Pat Patterson) reminisce. I asked to see all over the house. Never have I feasted my eyes on so many Impressionist paintings (can't wait to tell Bob Leylan), priceless jade, Ming porcelain, etc. It left me speechless but despairing. I would love to be rich and famous if I could be like Maureen, perfectly sweet and human. She radiates the most wonderful warmth, a perfect wife-and-motherliness.

I arrived at the hotel on Tuesday afternoon and have a lovely room. As the Farrows' guest I get VIP treatment, the maid asked if I was in films. The telephone operators are charming but can't cope with my name, Christie-Miller. They probably suspect that a Mr. Christie and a Miss Miller must be having a spree in Room 344. The pool is heaven with a bronzed, fair-haired, blue-eyed attendant.

On Tuesday I had supper at the Farrows' home, which is divine. I have never seen Maureen look lovelier and their six children are awfully sweet. Maureen took me to all their bedrooms to hear their night prayers starting with Mia who at sixteen is the eldest. While in the swimming pool, John Farrow talked about a film he was hoping to direct casting Claire Bloom as the Virgin Mary. I was charmed that he was so kind and genial to me. Maureen talks about you incessantly and loves you very much. She told me that your brother my uncle Bay had proposed to her once.

Darling, I'm sure you would anyway, but please write and tell her how ecstatic, appreciative and pampered I feel, though of course I said how overwhelmed and grateful I am for all her hospitality. She brushed it off, saying you would do the same for her children. [Later, the Farrows visited England, and when my mother entertained them, the children saw their first snow in my mother's garden.]

Yesterday Maureen took me to a charity lunch at the Beverly Hilton Hotel. I was terrified, sitting amongst the cream of LA society, wearing hats, dripping with diamonds, champagne flowing, watching a fashion show and ticking off Dior and Laroche numbers on their programs. Luckily, I was soon getting along fine with the ladies because thanks to Christie's, I could talk about Monet and current art market prices.

I can think of no lovelier part of the world for you and Robert to retire to. It has a perfect climate, sea and mountains within easy reach, gorgeous houses, golf courses, sailing, etc. All the women I met look wonderful with perfect complexions and girlish figures. People are courteous and friendly and seem happy. I could live here but I'd need to get a car first because distances are enormous.

After Hollywood, I stayed with my old friend Pat from Villa Beata and her husband, Chuck, in Pasadena. (Eventually they had nine children.) We drove many miles along the coast on Sunday just to see Los Angeles Harbor, Marineland, and Disneyland, and we spent a weekend sailing at Newport Beach.

Having researched some of the above-mentioned Hollywood celebrities many years later, here are some more details about them. Iris Tree, English poetess, actress, eccentric, a wit, and an adventurer, was at the party with her son Ivan Moffat. Lorraine Sherwood was the dialogue coach in *Gentlemen Prefer Blondes*. David McLean, movie and TV actor, was best known for his Marlboro Man ads in print and on TV. At that time, Caesar Romeo was the Latin love of many musicals and romantic comedies. Ida Lupino, English-born film and TV actress, was one of the first women directors and screen writers. She discovered Hugh O'Brian, who was also at the party, and opened the door for him to sign with Universal Studios for many movies.

During this time, my mother and stepfather, Robert Niven, were leading a rather glamorous life, attending receptions and dinners nightly among international diplomats and being entertained by the local inhabitants, university professors, and high-up civil servants in, of all unlikely places given recent history, Baghdad, Iraq. They traveled freely to the famous architectural sites: Babylon, Erbil, Sulaymaniyah, and throughout Persia, now Iran. My mother taught English to staff of the Chinese embassy in Baghdad. Robert loved his teaching job and bonded with his students. The country was run by Saddam Hussein's predecessor, a handsome man, Kasim, later assassinated. I still have a set of silver hairbrushes that he gave to my mother. The British government paid my stepfather's salary as Professor of Public Health at the University of Bagdad for the first year. The Iraqi government was supposed to pay the second year, but they reneged on the agreement. Robert was posted to Hong Kong as a brigadier general in charge of medical services for the military.

They were anxious for me to visit them while they were in Hong Kong, still a British colony. A spectacular white house in Stanley Fort, called Windsor House, went with the job, as well as two Chinese female servants, called amahs. The house had views of the South China Sea on three sides and hills behind it. Occasionally, packs of wild dogs appeared over the hills, but Sober, the Cocker Spaniel, was kept in the house. At that time, canine household pets were not popular among the Chinese, and occasionally my mother caught one of the servants giving her a kick. Also, when my mother went to buy food for Sober, she asked for "meat for dog." Had she said "dog meat," that is exactly what she would have been sold. After Robert's tour of duty ended and he and my mother returned to England, Windsor House was torn down. Apparently it was too large and no one wanted to live in it.

I arranged three months leave of absence from Christie's US office and found another English girl to take my place in the apartment on 67 Street with June. Her father was the head of British Airways at the time. June wrote to me in Hong Kong that she had not changed her sheets for six months.

After a cheerful send-off by friends, I boarded the night train from New York to Montreal and then took the Canadian Pacific across Canada. The rail journey was spectacular. I will never forget the incredible views from the observation car as the Rocky Mountains rose from the seemingly endless plains and the descent through the Fraser Canyon to Vancouver. I visited Agnes, widow of a famous artist cousin, Hughie Monahan, and spent a few happy days in that loveliest of cities. I flew to Seattle for the Pacific crossing. In those far off days, Pan Am gave its passengers a free hotel night and time on Waikiki Beach before embarking on the long flight to Hong Kong.

# Chapter Nine

On my first Sunday in Hong Kong, my stepfather kindly arranged for me to go waterskiing. A young officer approached me as I waited my turn on the beach and asked me if I typed. Most young women already knew the QWERTY keyboard long before computers came in. Men, except for journalists, had a harder time learning the finger work, because they would not have been caught dead behind a typewriter in those days.

I had barely answered in the affirmative when he told me to start work on Monday at SMISHK, which is hard to say after a few drinks (and Hong Kong was very social, with constant cocktail parties). It stood for the Special Military Intelligence Section, Hong Kong.

My brief career in this branch of MI6 always seems to interest people. However, most spy business is rather boring. There are long hours of not much happening. Bill Hood, who lectured at the New York Public Library on writing spy novels and was

Allen Dulles's biographer, as well as ex-CIA and author of many spy novels himself, advised us always to include the O.S.S. in our writing. The Obligatory Sex Scene was supposed to liven up our stories. Actually, I did not indulge in any on the job, because soon after being hired and put to work typing Top Secret documents, long before my positive vetting security clearance came through from London, I had met and fallen in love with my future husband.

Most of the time I typed long, boring reports on Chinese troop movements (this was still the Mao era and height of the Cold War), which were of great interest to the US and other NATO countries. However, it was exciting to be part of one cloak-and-dagger episode, more cloak than dagger because I never saw any weapons brandished. My boss changed out of his army uniform and we switched vehicles a few times as we drove round Hong Kong at high speed and eventually got into a small, fast boat, which took us to a remote island, a former leper colony, where a Chinese army deserter was being debriefed. He chain-smoked while he spilled the beans about military activities to an interpreter, and I typed up the report. I trust he was given a good job and a new life in the colony.

My godmother, Blanche Hanbury-Tracy, came to stay with us, originally for three weeks, but in fact she remained for three months. It took that long to get a visa for the People's Republic of China in order to reach the Soviet Union via the Trans-Siberian Railway from Vladivostok. In her attempts to obtain a Chinese visa, she was told to contact a certain Percy Chen. Intelligence being what it was, both my stepfather, as head of medical services for the military, and I, a junior clerk in SMISHK, were told that the Hon. Mrs. Hanbury-Tracy should on no account meet with Mr. Chen in our house, as he was a strong supporter of the Communist regime in the People's Republic. Somehow, she obtained that visa.

Another example of intelligence at work: I can remember my humiliation when one Monday morning, my boss reprimanded me for an injudicious remark of mine overheard at a cocktail party the previous weekend. It reminded me that Uncle Dermot, when we arrived in Indonesia, told me never to ask people for details about their jobs because they might be undercover intelligence agents. Maybe some corporate chap I was chatting up at that party was really CIA or MI6.

Then there was the spy from Central Casting. I asked to be demoted to work for a civilian intelligence officer who disseminated reports about real life in the People's Republic. Human interest stories were much more engaging than troop movements, but reports bore only "Secret" rather than "Top Secret" designations, hence the demotion. Peter was a delightful man, cynical, a good artist who drew comical cartoons. He deplored the shortcoming of the intelligence high-ups in London transferring him and colleagues from Berlin to Hong Kong at the same time. Of course the East Germans told their fellow communists in Peking (as it was then). We used to have a drink after work on Saturday mornings at the Cellar Bar in the Peninsula Hotel, later a gay bar. Ian used to meet me there for our Saturday date and wanted to know who the man was wearing the trench coat. For some reason, he did not buy the story that Peter was my boss.

We worked on Saturday mornings because the offices of SMISHK were not air-conditioned. To compensate, we had Wednesday afternoons off and used to go waterskiing off a beach in the New Territories. Our leader, a colonel, was particularly fond of ballet, as well as waterskiing, and was reputed to be an excellent dancer. He must not have been too concerned about security since the entire British contingent from the department water-skied together.

Because high winds off Hong Kong Harbor blew through our wide-open windows, sometimes sensitive documents flew out to the courtyard below, whereupon most of the SMISHK staff clattered down the stairs at high speed to retrieve them.

On the subject of dancing, I recently found in my five-hundred-year-old Tudor oak chest, where personal papers are stored in New York, an invitation card embossed (not printed) with the royal coat of arms:

*In honour of*
*Her Royal Highness Princess Alexandra of Kent*
*His Excellency The Governor and Lady Black*
*request the pleasure of the company of*
*Miss M. Christie-Miller*
*at a Ball*
*on Friday 10th November, 1961, at 9/30 p.m.*

*Evening dress,*
*Dinner Jacket or national dress*
*Ladies: long or short dresses*
*Decorations will be worn*         *RSVP, A.D.C.*
                                   *Government House*

The days of Empire had dwindled but not totally disappeared across the globe. At another less formal evening event, Princess Alexandra sat on the arm of my stepfather's chair after dinner, chatting amicably.

Hong Kong felt somewhat claustrophobic in those days. Maybe after two years in the US I was frustrated that one could not just get into a car and drive on long, straight roads. Ian used to drive almost the entire length of the colony, from the New Territories, near the Chinese border, by road and car ferry to my parents' house at Stanley Fort during our courting days. Roads in the New Territories and on the island were congested and hilly. I remember acrimonious bridge postmortems as he drove the switchback road to take me home following an evening of play when I had obviously made egregious mistakes.

There were some islands to visit on Sunday launch picnics or sailing jaunts, but the only foreign weekend destination was Macau, by ferryboat, later by hovercraft, still a Portuguese colony. It had a certain seedy charm, with picturesque old buildings, and it was known for gambling. The Chinese would play Fan Tan for hours and hours on end, betting whether the scoop would end up with three, two, or one button-like counters, which seemed so boringly repetitive. Bachelors favored Macau for all-male weekends, and Ian used to go with a group of brother officers who belonged to the FTA (Fuck The Army), an informal association.

My mother, being very hospitable, had many houseguests who were easy to accommodate in our large house. She enjoyed giving lunch and dinner parties and taking them shopping. Jade and pearls were popular, as were crocodile handbags. Mikimoto pearls were much in demand. I still have two double strands, one being often worn and occasionally restrung. Jade was tricky because soapstone was frequently substituted, and it took an expert to spot the fakes. Robert made friends with some of his Chinese medical colleagues who were collectors of fine antiques, which they brought out of China when they left. The Min Chu Society met once a month for a gourmet dinner in an apartment owned by the society, and members would bring priceless *objets d'art* for fellow members to admire. We were honored to be invited to one of these dinners. I still have a set of silver coffee spoons with jade pieces in the handles, a wedding gift from Drs. Phillip and Barbara Mao.

In February 1962, my mother, my stepfather, and I visited my uncle, who was British ambassador to Thailand. The *Times* in 1961 had written his bio in a nutshell: "Recently appointed British Ambassador to Siam, Mr. D.F. MacDermot, will succeed Sir Richard Whittington who is retiring from the Foreign Service. Mr. MacDermot who is fifty-four served as Ambassador to Indonesia from 1956-59. He has held posts in Japan, the Philippines and Formosa (now Taiwan). He has been Assistant Under-Secretary, Foreign Office, for the past two years. He was Minister to Romania, 1954-56."

There were rumors that his career might have culminated in the top government spot at the FCO, (Foreign and Commonwealth Office). He certainly loved his post as ambassador to Thailand. He wrote to my mother describing the Thais as "Asian Dubliners," high praise from this brilliant Irishman, a complimentary description implying that they were charming, sophisticated, gracious, fun-loving people who enjoyed partying.

Excerpts from my diary follow:

> The British Embassy is situated in a spacious compound containing the Residence, houses for the Counsellor, Head of Chancery, Chancery guard, wireless operator, servants' quarters and Gurkha guards' quarters. The latter are the sentinels at the main gate. I noticed that the soldier guarding the front door was knitting with maroon wool. An apologetic and remorseful Thai government gave this valuable land to the British

after a Consul had been murdered in Bangkok. A few years ago the entire compound was sold and must have been worth billions.

Bangkok is dead flat. Oh, the joy of long straight roads after Hong Kong's switchbacks. There are large trees everywhere; rain trees, banyans, a bo (temple) tree in the servants' quarters, bougain-villea, gorgeous red in front and purple at the back surrounding the small lake from which fish constantly rise. Many birds, kingfishers, Straits robins, coppersmith birds and others fly around the gardens and buildings. Tropical as well as English flowers and shrubs surround the lake, canna and spider lilies, weeping willow, marigolds, datura and others. There is a hideous statue of Queen Victoria as Empress of India.

The Embassy chef, who is head of the Cooks' Guild, produces the most excellent meals. He has wonderful ways of doing chicken and duck, makes delicious meringues, and there is always a succulent range of tropical fruits: mangoes, mangosteens, pineapple, papaya, a toffee-like brown fruit, bananas, etc.

The Residence boasts one of only two punkahs still in use in Bangkok. As in Djakarta, these fans wave from side to side, operated by a string attached to a servant's big toe.

There is actually a hearse stored in an Embassy garage.

> One evening after an early dinner at the
> Residence we drove to a huge, semi-outdoor
> theater to watch a review. The king's arrival was
> impressive. He seemed to be a solitary, dignified,
> rather morose man, who seldom smiled. We all
> rose and the women curtsied. He sat on a throne
> and anyone approaching him prostrated them-
> selves. Afterwards the theater was rearranged
> for dancing. We sat with the President and
> General Pissit, and I was introduced to Prince
> and Princess Chumbhot with whom we had tea
> in their gorgeous palace a few days later.

Tourists today visit most of the same "must-see" sights: the
floating markets, silk factories, the house of the famous Jim
Thompson (who made the world aware of Thai silk but who
disappeared mysteriously some years later in the Cameron
Highlands of Malaya) antique shops, workshops where temple
furniture is made. They visit the various wats or temples, Wat
Pho being the most famous. The Catholic church we attended is
irreverently referred to as Wat Ho, which has a jaunty ring to it.

We visited Wat Pho as the sun was setting over the temple
roofs, monks everywhere in saffron robes, crude animal statues,
many broken and half-buried, ugly mosaics of colored glass and
porcelain sparkling on the chedis. There were four large, quaint
statues of giants, one for each recent king, by the ancient teak
gates, wearing top hats. An inner courtyard housed a hundred
bronze Buddhas and the famous Reclining Buddha, over a hundred feet long. The Temple of the Emerald Buddha was built by

Rama I in 1785. The temple bell clappers are cut in the shapes of Bo leaves. There is a beautiful bell tower. Colorful statues of giants and pavilions surround the temple. The Emerald Buddha was carved out of a single piece of jasper, twenty-three inches high. He has three changes of vestments made out of gold cloth and precious stones.

We strolled around the grounds of the Grand Palace, the lying-in-state hall, Dusit Maha Prasad, full of thrones and golden Garuda birds. We saw the elephant mounting place and a little pavilion where the king sometimes sits. The walls are covered with delicate Thai designs of angels rising from lotus blossoms, giving a tapestry effect. Another palace, the Chakri, was designed by a British architect in Italian Renaissance style but with a Thai roof. It contains the Amarin Throne Hall, royal bedchamber, and coronation hall.

We were extremely fortunate to mingle with interesting people, distinguished Thais, members of the royal family and diplomats from many countries at receptions and dinner parties. We met Prince Dhani Nivat, who acted as prince regent for the king. Diplomats included the French ambassador and Madame Clarac, the British ambassador to Cambodia, and Mrs. Murray, the Vietnamese ambassador, and Madame Cao Thai Bao. At one dinner, I sat next to Nai Tula Bunnag, of the Thai Foreign Service seconded to the royal household. He told me he would be accompanying his majesty to Pakistan next month with a modest retinue of thirty-five. The Danish king and queen visited with an entourage of thirteen, whereas Lyndon Johnson as vice president brought 105. He misread the Thais or was improperly briefed by his staff. *The Ugly American* was a best seller at this time. My uncle was horrified that Johnson was late for lunch with the king at the palace, because he had been passing out ballpoint pens on a bus in downtown Bangkok, rather pointless since Thais would not be voting in the 1962 US General Election. The Thais do not approve of any lack of respect for their king. (In recent years, this has changed somewhat, and there has been much unrest and anti-royalty demonstrations.)

I danced with Dr. Chaleom Puranananda, a distinguished bacteriologist who invited us to dinner to see his Thai paintings. It was a memorable evening. After attending two or three diplomatic cocktail parties, we went to his house where the dinner was hosted by his mistress, his wife being away in Switzerland at a sanatorium. Other Thai guests included Jo Bunnag, scion of an old Thai family of Persian descent, owner of the Trocadero Hotel and a great gourmet, and his lady friend, plus two other couples. The second wife of one was the very lovely daughter of a former Thai ambassador to Russia and Pakistan. Dr. Puranananda was an excellent host. Onion soup was followed by fondue where we dipped prawns and meat on skewers from Switzerland into delicious mustard and mayonnaise sauce made by the host himself. Dessert was "Portuguese custard," coconut saturated in syrup with fried onions on top, which, surprisingly, was delicious. In Thailand as in other countries, at the end of dinner, women left the table to "powder our noses" and men stayed at the table and told dirty jokes or rearranged world politics over cigars, port, and brandy. As we followed our pretty hostess upstairs, she passed out on the top step. Nonplussed, we stepped over her and continued to the bathrooms before coming downstairs for coffee and liqueurs.

One evening, after an excellent dinner at the Erawan Hotel, we went to a famous bar called Chiquita's. My mother kept asking the talented pianist to play Irish tunes, but he did not know any. Dermot was eyeing two gorgeous call girls. He liked one in particular and tried to find out her price. My stepfather and priggish yours truly were rather embarrassed at what we considered unseemly behavior by the British ambassador and his sister.

Sir Stephen and Lady Weir hosted their New Zealand National Day on February 6, after which we dined at the Oriental Hotel overlooking the river, where Somerset Maugham wrote one of his novels. Later that week at our embassy, Dermot presented a large cup donated by Lord Louis Mountbatten to the deputy prime minister. Various military VIPs attended, duly surrounded by a barrage of TV and press photographers. Thailand was a military dictatorship at the time.

The promised tea invitation from Princess Chumbhot took place at the prince and princess' Suan Pakkad Palace. We walked around the garden where we saw a four-hundred-year-old lacquer pavilion, lovely lotus ponds, and King Chulalongkorn's houseboat. Their authentic Thai house was full of antiques, including gold lacquer shrines like miniature temples for royal ashes. There were collections of drums, other musical instruments, modern art, handicrafts, and Chinese porcelain, including fourteenth century Celadon. The princess' treasures also included red and gold ornate furniture, a cloth of gold stole and cape, family fans, medals, entire elephant trunks, and innumerable Buddhas.

On February 10, we went to the races and were invited to tea in the royal box. The king arrived in a yellow Daimler, followed by two red Armstrong Siddeleys containing staff in gold-braided white uniforms. Various people were presented to him, then he sat a few chairs away from us in a solitary state, while we drank too-sweet tea and ate sticky cakes. Shortly after the big race, the King's Cup, he and his entourage left, and the rest of us remained for more races and modest betting.

Next day, we drove for two hours across flat plains to Ayudhya, which was the capital of Siam in the fourteenth century and was built on an island surrounded by the Chao Phraya River. After visiting the ruined temple of Wat Yai Chai Mongkhon, another giant Buddha, ruins of the royal cremation grounds, we took a luxury launch belonging to Shell, six hours down river past wats, houses on stilts, fishing nets hanging up to dry or being thrown from boats, delicately carved houses with thatched roofs, floating logs, barges, and as many as thirty-one small sampans being towed by one barge.

We went ashore at Bang Pa-In, established in 1630 as the country seat of the king of Ayudhya. There was also a Chinese palace and a temple built in Gothic style like a Christian church. We visited an amazing stork colony where Dermot dared me to climb a ladder for a better view, but halfway up, I was stung by a swarm of bees. One got me on the eyelid, which was very painful.

Most of us can still remember the movie *The Bridge on the River Kwai*. We arrived at Kanchanaburi after about two and a half hours' drive from Bangkok, then took a launch upriver to the war cemetery at Chungkai, containing seven thousand Dutch, British, and Australian graves, passing elephants towing rafts and teak logs. We saw the remains of the railway bridge immortalized by Alec Guinness, its rails and sleepers riddled with bullet holes, as well as the new bridge in current use.

My final happy event in Bangkok was the consecration of a Buddhist monastery. Lunched with Guy Micklethwait, embassy staff who had served with Dermot in Indonesia, and Ronald Steed, Southeast Asia correspondent for the *Christian Science Monitor*, and then drove out to Nonburi, where a Buddhist assembly hall, or bot, was being consecrated. We met the abbot and two Englishmen who had become Buddhist monks, as well as the president of the Buddhist Association. People were burning offerings: pencil and paper representing learning, needles and thread for wisdom and longevity, and sticking gold leaf on stone balls around the temple. Busloads of monks arrived, went into the bot, chanted, then came out and stood on the surrounding terrace, chanted, and moved slowly until every bit of stone had been trodden upon by their feet and was therefore consecrated.

We departed by night train for a visit to scenic Chiang Mai, in the mountains, also a popular haunt for hippies and tourists. A memory has stayed with me of a Hmong silversmith who was an Anglophile and slept in his coffin wrapped in the Union Jack.

Dermot retired after serving his tour as British ambassador to Thailand. He was knighted by the queen but did not receive the usual tap of the sword on his shoulder at Buckingham Palace. Rather unceremoniously, his "K" was mailed to him in the diplomatic bag.

Unlike most diplomats, he and Betty never invested in a home, which would have paid for itself with rentals while they served abroad. Upon retirement, they rented houses in Ireland, which Dermot loved, but Betty wanted to live in England. They tried for a while, but Dermot was miserable. They compromised by renting in Malta for a few years, then returned to Ireland.

The last time I saw them was when Charles and I visited them in their rented house in Oughterard in County Galway, where they seemed happy. Recently, my godson Rory told me about playing chess with his grandfather around the time of the famous 1972 match between Bobby Fischer and Boris Spassky. Betty was a big bird watcher and belonged to a bird-spotting organization. According to Rory, Dermot drove her all over the countryside while she enumerated bird species, drank his gin, and enjoyed picnic lunches when the weather cooperated.

Conor, who worked for the Irish Geological Survey, bought a house, which they shared with him until they died in their eighties. Conor never married and died much too young in his sixties. He had a distinguished career in the Geological Survey of Ireland and was a dedicated and knowledgeable scientist. Quoting from an obituary speech given by the director, Peadar McArdle, "His passion did not stop at geology, it embraced every aspect of nature. He got this broad interest from his mother. It made him a wonderful and inspiring field leader. He had a real appreciation of his family's heritage and was concerned that memorabilia would be conserved." Happily, several members of our family have seen to this, particularly his older brother Hughie.

Dermot's crowning achievement, which brought great satisfaction in his later years, was an enormous family history in two volumes, *The MacDermots of Moylurg*, which traced our family history for over a thousand years. Betty wrote her own history of the O'Rourke family, from whom she is descended. I had given my hefty two volumes plus my copy of the family tree, many pages long, to my godson, Fergus MacDermot, grandson of Dermot and younger son of my first cousin Hughie. Fergus emailed me from Hong Kong that the earliest recorded ancestor died in 195 AD, but a more reliable starting point would be 956 AD.

When Uncle Bay died, Dermot inherited the title The MacDermot, Prince of Coolavin. He liked to use it rather than the British Sir Dermot, though they never moved to Coolavin. The dowager Felicity Madam MacDermot spent the rest of her life there. Betty much preferred being Lady MacDermot.

Many people remember the romantic moment they met the love of their lives, across a crowded room, as the song goes. I do not, but during the course of that year, working at SMISHK, Ian and I must have met at one of the many parties we attended. He was the dental officer for a Ghurka regiment stationed in the New Territories. He appealed to me because he was different from the other young men I went out with, who seemed frankly boring and insular after my two years in New York. Their recreational interests mostly were sports, going to parties, cars, and drinking excessively. Ian took the trouble to learn Cantonese, which none of the other young Englishmen did, and went into the countryside to photograph local Chinese peasants after obtaining their permission. He was very talented, and those portraits were artistic. He took a moonlighting part-time evening job as an announcer for Radio Hong Kong. He recorded many tapes from their extensive collection, from classical music to current comedians, Tom Lehrer, Mort Sahl, and others. For many years, we played those tapes and were glad to have them when we went to the Canadian far north, where there were only a few hours of television each day, one radio station, and no classical music station. The theme song of our courtship was "Moon River" from *Breakfast at Tiffany's*.

The romance blossomed, and we became engaged. Plans for our wedding on November 7 went forward. About two weeks before the big day, a typhoon hit Hong Kong. The small sailing junk we had been given when we got engaged was swept up a hillside, dismasted, and the engine and some of the superstructure destroyed. The insurance company reimbursed us, then an American visitor to Hong Kong bought the remaining hull from us to ship to a lake somewhere in Minnesota where he planned to rebuild the junk. There was not a flower left in the colony, so my mother reordered the wedding flowers all the way from Japan. Although many ramshackle buildings were destroyed, thanks to the existence of transistor radios, most boats made it safely to typhoon shelters and there was no loss of life. The transistor radio was the technological equivalent during that era of today's cell phone.

Ian's military service in Hong Kong was completed soon after our wedding, a major military social affair, which was attended by my stepfather's colleagues, subordinates and their wives, plus some Chinese medical associates, a few government and civilian friends. I recognize few faces in the wedding album so many years later and still feel badly that so many junior officers reporting to my stepfather felt obliged to buy us wedding presents.

The best man, like other officers, wore dress uniform. During the ceremony, he fainted because the garrison church was so hot. Someone forgot to open the windows, plus he was suffering from the excesses of the bachelor party the night before. He fell to the floor, spurs clattering, causing my child bridesmaid to burst into tears. Happily, everyone recovered quickly and thoroughly enjoyed the wedding reception in Windsor House. This incident presaged later tragedy, if one is superstitious as I am and believes in omens. Back in England some years later, I was told that the church had to be reconsecrated after the war because New Zealand nurses had been raped and murdered there during the Japanese occupation. Within five years of our marriage, Ian was dead, my mother terminally ill, and the mother of my child bridesmaid, her unborn baby, and the little girl herself had been killed in a car accident.

For our honeymoon, we visited Saigon, first having flown on one leg of the famous Pan Am Flight 1 around-the-world flight. I remember a fellow passenger asking, "How many hours have you been married now?" Luckily, I remembered the brown paper package of saris in the overhead luggage rack, which Ian's Indian tailor in Hong Kong had given him for his brother in

Saigon, having done Ian the favor of producing some Vietnamese currency after the banks had closed the day before our wedding. What was left of our wedding night was spent in the Intercontinental Hotel, both of us rather the worse for a post-reception alcoholic send-off at the airport. Sometime later the next day, we surfaced and delivered the package to an assistant to the tailor-brother whose shop was just around the corner from the hotel. The proprietor, a portly Indian, came to the front of the store beaming from ear to ear and insisting we dine with him that night.

He collected us from the Intercontinental Hotel with his plump wife and his slender, nubile mistress. We drove to a splendid French-Vietnamese restaurant on stilts some way from the center of Saigon. After the meal, our host suggested a drive. His chauffeur looked anxious. Ian had been briefed earlier in the day by the British military attaché and told not to leave the city limits, so he asked if they ever met the Viet Cong. The answer from our ever-genial host was, "When they see I'm an Indian gentleman, they don't bother me, but with Americans it's different." He made the universal throat-cutting gesture. We doubted the VC would bother to ask if we were Brits, so were relieved when the chauffeur insisted we return immediately to the city center.

We explored Angkor Wat in Cambodia before there were many tourists, staying at the only seedy hotel that existed at the time, where we found weevils in the bread. After a few days amongst the magnificent ruins, having temporarily run out of money, we took a bus instead of a plane in which the local Cambodians shared sticks of sugar cane with us, reaching Phnom Penh that evening. As we took off in our DC3 en route to Bangkok, we were amused to see a sign at the end of the runway: "Pilots beware of ditch."

This was my second stay at the embassy with Dermot and Betty. After some happy days there, we took the train south into Malaya, stopping in Penang, visiting Hong Kong and Shanghai Bank (now HSBC) friends in Kuala Lumpur, who opened the bar mid-morning and kept on drinking late into the evenings. From KL, we took a long-distance cab driven by an Indian accompanied by family members all the way to Singapore, where we finished our honeymoon by staying with my lifelong friend Wanda, now married to John Rix, with two small children.

# Chapter Ten

Ian was posted back to England at the end of 1962 for his final two years' commission. When he retired with the rank of major and received a gratuity, he invested half of it in vintage wines with Justerini & Brooks, to be held in their cellars under the Thames. After a certain time, when the wines were at their peak, half would be sold at a profit and half returned to the investor to consume.

England in 1963 was a rude awakening for a spoiled young couple like us. Besides the horrible climate, we were meeting each other's friends and families for the first time. I have never been so cold in my life as I was in Edinburgh staying with a young doctor and his wife, a nurse, who had no heating in their flat. We would get out of bed in the morning, put on all our clothes, coats, and scarves and head down to a cafe on Princes Street for breakfast.

The two years in Hampshire with the Rifle Brigade, otherwise known as the Green Jackets, passed pleasantly. When Ian was posted to their depot in Winchester, the army paid our rent for a charming seventeenth-century thatched cottage in the village of East Stratton. I remember I was in its quaint, impractical kitchen, looking out over the half-door when I heard the news of Kennedy's assassination.

While we were living at Stratton End, my cousin, Caroline Christie-Miller, used to visit us for weekends. Caroline is my closest first cousin, for whom I have great affection and admiration. She graduated from Badminton School in Bristol and then went to Manchester Art School where she won a painting prize. She chose the Courtauld Institute of Art over the Chelsea Art School, after a year in Florence, because she wanted to explore museum work.

Anthony Blunt was director of the Courtauld from 1946 and surveyor of the king's, subsequently the queen's, pictures. Caroline and Peter Cannon-Brookes who met at the Courtauld were both taught tutorials by him. His relationships with Burgess and Maclean, the two famous spies, were already known to MI6. Donald Maclean, by now exiled in Moscow, had been a friend of Peter's father during their college days at Trinity Hall. At the Courtauld, Peter sensed that Blunt was wary of him because his father had been head of the private office of Lord Selborne as minister for economic warfare and secretary of the SOE Council. As a research student, Peter got to know Blunt very well. When he traveled in Eastern Europe in 1963, Blunt gave him letters of introduction. This upset the Foreign Office because, unknown to Peter, his father was still deeply involved with MI6. After Kim Philby (the "third man") defected from Beirut to the Soviet Union, Peter was interviewed by security services before driving to Budapest for the British Council.

Caroline was offered a lectureship at Leeds University, a post that was confirmed by Quentin Bell (son of Vanessa Bell and nephew of Virginia Woolf). She and Peter married in 1966 and, as they were friends of Peggy Guggenheim, she invited them to stay with her in her palazzo in Venice on their honeymoon. On one occasion, they accompanied her to dinner with Andy Warhol in that city. Andy sat at the head of the table between the host, John Richardson, and Peggy. He did not speak, eat, or drink the entire evening. Peter concluded that he was totally stoned. When he and Peggy ran into him next day on a vaporetto going out to the Lido for a film premiere, he had no idea where he had been the night before. She visited them in Birmingham and became godmother to their son Stephen.

Caroline taught history of art for Birmingham University extramural department to adults and later in Cardiff. Peter was keeper of art in the Birmingham Art Gallery, then keeper of art in the National Gallery of Wales from 1978 till 1986. He and Caroline founded the *International Journal of Museum Management and Curatorship* as joint editors. They moved to Oxfordshire in 1986, where she continued to teach history of art in the Oxford University Department for Continuing Education, now part of Kellogg College.

Peter and Caroline have always had close connections with the Czech Republic, where Peter was awarded a medal by the Masaryk Academy. He had devoted much energy to keeping channels of communication with the Czechs open while they were under communism. Caroline and Peter wrote *Baroque Churches* together. Caroline was a lecturer for Martin Randall Travel cultural tours in Prague, Bohemia, Moravia, and Sicily.

Peter had a distinguished and interesting career. A few other facts: In 1989, he set up for the University of Manchester the Tabley House Collection as a country house museum and continued as its consultant curator until November 2020. Also, as consultant curator, he organized and cataloged the Atelier sale of Franta Belsky and Irena Sedlecka in Oxford in 2017. He is writing a book on the life and sculpture of Irena Sedlecka, and Czech TV wants him to write one on Franta Belsky. He has written other books, all listed in *Who's Who.*

On behalf of Count Natale Antonio Diodato "Luccio" Labia, the grandson of the South African diamond and gold tycoon who owned ten miles of the Rand, he organized the major sale of paintings from the J. B. Robinson collection at Sotheby's and has remained a consultant to them ever since. A small group of the finest paintings, which were not in the sale, were on loan to the University Art Museum of Princeton. Peter visited them (and us) regularly until after the death of Luccio Labia.

During those two years in England, we visited Ian's family in County Durham, friends in London, and elsewhere. We attended the weddings of many friends and relatives. My New York roommate, June Hare, married Howard Dickinson in Devonshire and subsequently lived in Conway, New Hampshire, after he had graduated from the Yale School of Forestry, where they owned many acres and had three children. After their divorce, June moved to Santa Fe, New Mexico. I am godmother to their son, Alexander ("Mouse").

In June, Jenny Hanbury-Tracy married Martin Morland in All Saints Church, the chapel of Wardour Castle, the former ancestral home of the Arundel family. Her mother, the Hon. Blanche Hanbury-Tracy, was the daughter of the 15th Baron Arundel of Wardour and my mother's greatest friend. I wrote about their life in London in the early thirties. Blanche was also my godmother, and the previous year had stayed with us in Hong Kong for three months.

Martin Morland was the son of Oscar Morland, whom my uncle Dermot succeeded as ambassador to Indonesia. Like his father, Martin had a distinguished career in the foreign office, becoming British ambassador to Myanmar in 1986, where he was a strong supporter of Daw Aung San Suu Kyi in her struggle for democracy.

We also attended the wedding of Michael and Anna Prince. Michael and Ian became friends when Michael was studying accountancy in Edinburgh and Ian was doing dentistry at Edinburgh University. Michael and Anna remained close friends, and since Michael died, she and I have kept in touch, occasionally meeting in London. She lives in France in a large, old manor. Her daughter, Auriole, with her husband and her children have stayed with me in East Hampton while they were living temporarily in Brooklyn.

While still living in England, we took a trip to France by car ferry and toured the magnificent Châteaux of the Loire Valley. We spent a night with Michael Prince's parents. His father, formerly with ICI and later the United Nations, and his French wife had an unusual house near Tours, consisting of rooms that were partial caves set into the hillside above the river. One entered and left by plate-glass sliding doors in front of the caves. A pre-dinner ritual was observing a grandchild being breastfed, which caused Ian huge embarrassment, but he was rewarded with a superb dinner. We drove further south to Sarlat, a medieval walled city in the heart of truffle country. I have a vague memory of running out of money when we reached Paris and spending a night in our car.

For our second year, we moved to officers' quarters in the city of Winchester, but Ian was restless. He did not want to stay in England but could not decide on another country, though he investigated many options. I got fed up with his indecision, so I went to Nerja near Málaga in Spain to stay with my godmother, Blanche Hanbury-Tracy, promising to come home when he made up his mind. No email or texting then, but I got a telegram saying we were going to Canada, to Vancouver, British Columbia, which was wonderful news to me. When Ian left the army, having completed his five years, we went back to Nerja in Spain in the early fall, where we could live on pennies a day in a tiny little apartment, so he could study for the British Columbia dental boards and I could go to the beach until it got too cold; though a girlfriend and I were almost raped by a guardia civil. My mother never got over being approached by a man brandishing a sword on a deserted Iranian beach. She screamed and he ran away. She admitted that the fear of being slaughtered was far worse than that of being raped, and ever after sat near groups on any beach.

I remained with my mother and stepfather while Ian flew to Vancouver and stayed with our cousin Agnes Monahan. We were part of the brain drain from England, and we were welcomed in Canada as landed immigrants, not resident aliens, the US nomenclature for immigrants. However, the cabal, consisting of prosperous dentists in Vancouver, was determined to keep a good thing for themselves and failed all the aspirants who took the board exams, unless a dentist was willing to go to Prince Rupert in the far north and treat the indigenous population.

For three winter months we drove across the prairie provinces, which were very cold and very flat. Though offered many jobs, Ian declined them all. Apocryphal, perhaps, but it makes for a better story: We were staying in a motel in Edmonton, down to our last hundred dollars, so I took a job typing in a warehouse. We were not about to return with our tails between our legs after we had told our families and friends we were going to leave boring old England to make our fortunes in the New World. Ian got a call from the mayor of Yellowknife, situated on the shores of Great Slave Lake, population five thousand then (forty thousand now) and home to two major gold mines, Cominco and Giant Yellowknife. They needed a dentist. The practice was geographically the largest in the world, stretching from Hudson Bay in the east to the Yukon in the west, from the Canadian provinces in the south to the Arctic and the North Pole, over a million square miles but extremely sparsely populated. The Northwest Territories was a huge expanse of land, about a third of the whole of Canada. Years later, it was divided into two geopolitical areas, the Northwest Territories and Nunavut.

Ian flew there for the weekend, came back on Monday, and told me we were headed for Yellowknife. We were to receive an apartment, a fully equipped surgery, and a warm welcome. He had called me his first night when he went to the only bar and met a real-life prospector, a very large man called Smoky Heal. Smoky had his Saint Bernard dog Barney by his side at the bar, and Ian decided we should acquire one too. Smoky had shown the true northern spirit of welcome by requesting that the plane wait until he had given Ian a meal at his home. Ian thought he was in a time capsule transported back to the Gold Rush. It was still a frontier town not so far removed from the nineteenth century. I have never lived anywhere so truly democratic: Professionals and underground miners speaking little English ("straight off the boat" from Ukraine or Italy) partied together. The common enemy was the weather. We endured nine months of winter when the temperature often dropped to fifty-five degrees below zero Fahrenheit, and three short months of summer when the sun barely set, good for fishing, sailing, camping, and waterskiing, but the mosquitoes were awful.

We drove a thousand miles north from Edmonton along the Mackenzie Highway, nearly seven hundred miles of which was unpaved, in a temperature of forty below zero, through stunted pines, spending a night at the hotel at High Level, with its noisy beer parlor, unshaven construction workers in heavy boots, farmers, and indigenous people. On again in the morning after breakfast, passing indigenous settlements, we stopped for tasteless coffee, helped ourselves to condensed milk out of the can, more uninhabited miles, and then a left turn at Enterprise and eighty miles to the ice road, crossing the Mackenzie River where tiny fir trees stuck in the ice marked the road. The huge river was about a mile wide, and to the right and left of us, the ice was frozen into waves, whiteness under a gray sky, and suddenly we saw perched on a skeletal tree an ookpik, or Arctic owl, surely symbolic that we had reached the far north. Driving the last two hundred miles we saw the Northern Lights, a great green arc like a giant waving curtain, the epitome of cold and relentless beauty, and so we eventually arrived at the Gold Metropolis.

Once we settled in, we became proud of our pioneering spirit, like the old-timers. Also, we got "bitten" by the far north. There is something undefinable about the force of nature, the wilderness, the vast spaces, the wildlife, caribou, moose, polar bears, the lakes and rivers teeming with fish.

In town, there were no bus queues, indeed no public transportation, no traffic jams, crowds, coal dust, fog or smog, only unlimited open spaces, excellent views of Great Slave Lake (about the size of Belgium), well-heated houses and apartments, and most of the amenities of a provincial capital, one of the most northerly and smallest in the world, on the same latitude (north of the 60th parallel) as some towns and cities in Alaska and Siberia. The economy depended mostly on the two goldmines,

Giant Yellowknife and Cominco, known as Con, and several outlying small "bush" mines on the tundra, and the government represented by the Department of Northern Affairs. Many civil servants and their families lived in Yellowknife to administer the Eskimos (in present times "Inuit" is the politically correct term, so I will use it from now on), indigenous tribes, and Metis, or mixed breeds (indigenous people). For four months of the year, we were cut off except by air while the Hay River froze or thawed (freeze-up and break-up), which meant prices of supplies rose in the supermarkets and other stores.

Spring came, not as it does in temperate climates, but suddenly, with bright sunshine and long hours of daylight and slush. The evergreens in their millions took no notice, the willows bravely put forth new leaves, their roots still snow covered. There is no smell in winter, but with the thaw, one could smell mud and shrubs.

People of many other nationalities lived and worked in Yellowknife: Central Europeans, Italians, Germans, Russians, Scandinavians, Ukrainians, Chinese, Japanese, Americans, English, Scottish, Welsh, and Irish. Actually, there was only one Arab family and one Jewish family. One day during the Six-Day War, Max, who owned the only laundry in Yellowknife, came to deliver our white coats and clean towels. Ian's Arab patient was leaving the surgery and he and Max had an amiable chat about being the sole representatives of the two sides. Our Anglican bishop, Henry Cook, was the suffragan bishop of the Arctic, and there were priests and ministers of many denominations, a convent, four large schools, three doctors, one dentist, the mayor, a few thousand miners, civil servants, merchants, bush pilots, and prospectors, some of whom were old-timers who could remember when there was no road to "outside." Boats brought supplies once a year, and there were no white women. Some were still waiting to stake the claim, which would make them millionaires.

Ian's practice was so busy that we seldom left town. Visits to Dogrib Indian and other indigenous (probably Dene) villages usually were combined with fishing trips, catching trout weighing up to forty pounds and arctic char, which tastes even better than salmon. Early in May, we had supper with a young doctor and his wife who had a cabin built on the rocks by the shore of Great Slave Lake. The mosquitoes were just beginning their annual assault, as we sat on the rocks basking in the sunshine, looking at the ice that had only melted a few feet from the shore. There was a simple nine-hole golf course with sanded greens in Yellowknife, and an annual match with tee-off at midnight on June 24 during our twenty-four hours of daylight.

Later in May, we flew to our first Arctic settlement, Cambridge Bay, on Victoria Island, at the time of annual betting on break-up. Inhabitants bought tickets for a specific date, and the lucky winner was whoever predicted the day when the sea ice candles broke up with loud cracking.

Approximately two hundred civil servants were stationed in Cambridge Bay or Coppermine or other settlements to administer the same number of indigenous Inuit. Igloos had been replaced with shacks and huts, and children were happier eating ice cream and candy than muktuk (whale blubber), though there is a photo of Ian building an igloo. A few families still lived off the land, hunting or trapping in winter and fishing in summer. Most were happy to live in the settlements on grandmother's old-age pension and welfare, so no longer were the aged Inuit put out on the ice floes to die of cold and starvation. Houses and apartments tended to be overheated. We used to hang game birds on our outside balcony during the winter until we were ready to thaw and eat them. Fresh meat and vegetables were flown in once a month. During the two or three months of Arctic summer, a hospital ship visited the settlements in the eastern Arctic, but in the west, patients requiring critical care were flown to hospitals in the provinces.

The midnight sun was so bright when we first visited Cambridge Bay, its brightness heightened by the whiteness of snow, ice, and no trees. Sometimes we stayed up till 4 a.m. playing chess and talking. In my diary, I wrote that I climbed on a chair to drape blankets across the gap between the curtain pelmet and the wall to try to get some sleep. "The sun has made its obeisance, a sort of stiff curtsey just above the horizon, and some visitor from 'Outside' is painstakingly poised behind his camera taking time exposures of the sunset and sunrise to impress the folks back home," but I forget who I am quoting.

On one plane trip north, many Inuit children were returning home from boarding schools in Alberta for the summer holidays, rejoining their families before break-up when planes could no longer land on the ice. The fishing season was beginning. Some were bound for remote settlements on Victoria and King William Islands and would have to continue their journeys by dog team. A few older children were destined for arranged marriages.

There is a story about an Inuit who had nightmares after hearing that people lived in blocks of apartments on top of each other, and he imagined them suffocating, which is understandable for a member of a race where the population ratio was approximately one human per fifty thousand square miles. However, only a small area is populated. Most of this vast territory, the Barren Lands, consists of tundra and many lakes where only muskeg grows above the permafrost, and herds of caribou and muskox roam. We got used to perpetual daylight and a bright glare off the snow and ice. There were no tarmac roads, just rocky tracks. Nevertheless, intrepid indigenous people, Inuit, and white trappers had traveled hundreds of miles inland by dog team. Survival always depended on the appearance of caribou for food and clothing. The trappers also snared white fox and harpooned seals through the ice. They traded skins, ate the seal meat, and gave the leftovers to their dogs. Walruses, polar bears, and narwhals were hunted too, though the latter were rare. Ski-Doos abounded and made hunting easier in many ways, except, as the hunters would say, when you were stuck in the freezing wilderness you could not eat your Ski-Doo, but one of your dogs could save you from starvation.

We greatly admired the Royal Canadian Mounted Police (RCMP) and the oblate missionaries. These priests were sent from their native Brittany to remote Arctic settlements. The priest at Cambridge Bay was a delightful man. He originally lived at Bathurst Inlet, where he used to go fishing for six weeks at a time and stayed there for eleven years, building a church out of the local rock with his own hands. He said Mass in a mixture of French, Latin, English, and Inuit, providing coffee afterward for the congregation. The priests operated their short-wave radios in their native Breton patois and also ran a thriving business selling Inuit ivory and soapstone carvings all over Canada. Carvers "see" in a block of soapstone the polar bear, the man hunting, or the mother and child, and then carve away the surplus material until a beautiful work of art appears. We once owned a unique carving of a walrus and a polar bear. It broke in half during its Atlantic crossing from England. An expert in Inuit sculpture wrote a letter explaining that in Inuit lore the walrus was mightier and larger than the majestic polar bear, so the insurance company reimbursed us because the two pieces after being separated were valueless.

The Mounties had a rather unusual duty in Yellowknife besides keeping the peace, which was to go after the bootleggers. The government-run liquor store kept regular hours so miners coming off late shifts needed to buy from the taxi drivers who kept bottles in their trunks along with an extra battery to prevent them from freezing in extreme below-zero temperatures. There were twelve taxis in the fleet, and if one happened to spot the police patrolling, they radioed to the other drivers that cab thirteen was out so they could take evasive action.

Our Saint Bernard puppy, Marcus, arrived by plane from Edmonton on the same flight as the canoe Ian had ordered during the spring of 1965. The canoe came all the way from Prince Edward Island. It was green when it arrived, became orange the next year, and scarlet the third.

As Marcus grew through puppyhood, he was much loved and petted by children and adored by us. We acquired him with the help of another Saint Bernard owner, George Dundas, manager of one of the gold mines. He came from the same kennels as George's Rheso, by mail order like everything in the north, including boats, pets, books, and, for some lonely miners, even brides. I befriended one of them, a beautiful young woman from Germany married to a much older man. Christa and I used to waterski together in the short summer.

I mentioned Smoky Heal and his Saint Bernard Barney, whom he used to take everywhere, including bars. One evening, we went to the Old Stope with Smoky, his wife, and Barney. As Barney wended his way through the tables, he caused more than one inebriated customer to fall off his chair with a wave from that huge tail. Once, after a night of heavy drinking when the outside temperature was thirty below zero, Smoky passed out in his truck. He would certainly have frozen to death had Barney not lain beside him all night.

On our first Christmas Eve, we gave a party, and put Marcus's wooden barrel purchased from Hennessy's in New York filled with brandy around his neck. There was pretty heavy drinking at Yellowknife parties. Over-proof rum was sold legally in the Northwest Territories. People were looking at each other wondering if there really was a second Saint Bernard in the room. They were not seeing double, which some feared they were, for Smoky had arrived with his dog Barney. The party was in full swing. I had not noticed that Marcus had retired to the kitchen where he managed to chew through his wooden barrel. The kitchen smelled strongly of brandy. Later in Monterey, California, we found a replacement, bound in Mexican silver, but it was too heavy for Marcus to wear.

Marcus was so devoted to Ian that he used to sit all evening on his haunches with his chin resting on the arm of his chair while he read. Occasionally, he would grunt, turn on his back, and lash out playfully with one giant paw to have his tummy rubbed. When Ian sat up in bed reading, Marcus would leap onto the bed and gnaw the handkerchief in his pajama pocket, or the top of the sheet or the blanket, long after puppyhood, indulged by his doting master. When I got into bed, he got off disdainfully. When Ian was away on an Arctic safari treating Inuit patients, he never entered the bedroom. He chewed his way through many a candlewick bedspread, dish towel, moose-hide slipper, and mitten.

After Christmas, we attended a very lively party given by four couples who served Ukrainian delicacies, including cabbage rolls and reindeer meat, plus plenty of liquor. The bank manager arrived wearing Ukrainian national dress, including a blond wig and his wife's boots. Ian could not remember anything the next morning, so I told him he had spent most of the evening sitting on top of a clothes washer, expounding on Communism (he was a professed humanist at the time) and flirting with one of his most tiresome female patients. He amused our host by requesting a "doggy bag" to take home to Marcus. Our doctor telephoned to ask us if he had misbehaved. I assured him that he had not, other than sitting on a Christmas ornament, which he broke.

We gave a farewell dinner party for our friends, George and Elda Dundas, who were retiring to Ontario following George's long career as a mine manager. Their Saint Bernard, Rheso, and Marcus got into a fight after dinner in the middle of the sitting room. There were no serious injuries, though Marcus had a bald spot above his right ear where Rheso had removed a chunk of hair without drawing blood. We inherited Rheso's crate in case Marcus ever had to be flown to Edmonton to a vet. We never needed to use the crate for a vet visit, but sometimes the Edmonton Zoo would borrow it because it was large enough to transport the occasional polar bear from the wilderness to the zoo.

Every afternoon in winter, regardless of temperature, I donned a pair of snowshoes made by Dogrib Indians at Fort Rae and strode forth across the nearby lake and low hills, skimming the snowy surface while Marcus foundered up to his shoulders, great exercise. In summer, I would take him to a small lake beyond the airport where I paddled around on an air mattress and he splashed through shallow water, for he hated swimming. Sometimes I tied him to a shady tree while playing tennis, or he accompanied a girlfriend and me around the golf course at uncrowded times.

There were no domestic livestock in Yellowknife because there was no grazing for cattle and it was too cold for pigs or chickens. Milk, meat, and eggs were expensive in the only supermarket. During break-up and freeze-up, prices for fresh produce soared because they could only be supplied by air while the one road to Edmonton was unusable. Our one airline, Pacific Western, had a daily flight to and from Edmonton. Ian used it to deal with his dental lab in that city for dentures, partial plates, and bridges. There was plenty of wildlife, caribou, moose, fish, and game birds to supplement supermarket wares. Caribou was delicious, so tender one could almost eat it with a spoon. We shot wild duck, geese, and ptarmigan, which we cooked, but it tasted fishy because there was no grain for them to feed on so far north. Wild berries helped to improve the flavor.

The next Christmas, we cooked a goose in our apartment, which we planned to eat with our Dutch friends, the Vanderbies. He worked for Radio Canada. They had eloped and emigrated from the Netherlands because Teresa's family considered she was marrying beneath her. Because they did not speak much English on arrival in Canada, they worked in menial jobs in hotels before they came to Yellowknife. By the time we had driven across town to their apartment, the goose had frozen. It was fifty-five degrees below zero that week.

We unbundled from our boots, layers of sweaters, and double-lined parkas with wolverine hoods. After putting the goose back in the oven, we admired the tree decorated with old family ornaments from Holland. On the previous Sunday, we had packed a picnic lunch and trekked across a frozen lake on our snowshoes to cut the tree from a small forest. Though only five feet high, it was many years old, its growth stunted by the inhospitable climate of the tundra. We unwrapped our presents, books, and records from Amsterdam, London, Vancouver, and Toronto. We exchanged Inuit carvings and mukluks whose soft leather soles and colorful felt legs are ideal footwear. My most treasured gift was a unique blanket made by Dogrib Indians at Fort Rae, crocheted from thin strips of rabbit fur. Sadly, it disintegrated some years later.

When we went to other peoples' homes for a meal, we would park our cars and plug a cable into sockets on the walls of buildings or their perimeter fences so that our batteries would not freeze. At home and work, we kept them plugged in. About half an hour before leaving a dinner party, one of us went out to turn on the car heater so it would be warm for the drive home. We took nature and the climate very seriously. On the only road out of town, a large sign told drivers to check that they had spare gas, blankets, an axe, some food, and matches. If you broke down, you were supposed to cut small trees and light a fire until help arrived. There were stories of bush pilots forced to land in the wilderness, surviving for days until they were rescued.

As a European woman, I had to learn to become involved in volunteer work in good North American tradition. I was unimpressed by the Handicrafts Guild and have never been handy or artistic. Opal Cook, the bishop's wife, suggested I might help at a crèche at the local hospital for mothers who were helping to ease the nursing shortage, but the idea of dozens of strange babies, mostly Inuit and indigenous people, terrified me, so I opted to work in the kitchen. At that time, the new correctional institute was offering high salaries to probation helpers, but again I worried that I might not be good at restraining drunken ladies, so I embarked on writing a novel. During our first months, I had worked with Ian in the surgery and office, but the practice prospered, and Ian was able to hire a charming and efficient dental assistant, so I just did the billing and bookkeeping. Sometimes it was embarrassing to have to socialize with deadbeat patients who had not paid their bills, but that was a hazard of small-town life.

Compared with stratospheric twenty-first-century dental costs, our charges were modest, and Ian did everything: extractions, fillings, cleaning, dentures, plates, bridges, etc. Implants had not yet been invented. In addition to private patients, the Canadian government paid for every indigenous patient and Inuit whom Ian treated, starting with five dollars for an inspection. An extraction cost the taxpayer fifteen dollars.

Every year in April, a Dog Derby was held in Yellowknife. This was an annual fiesta consisting of three days of dog sled racing; squaw wrestling; ice-jiggling (fishing through the ice); bannock, bacon, eggs, and fish frying on fires on the ice; indoor fancy dress parades; figure skating on the indoor ice rink, usually used for endless curling matches; and dancing. Preparations started in January when true northern males started to grow beards. The thickest and bushiest won a prize. A carnival queen was chosen from high-school girls, the winner being the one who had sold the most raffle tickets, but I thought they should crown a carnival king in all his bearded glory.

The mayor opened the Derby with a few well-chosen words as he shivered by the flag on a wooden dais, the temperature averaging forty below zero. The first day was a half-holiday and children showed up in fur-trimmed parkas, sealskin or embroidered mukluks, fur mitts, and lots of cameras. Usually about six dog teams entered, driven by indigenous people or Inuits, and an umpire went along in a yellow Cat or snowmobile to see fair play. There were no "bloodstock" sales, but a few leading sled dogs changed hands over beers at the Old Stope Bar. They were a mix of Samoyed, Alsatian, and Eskimo husky, and ranged in color from pure white, gray, brindled, and salt and pepper to jet black. Any underfed dogs showing their ribs were eliminated before the races started. They tore off across the snow-covered frozen lake, their owners brandishing moose-hide whips decorated with multicolored woolen tassels. The competitors spread out as they scrambled up the shore of the lake, raced through the middle of town past an abandoned mine, and onto the big lake, followed by photographers in cars. The racing was repeated for two more days.

Another annual event in Yellowknife was June 21, or Saturday nearest, the only golf match in the world that started at midnight. Golfers could blame bad scores on the long twilight rather than alcohol consumed beforehand. The fairways consisted of rocks, scrub, and pine trees, and the greens were oiled sand. It was preferable to lose one's ball to Raymond, the sporting raven and town emblem, than to suffer the ignominy of one's too-low drive boomeranging back to the tee after colliding with a chunk of Precambrian rock.

In summer months, we went camping by canoe with our tent and sleeping bags, food, and Marcus, enjoying the vast open spaces of lakes, rivers, and forests. We usually camped on islands and hoped that marauding bears would not swim out to pay us a nocturnal visit, for they were reputed to smell food from far away and had been known to open cans with their claws and devour the contents. We often portaged our canoe, that is, unloaded it and carried it upstream over rocks and fallen trees. Going downstream, we would sometimes shoot the rapids, which was mildly dangerous but very exhilarating. We often camped in places where we felt no human beings had ever been before. However, we often chose indigenous peoples' campsites and lit our fires where large bones bore witness to the remains of a caribou feast.

Sometimes we explored Great Slave Lake for old forts and trappers' cabins. We used to dig for old copper pots and antique rifles as well as looking for eagles' nests. I still have a couple of those pots, which I use to collect the ashes from my fireplace in East Hampton. Sometimes Peter Bromley joined our weekend camping trips, Barbara and the children preferring day trips.

Marcus grew up with the canoe. As a puppy, he presented no hazard to stability but had to be lifted in and out of the canoe. Trouble started in our second summer. We ventured up the Yellowknife River to the rapids. The air was chilly but the water was ice free. On the way back, Ian cut the engine to observe a flock of trumpeter swans. Marcus stood up to have a look, causing the canoe to turn turtle, to the amusement of our friends in another canoe. Luckily, we were in shallow water at the end of a sandbar and were able to right the canoe and replace our sodden selves and dripping dog into the boat, but it was the coldest, wettest five miles I have ever navigated. Marcus never set paw in the canoe again.

During our three years in Yellowknife, Ian's dental practice grew, as did Marcus. Ian treated everyone, private patients and indigenous people. Most of the Dogrib Indians came to our surgery, but to treat the Inuit, as I already mentioned, we traveled by small plane to settlements on the Arctic Coast during summer when we endured twenty-four hours of daylight.

We usually treated the indigenous patients and the workers from the outlying mines at the end of the working day because the former smelled so strongly of fish and the latter of booze. They told us that we white people smelled to them like mothers' milk. The miners who worked at dry mines way out on the tundra wanted to visit Yellowknife for wine and women, but this required a doctor or dental visit. They had to show a receipt when they returned. Sometimes they would insist on a tooth being extracted without Novocain because they were feeling no pain. To our amusement and their embarrassment, they would occasionally give me their room number at Yellowknife's only hotel and ask me to meet them later for a drink before Ian or I explained that I was his wife!

One winter, we took a trip to Calgary then Las Vegas, and drove north and west through California, staying at a dude ranch where we rode horses with a famous TV anchor and his wife, then through mission country to San Francisco. Listening to Thelonius Monk in a nightclub there was a special memory.

In the summer of 1966, Ian's parents came out from England. We drove through the Rockies to scenic Banff and Lake Louise, staying in lodges so they could see more of Canada than Yellowknife.

Princess Alexandra and her husband, Sir Angus Ogilvy, visited Yellowknife in the summer of 1967. He was intrigued by Ian's planned canoe expedition and would have happily joined, but his wife reminded him of many upcoming royal engagements. This was indeed fortunate in view of what happened. They were anxious to experience a dog-sled ride, which we were able to arrange.

Later that summer, a delegation from Siberia came to visit Yellowknife. We shared similarities of climate and geography, tundra and taiga, mining, etc. A dinner was arranged, and it was decided that the owner of Yellowknife's only taxi company should sit next to the leader, because he spoke Russian. The Siberian Communist complained that he considered himself socially superior to a taxi driver.

We flew in small planes piloted by legendary bush pilots to various Inuit settlements on the shores of the Arctic Ocean well north of the Arctic Circle. Lacking necessary equipment for fillings or more elaborate dental work, Ian was only able to do inspections and extract teeth on site, referring other patients for treatment "outside," as we called it. He was an excellent photographer and very interested in the Inuit people. He collected many soapstone, whalebone, and narwhal tusk carvings as well as prints.

There are many stories about these intrepid pilots, some of whom had nicknames. Moosey Brown, a first-rate flier, was so called because of his elongated face and Roman nose, the Arctic Fox for his grey hair and beard, and there was a Red Baron. We chartered Silent Bill to pick us up at an appointed spot on the Yellowknife River after a five-day canoe trip. He said not a word as he tied the canoe to the plane struts and lifted an adolescent Saint Bernard into the cabin, but his expression said enough. There were hair-raising stories of hazardous flights, a pilot following what he thought were DEW Line beacons (Distant Early Warning stations, a feature of the Cold War), only to discover that they were stars. One pilot considered it a joke that he had to hold the cockpit door shut, and another found landing sideways on a runway hilariously funny.

A man must have a bit of daredevil in him to become a bush pilot. There are easier ways to make a living than flying around the north in all weathers, whether with skis or floats, in fog, snow, freezing rain, and whiteouts, with limited radio communication and practically no instrument flying. Pilots often had to do their own mechanical work in small settlements, turning out at all hours of the day or night, to fight a forest fire, rescue a sick Inuit, search for a missing comrade, fly a party of government officials to a conference, and so on. Like most jobs, much was routine and dull, regular runs flying freight, mail, and passengers to Arctic settlements and outlying mines, often under contract to mining companies engaged in exploration.

During the summer, besides sailing our lightning-class sailboat, North Wind, purchased from friends partly to accommodate Marcus, we did a lot of canoeing. In the summer of 1966, Ian and his good friend Peter Bromley canoed all the way from Great Slave to Great Bear Lake (Port Uranium), portaging the canoe when the river was not navigable. This was good practice for their Centennial project, which they spent a long time planning.

# Chapter Eleven

The year 1967 was Canada's Centennial, so Ian, Peter Bromley, and Peter's sixteen-year-old son Bob decided on a special project. The mid-nineteenth century represented the height of Victorian imperialism. There had not been a major British naval event since the Battle of Trafalgar, and the British wanted to be world leaders during this era of naval exploration. An important goal was to find a route through Arctic waters to the Pacific. Sir John Franklin, the famous British explorer, went in search of the Northwest Passage with two ships, HMS *Terror* and *Erebus*, but never returned.

When the *Erebus* and *Terror* failed to sail back to England, rescue expeditions were sent to the Canadian Arctic. Sir George Back led one of many search expeditions, but there was little hope of finding survivors. He navigated a river called the Great Fish River, subsequently named for him as the Back River, which flowed from the Barren Lands to its estuary in the Arctic Ocean. He found no traces of the Franklin expedition but brought his crew safely back to England. A few years ago, wreckage of one of the Franklin ships was actually discovered, though over the years there had been traces of men and their possessions who had abandoned the ships but did not survive. I have a leather-bound copy of Back's *Narrative of the Arctic Land Expedition to the Mouth of the Great Fish River, and along the Shores of the Arctic Ocean in the Year, 1833,1834 and 1835* dedicated to the Earl of Ripon, Secretary of State for the colonies.

Ian and Peter decided to follow in the footsteps of the Back expedition as a Centennial project, described thus in the *News of the North*: "Peter Bromley, his son Bob and Dr. Ian Calder took off this week on a wilderness trip following the route of an earlier explorer. They flew from Yellowknife Tuesday for Tundra where they will start their canoe journey toward the Arctic coast following routes covered by Capt. George Back, during his search for survivors of the Franklin Expedition. They expect to reach the Arctic coast in about three weeks. They will have with them Back's account of his trip and will be following it with interest."

When preparing for their journey, they knew they would have to portage the canoe and all their equipment, so they packed very carefully, eliminating superfluous material. Finally, they settled on their canoe, paddles and spares, a small yellow nylon tent, cameras and film, sleeping bags, extra sweaters and socks, a twelve-gauge shotgun to shoot their fresh meat, a thirty-five-day supply of concentrated and freeze-dried food, a sack of bannock, a slab of bacon, a tiny stove and fuel supply, fishing tackle, plenty of matches, and sundries for emergency use. They allowed themselves one book each, so Ian chose Dylan Thomas's collected poems. They did not take a radio, because apart from the weight, they did not want us to worry about them if it malfunctioned when we expected to make contact. Also, there was no fear of getting lost since they would be on the river or crossing lakes where it widened, and we would spot them from the air if they did not reach the estuary on the Arctic coast. They planned to supplement their diet by living off the land, and they expected to find musk oxen, caribou, wolves, wolverines, foxes, rabbits, Arctic hares, ptarmigan, duck, geese, grouse, trout, and grayling in the river. Back, in his journal, described being held up by ice in July, so they postponed their start until August 1 and expected to reach a summer Inuit settlement at Chantrey Inlet on the shore of the Arctic Ocean by September 2, allowing for delays due to storms, especially when crossing large lakes along the route.

On August 1, a Wardair Otter flew them to Muskox Lake via Tundra Mine where freight and passengers landed, and Ian and Peter collected their canoe, which had been flown in on a Bristol a few days earlier. They were much more fortunate than their nineteenth-century counterparts, for Back and later Anderson had to reach the source of the river traveling overland, and in addition they had to cache provisions for the return journey. I had a last-minute seat when a passenger failed to show up at Wardair's Yellowknife base. After leaving the tree line, we flew over the land, which Ernest Thompson Seton described as "a million unnamed lakes and rocky heath." Ian often quoted Seton, who wrote, "Nature when she set out to paint the world, began on the Barrens with a full palette and when she reached tropics had nothing left but green." After taking pictures, I handed over Ian's camera, and Bill Hines, the pilot, and I prepared to return to Yellowknife. As we took off, the three canoeists raised their paddles in the air in salute.

Here are some excerpts from Ian's and Bob Bromley's diaries. At the end of the first day, Ian wrote, "A perfect peace is in the air, the sun is setting in a purple flash, we hear the cry of a loon."

By the third day out, they had seen muskox, geese, grouse with young, ducks, and loons, and, swimming in the river, a caribou and her calf. On August 5, they built their first cairn, and on turning into Beechey Lake, saw their first wolf. On August 6, they passed the abandoned camp of the 1961 Geodetic Survey, where they obtained additional fuel. Next day, they completed the mile-long portage of the first Cascades in about four hours. In open water, navigation was assisted and accelerated by the use of a polythene sail when wind direction permitted. At the end of Beechey Lake, they found the remains of an Inuit camp. The rocky landscape gave way to large sandstone hills, as described by Back, and they ran the second Cascades with no difficulty. On August 8, they saw large flocks of geese, also a herd of a dozen muskox including a bull in the Baillie's River area. At Hawk Rapids, they actually saw hawks as had Back, who named the place accordingly. August 10 was their first hot day, and they observed the Inuit people as described by Back in his journal. Next day, they were forced ashore twice by cloudbursts, high winds, black clouds, and lightning, referred to by Back as "fierce electrical disturbances."

In twelve days, they reckoned they had reached the halfway point but were perturbed by the prospect of four large lakes to cross. On August 13, they sailed and paddled down Pelly Lake. Ian noted, "Here loons do not laugh, but emit a croak." They saw large quantities of wild lupins. The weather continued wet and stormy, and all three suffered from stiff joints and sore backs due to cold, constant dampness, and strenuous paddling. Bob Bromley remarked on the difficulty of dealing cribbage cards with wet hands, while resting storm-bound in their tent. The explorers of both centuries dwelt obsessively on food, deploring its sparsity and monotony. On August 18, they wrote of cold, piercing winds and took a wrong turn but eventually regained their proper route. On August 19, they endured their first frost and reached the abandoned mission on Garry Lake. Ian caught four trout and a grayling, and they saw plentiful wildlife on the island. He wrote, "The ghost of Father Buliard is in evidence. Little has changed since he was murdered. Everything is in an excellent state of preservation, his medicines above the bed, a glass vial for holy water." They also saw what they presumed to be the priest's grave.

On August 22, in calm weather, they paddled through the Third Narrows, made another cairn, entered Buliard Lake, and spent some time repairing broken paddles and catching fish. On August 24, they encountered snow, navigated McDougall Lake, building a cairn on the south shore of Upper McDougall Lake, and on August 26, passed through Escape Rapids.

On September 5, Peter's wife, Barbara, and I chartered a twin-engine Beechcraft from Bob Engle of Northwest Territorial Airways, piloted by Rocky Parsons and his assistant Alfie, bringing Stuart, a younger son, with us to fly north to collect them. We were weathered in at Contwoyto Lake and were lucky to overnight at Gerry Bruce's camp on an arm of Pelly Lake. The next day we flew on but again had to "sit down" on McDougall Lake. In the afternoon, our wise bush pilot insisted on flying low well before reaching the mouth of the river in case they had weather delays and had not reached their destination.

Our first sighting was a tent and a figure waving his arms. I had a horrible premonition not shared by the others. I knew something was wrong, though I could not explain why. When we landed, Bob ran toward us crying, "They're gone." Bob told us through his tears that on August 27 they were following a fast current downstream and saw deceptively mild-looking white water ahead. They were through the worst when a rock and waves five feet high swamped the canoe and it tipped. They clung to the boat, but the swift water was cold, and they were not getting nearer to land. Bob, encouraged by his father, managed to reach the shore where he collapsed from exhaustion and passed out, having last seen his father and Ian still clinging to the boat and trying to right it. When he came around some hours later, he searched and called until he dropped in his tracks for a cold, restless night. His clothes were sodden and he was practically barefoot.

The next day, he continued to search for the two men and fortunately discovered that the tent and their three sleeping bags had washed ashore near the rapids. He also found his father's knapsack with seven cans of meat and extra matches in plastic bags. He made two poles to support the tent and placed a space blanket as a signal flag on top of a hill. He pegged out a sleeping bag with an SOS in stones. His feet were bruised and swollen, and although on August 29 he heard a plane overhead, he could not move his legs to leave the tent. The next day he felt better, and walking along the shore, he found two paddles, a life preserver, some more food, and wood. He managed to light a fire every second day. He possessed such amazing presence of mind knowing that we would come to rescue him within days.

From the air, we searched the riverbanks but found no trace of the men. However, we located the canoe with the gun, more knapsacks containing Ian's diary, and the photographic equipment. The film was recovered and viewed by many people. Sadly, their bodies were never recovered. Years later, though lacking any professional training, I was asked to counsel a young woman who lost her fiancé in the Twin Towers disaster, hoping to help her with her grief when there was no body for closure.

In a state of shock and sadness after flying up and down the river searching for a few hours, we returned to Gerry Bruce's camp before dark. We were deeply indebted to Gerry and his two companions, Buddy Downs and Freddy Furlong, who again gave Barbara, Stuart, and me their sleeping quarters. Gerry planned to fly up the next day to search some more, and by now the authorities had been alerted, Search and Rescue, and also the RCMP, but we all knew they could not have survived the cold and ice of the river and had died of hypothermia. Grieving deeply, I gave my cigarette lighter to Gerry to drop near the rapids. We flew back to Yellowknife the next day. To our horror, poor young Bob was interrogated by the RCMP, because he was the last person to see his father and friend alive. They were practically accusing him of homicide, which seemed so insensitive, but apparently they were following police procedure.

The Bromley family lawyer appealed against the traditional seven-year wait for declaration of death because no bodies were found. They were in a frozen, uninhabited wilderness. They would never have left the riverbank if they were alive. The case went to the Supreme Court of Canada and was resolved in favor of immediate declaration of death so their estates could be administered.

Some weeks after Ian's death, and after I had sorted things out, I was ready to return to England. Before I left, I went to Bob Engle's office (he was one of several Americans who avoided the Vietnam draft by moving to Canada, where he started a local air charter service, which grew to become a successful commercial airline) to pay my share of the charter we had hired to fetch Ian, Peter, and Bob Bromley from what we hoped would have been the estuary of the Back River at Chantrey Inlet. There were also voluntary subsequent searches in the area by other pilots in planes owned by him. I was speechless when he replied, "There is no bill. This is the north. This is what we do when people are lost in the Arctic."

In addition to our gratitude to Bob Engle and his airline, we thanked Gordon Hornby, who conducted a private search, and to those who went with him as spotters; the citizens of Yellowknife, who contributed generously; the RCMP in Baker Lake, who spent many days in the locality; and countless others for their sympathy and kindness.

Another kind gesture came from the mayor of Yellowknife, who told me I could stay in our apartment for as long as I needed to. At the time, another government-appointed dentist was anxious to take it over.

Indeed, I was the recipient of so much goodwill. Many friends, Joyce Jarman, Harry and Opal Cook, Audrey Rivett, and others rallied around this young, childless widow with no family in Canada. Bishop Cook conducted a memorial service for Ian who, although never a churchgoer, would have appreciated it.

Ian and I had wanted children, and I had been seeing a specialist in Edmonton who could find nothing wrong with either of us. Those were the days before in vitro or surrogate parenting. Shortly before Ian left for the Back River, a local social worker had been trying to interest us in adopting. There seemed to be a degree of infertility among some of us young professional couples. Was it the arsenic from the mines seeping into our drinking water? Probably not, because the birthrate among the underground miners' families and the indigenous population was very high. Those Inuit babies were adorable. Had we in fact adopted one of them before Ian's tragic death, my life would have been very, very different. It would have been virtually impossible to return to England or go to live in the US as a single mother of an Inuit baby.

The day after we returned to Yellowknife from the Barren Lands, which was a Saturday, our bank manager came to my apartment during the afternoon. He produced some papers for me to sign, explaining that there were a few thousand dollars in our account. He was opening a new account in my name and transferring the balance except for five dollars, because it was likely that on Monday, Peter and Ian would be declared missing, presumed dead, and all accounts would be frozen until further notice. No local branch manager in this day and age would take care of a customer in such a personal, caring manner!

Ian and I had acquired three polar bear skins. He had also bought me a gorgeous wolf parka, which somehow he intercepted and purchased from a patient who was hoping to sell it to the premier's wife, Margaret Trudeau. Two years later, walking through Rockefeller Center in New York, a stranger, a gay man, offered me $1,000 for it. Also in New York, a saleslady at the formerly famous B. Altman department store was startled when she saw it on the floor of a changing room while I was trying on a dress, thinking it was alive. At that time, those furs were not endangered.

One of the polar bear skins was acquired in exchange for a set of dentures, which Ian made for a cash-strapped patient. The other two were probably acquired during trips to Arctic settlements. Joyce Jarman, wife of a bush pilot, accepted one of them, my thank-you gift for all her help, along with my white-and-silver wedding dress, which had been made for me in Hong Kong by the dressmaker to Miss World. Joyce offered to sell the second skin and I kept the third, which came to England, then New York, where after a few years it disintegrated during dry cleaning.

Inuit skin curing was somewhat primitive. Joyce found a buyer, our local Member of Parliament, who told her he wanted to make thousands of fishing flies from the sturdy polar bear hairs. He was slightly indignant, given his position, when she insisted he pay cash.

So many years later I am still in touch with Joyce, who lives in British Columbia near her children, grandchildren, and a great-grandchild. I have two goddaughters from the Yellowknife era, Maria Vanderbie, daughter of Teresa and John, both now deceased, and Ceri Lovell, daughter of good Yellowknife friends Julie and Neville DePass. We met Julie the night we arrived in Yellowknife and were surprised to encounter a charming young woman at what seemed like the ends of the Earth who knew Ian's brother Keith in Darlington in England. She was teaching school and married Neville, a banker who originally came from Jamaica. They also have a son and grandchildren and live in Ontario where I have visited them, and two years ago I saw Julie, Ceri, and her daughter Gwyneth when they visited me in New York.

During those weeks, I had tried to be brave and not cry much so as not to worry my friends, a process I repeated forty-three years later when I was widowed for the second time. I had found an excellent home on a farm in Ontario for our beloved Saint Bernard, Marcus. He and I left Yellowknife together on the same daily flight run by Pacific Western to Edmonton. He traveled in the crate that the Edmonton Zoo sometimes borrowed for polar bear transportation. That October afternoon, it required three Dogrib Indians to carry the crate to the plane. When we landed in Edmonton, my last glimpse of Marcus was being carried to another flight for Toronto. I spent the evening with old friends who poured me onto Air Canada's London flight, having plied me with alcohol over dinner to cheer me up. Once aboard, I started to cry and wept the whole way across the Atlantic. When a kind flight attendant asked what was wrong, I told her I felt ashamed, because my husband had drowned six weeks earlier and I was really crying for the first time because I had just said good-bye to our dog. A few hours later, having been met at Heathrow by my mother and stepfather and driven to the house they lived in part time in Aldershot because of his army medical position, Robert closed the living room door while my mother went to fetch champagne and informed me that she had inoperable lung cancer but was in remission and did not know. Apparently she convinced herself that she had tuberculosis. Pleading jet lag, I retired to my bedroom after lunch to cry my heart out.

Many years later, the Canadian government named two lakes in the Barren Lands after the explorers, Calder Lake and Bromley Lake, and also two streets in Yellowknife. Kayla Sanderson, aged ten, who lived in Calder Crescent was curious about the name of the street. I sent her photos, old newspaper articles, and correspondence, and she also interviewed Bob Bromley and worked with the archivist Robin Weber of the Prince of Wales Northern Heritage Centre to produce her prize-winning project "Qui Était Ian Calder?" Her research told the story of Peter, Ian, and Bob, which won her the Yellowknife Heritage Award in 2012. She felt that Calder was an important figure in the sixties for being a dentist who served all the Northwest Territories and Nunavut. His photographs allowed many people and places to be documented during those years. She also went on to win the Primary Research Award at the territorial heritage showcase held at the Prince of Wales Northern Heritage Centre. I could not be prouder of her.

# Chapter Twelve

Difficult months followed my return to England. It was not easy being a twenty-nine-year-old widow at the best of times, especially in a country without a war. In America, men were dying in Vietnam, leaving wives, mothers, sisters, daughters, and girlfriends to grieve. I lived at home at Stratton End with my mother and stepfather and visited family and friends around England and Ireland.

Ian's mother preempted the role of principal mourner, but his brother Keith was very supportive. His parents never really appreciated Keith, their eldest son, who stayed close to home to care for them in their old age, though he would have loved to have led a more cosmopolitan life like his younger brother. Keith was also a dentist, a good husband to his wife, Helen, and father to his daughter Fiona and son David. As I matured, I could better understand how terrible the loss of a child is and became more forgiving of my mother-in-law, who was adamant that she did not want a memorial service for Ian in England. At the time,

I felt my life was over. Happily, my mother's cancer went into remission for several months.

I have already mentioned that I was the unwitting victim of disinheritance by mother and grandfather. Ian had a guilt complex about his parents, who reminded him constantly of the sacrifices they made to put him through Edinburgh University. He was persuaded by our lawyer to make a will the morning he left Yellowknife for his Canadian Centennial expedition. He did not take it seriously, foreseeing no danger in their voyage. He joked with me as we flew to the source of the Back River at Musk-ox Lake that he had left his life insurance and his collection of fine wines purchased with his army gratuity three years earlier to his parents. "After all," he said, "you're young, you can work, and you'll marry again." Prophetic, as it turned out.

I did not resent my parents-in-law inheriting a few thousand Canadian dollars, although our lawyer said I could contest the will. They installed a downstairs bathroom and added a few other amenities to their home. However, the wine was another story. Ian's mother drank the occasional glass of sherry and his father enjoyed a few beers in the local pub. Neither of them cared about the magnificent claret maturing under the Thames in London with Justerini & Brooks, so they ordered it to be sold. Keith Calder managed to persuade them to give him and me a case each. It was superb.

During that winter, I worked on a manuscript given to me by our Yellowknife lawyer. Very few Inuit had any assets, but a certain Charlie Smith owned a boat and therefore an estate, which the law firm was handling. He left an incomplete manuscript of Eskimo legends, partly in English and partly in French. Malcolm suggested I rewrite the stories as a children's book, which I did, and try to get it published, splitting royalties with the daughter and any other descendants of Charlie Smith. When I met Alan Figgis, the Irish publisher, in 1970, he decided to publish it and hired an artist who proposed to illustrate the stories with woodcuts. After sending me a contract, Alan realized the Irish market was too small and it would be an impractically expensive children's book. At the Frankfurt Book Fair, the English publisher, The Bodley Head, took it over for their much larger market, sending me another contract. *The Stories of Charlie Smith* appeared on their forthcoming spring list with a first printing of ten thousand copies.

By this time, four years later, my second husband, Charles, and I were married, and he suggested leaving out the name and just calling it *Eskimo Legends* since the stories were in the public domain. We should have listened to him. At some point, we were contacted by the department of northern affairs in Ottawa. A lawyer representing the family of Charlie Smith wanted to halt publication, stating that the family had been exploited by white people, south of the Canadian border and on the other side of the Atlantic Ocean. A staff member of The Bodley Head and I flew to Ottawa for a meeting. I had already offered to split royalties with the Smiths. They needed money, and in fact, I would have given them more than half, but their lawyer prevailed; so The Bodley Head asked me to release them from their contract, which of course I did. This could have been a win-win situation. Without Charlie Smith, there would have been no manuscript, but without the publisher and me, there would have been no book. It ended up being lose-lose on both sides.

Returning to the winter of 1967 and early spring of 1968, I took up again with old friends in Hampshire and also drove my mother and stepfather to dinner parties as the designated driver. At one dinner, I met a Royal Navy couple. The husband,

Tom, and I then had a brief but passionate affair. We used to meet either aboard his ship docked in Portsmouth or in London. Given his position as a captain in the Royal Navy, my stepfather's senior army job, the fact that Tom was otherwise happily married, and because of my mother's advanced illness, I respected her wishes and ended the affair. Soon afterward, he was posted to Copenhagen as naval attaché to the British embassy. To this day, I remember him as the funniest man in my life, along with my erstwhile fiancé, Ben Gingell.

I saw old friends Susannah (Begg) Hardman and Wanda Rix while I was still living with my parents in their seventeenth-century thatched house, Stratton End, which Ian and I had found for them on their return from Hong Kong in 1964. I visited Wanda and John in their house near Liphook for dinner parties and to play tennis. Wanda asked me to mind the three children and drive them to school when John commuted daily to his job in London, while she was giving birth to her fourth child in the local hospital, Christopher, known as Kip, who now runs a lodge in Scotland.

The Labour government at the time imposed a ninety-five percent tax on unearned income. Wanda benefited from the Pearson family wealth but maintained a low-key lifestyle. John rushed into her hospital room shortly after the baby's birth and announced that they must move to a tax haven like the Isle of Man or the Channel Islands. Wanda said she was too exhausted to contemplate anything of the sort, and indeed they live happily in the same house in Hampshire more than fifty years later.

Having given some of Ian's Inuit artifacts and photos to the Yellowknife museum, I took several more plus their film and Ian's diary to the Scott Polar Research Institute (SPRI) in Cambridge, England. Ian's records of their expedition joined those of truly famous polar explorers, Scott, Franklin, Shackleton, and others. Then the director, Dr. Robin, realizing that I was still heartbroken over Ian's death and with no immediate plans, changed my life. Once again luck came my way.

He hired me, although I was no scientist or academic, to manage the Second International Symposium on Antarctic Ecology. Scientific Committee on Antarctic Research (SCAR), which was founded in 1958, initially had twelve member countries: Argentina, Australia, Belgium, Chile, France, New Zealand, Norway, Japan, South Africa, UK, US, and USSR. (Fifty years later, in December 2018, I realized my dream and went to Antarctica on a Norwegian expedition cruise.) My assistant was a young woman with a PhD in classics, whose father was the Master of Jesus College. When I suggested that she might be overqualified, she replied that it was much better and more interesting than her present job behind the counter at Woolworths.

As it was still the height of the Cold War, only politically "safe" scientists from the USSR could travel to international conferences, where they read the papers of more erudite scientists in their respective disciplines but were not allowed to go abroad lest they defect from the Soviet Union. There was a group minder among the Soviet delegates. When we were entertained for supper by one of the Cambridge professors, at the end of the evening they all got up at a given signal, which was invisible to us, and left. The young men of the British Antarctic Survey and others at SPRI found the Russian girls rather attractive, whereas we fancied a handsome young Russian who was the nephew of the famous writer Boris Pasternak.

While living in Cambridge and working for SPRI, I frequently visited my cousin Niall MacDermot, his wife, Jan, and my godson, Rory, and their lovable overweight golden retriever,

Seamus, while he was serving in the Royal Air Force at RAF Bassingbourn. Niall had studied nuclear physics at college in London and joined the air force where he won the Glen Trophy for best student and the Aerobatic Trophy for his flying skills. During his career, he flew Hunters, Valiants, and Vulcans. He was a member of the Black Arrows while he was flying Hunters in the late fifties. In the early sixties, he was captain of a bomber with the nuclear bomb aboard, but luckily the situation deescalated and World War III never started.

He left the RAF in 1970 and worked for Neve's, an electronic sound recording company in Ireland. His daughter, Siobhan, was born in 1972. My stepfather, Robert Niven, was her godfather, but she was only four when he died. A notable achievement by Niall for the firm was designing the Angelus Bell for RTÉ, Ireland's national television station. He and Janet retired to Cyprus, where many former colleagues lived, because they wanted to escape the Irish climate. Niall died in Ireland surrounded by his immediate family. Janet lives in County Wexford with her son Rory. Siobhan, her husband, Dominic, and their children, Niall, Moira, Sally Felicity, and Hugh, live about five minutes away from them.

During my time in Cambridge, thanks to Susannah Hardman, I became friends with Michael and Tessa Till. He was the chaplain of King's College, so I spent many hours of my free time listening to the world-famous choir and helping Tessa feed choristers large suppers on a very small budget. Tessa was the daughter of Stephen Roskill, the distinguished naval historian.

My mother became seriously ill in December 1968, so I gave up my job at SPRI. By that time, we had wrapped up the symposium's loose ends and published the papers. By then, I was working with the Law of the Sea and had completed the job I was hired to do. I returned to Stratton End in December 1968 to care for her. At her request, we spent Christmas in London, but she was too infirm to enjoy herself. I tried valiantly to keep the Christmas cheer going, which resulted in my acquiring a lifelong aversion to champagne.

After my mother died in April 1969, I stayed at Stratton End to take care of my stepfather. He was commandant of the Royal Army Medical Corps at Mytchett, near Aldershot, and I attended several functions with him. The queen mother, as honorary colonel of the regiment, inspected the headquarters. The ladies room in the officers' mess was repainted in honor of the royal visit. When we repaired there after the parade and before tea, Her Majesty, her lady-in-waiting, and I discussed the weather and the traffic from London.

Robert purchased an expensive antique goblet from Spinks and commissioned a famous artist, Honoria Marsh, to engrave scenes of my mother's life on the commemorative glass. A very talented lady, she etched scenes of my mother's life: Coolavin, Stratton End, their thatched house, the ruined castle on Loch Key, a side-saddle for her riding days, a microphone representing her radio broadcasts in Hong Kong, and her last dog, a Cavalier King Charles, Rupert. The two houses were framed, respectively, in common yellow bog iris and bog cotton. Honoria rather set her cap at Robert and requested more visits to sketch the house and go through photographs than were strictly necessary. He was after all a recent widower, handsome, and charming, but he was uncomfortable and liked me to hang around during her visits. After his death, I brought the goblet back to New York but eventually took it to Ireland because I felt it should be with MacDermot descendants. I gave it to Siobhan Ryan, my first cousin Niall MacDermot's daughter and Robert's goddaughter, mentioned earlier.

Sallie and Jimmy Warden and their two boys, James and Andrew, visited us from London, where he was running the London branch of the Philadelphia National Bank. The bank allowed him to buy a house for their London representative, so the family was able to live in the house they chose in Chelsea.

A friend of the Tills, Elizabeth, who lived nearby, had inherited a tiara that once belonged to her godmother, Queen Mary, which she sold to install a swimming pool. I spent time there with her during that rare warm summer in England and knew she was anxious to have a child.

We lost touch when I went to the US, but one Friday night, driving from New York to East Hampton for the weekend, I heard on the radio that a cousin of the queen's had killed her baby by starvation because she had been born with a severe mental disability. She was acquitted due to extenuating circumstances, a brilliant barrister, and the right connections, and remanded in custody to the Tills. What a tragedy for Elizabeth and her family.

In 1969, I became godmother to the Tills' son Tobias, now a distinguished artist, expert print maker, and lithographer, father of two boys, and married to Cynthia Westwood, an American and also a distinguished painter. They live in England. Tobias's sister, Sophie, a wife and mother, lives in upstate New York. As a world-class violinist, she travels widely giving concerts and master classes.

In 1968, the Tills had taken the choir to Africa for summer concerts, and I was checking their Cambridge house once a week after work. One evening, I discovered it had been broken into, so I was able to deal with the police, clean up the mess, and let Michael know so that he could break it gently to Tessa. She was pregnant after several miscarriages. Michael claimed that I saved her from what might have been a severe shock and possibly another miscarriage, and Tobias was safely born in April 1969. I think this may have been the reason I was asked to be his god-mother, and I also had the honor of holding him over the silver monteith (large ornate bowl) during the christening, because King's College Chapel had no baptismal font and this was the first baptism in a hundred years. Two christenings were held on that day: the chaplain's son and his very upscale family, friends, and academics; the other baby was the son of the verger or grave digger, surrounded by all their relatives and friends.

Michael continued his distinguished career in the Anglican church. After being chaplain of King's College, he became dean and a fellow. He was vicar of Fulham, then archdeacon of Canterbury, where we visited the family living at the time in a thirteenth-century house. His last position was dean of Winchester, after which they retired in 2013 to Petworth in Sussex. He died very suddenly in 2012, followed shortly afterward by Tessa.

So many events in my life have been happy accidents. It could be karma or mere lack of planning on my part. When asked how I felt about moving to the far north of Canada, I always replied, "Why do you ask?" In those days, we followed our husbands, as did my mother, sailing to India with my father and later with my stepfather to Singapore, Hong Kong, or wherever in the UK the army designated.

I am a great believer in silver linings and also in the road not taken. Had my father not married Hilda and disinherited me at the age of sixteen, I think I would have been boring and horsey. As life turned out, I had to go to work while my stepbrothers were set up in businesses by my father, all of which subsequently failed, and his wife drove Jaguars and owned show horses. My mother said to me on reading the fateful disinheriting letter, "Look at it this way, darling, now no one will marry you for your money, only for love." She was right.

On July 20, 1969, the world was watching Neil Armstrong and Buzz Aldrin land on the moon. I remember staying up most of the night following the events on TV.

That summer, I attended Lydia and Ian's wedding at Firwood, where John and Bridget were still living. Fifty years later, I was invited to their golden wedding aboard HMS *Drake*, which, alas I was unable to attend, as I was convalescing after major surgery.

Lydia joined the British Red Cross Society and trained initially at the Cambridge Military Hospital in Aldershot where she met my stepfather, who was the brigadier in command. He and my mother invited her for a weekend "which did a lot for my credibility with my superiors," she wrote me recently. She was posted to the Royal Naval Hospital in Plymouth, where they worked as almoners, occupational therapists, and librarians. She met Sir Francis Chichester in the hospital and watched him set sail on his around-the-world solo voyage.

Her next posting was to the British Military Hospital, Singapore. She was invited to a party on board the brand-new royal navy-guided missile destroyer, HMS *Glamorgan*, where she met Ian and they were engaged by Christmas.

After their marriage, the navy sent Ian to learn Russian, and they spent six months staying with a white Russian émigré couple in Paris. He then became supply officer on HMS *Danae*, and Lydia moved to their house, Ludbrooke Farm, in Devon. She joined him in Singapore, where the ship was being handed over to ANZUK, and spent some time in Hong Kong, where she found it difficult to climb to The Peak, being seven months pregnant. Henrietta was born in 1972, and Alastair two years later.

She became involved in a "twinning" exchange with a village in Normandy, which lasted twenty-five years. They visited various wartime sites, D-Day landing beaches and memorials, and had a revered veteran, Major Mott, in their group. She also worked for the Citizens Advice Bureau and the National Trust Saltram House in Plymouth. She was invited to become a freeman of the City of London and a liveryman of the Feltmakers. Before the coronavirus pandemic, she enjoyed dinners in various livery halls and the Mansion House. She attended the Lord Mayor's Show in 2018 and watched him ride in a golden coach.

Ian was posted for six months to the Ukraine, and subsequently they supported a Lifeline for children affected by radiation from the Chernobyl disaster. They visited their son, Alastair, when he lived in Ecuador. He has two daughters, Jasmin and Pacha. Henrietta and Paul live in Scotland facing the beautiful island of Arran. They have a son and daughter, Conn and Tamara.

Before I left for New York, Robert decided to find a new home for Rupert, my mother's Cavalier King Charles spaniel. My uncle and aunt, David and Joan Christie-Miller, owned one named Carmel and thought Rupert would be good company for her. Shortly after Rupert moved in, they returned from dinner one night to find Carmel lying dead across the lintel of the door. She had had a heart attack, to which the breed is prone, but they blamed Rupert for causing it. Another home was found for him with army friends of Robert's.

# Chapter Thirteen

Having sailed to New York in 1959 on the French Line's *Liberté*, I chose another ocean crossing ten years later on Cunard's *Queen Elizabeth (QE) 2*. Waiting in line for table seating, I met a charming man who became my "date" for the five-day journey, a gay hairdresser from California, a wonderful dancer, though he was always reticent about his family connections to the Genovese family. We shared a table with a young banker and his English wife, who remained friends in New York for many years.

For the first few days on dry land, the ground swayed beneath my feet, due to joy at being back on US soil, reuniting with old friends, plus the effects of five evenings dancing our way across rough Atlantic waters. On the day I arrived, my friend Lucia Woods took me to lunch at the Four Seasons.

Fall and winter passed happily, visiting friends, traveling, house-, cat-, and dog-sitting, a few "off-the-books" jobs because I had a six-month tourist visa, my original green card having expired. A close friend from my previous life in New York, Karen O'Brien, gave me a terrific welcome, which included passing along some boyfriends in whom she was no longer interested. It worked the other way too. We met a Californian at a cocktail party who ran a successful canine shampoo company and was in New York for the Westminster Kennel Club Dog Show. He and I spent a couple of evenings together, and of course I was thrilled to go to the dog show, but when Karen admitted she had rather fallen for him, I was "busy" the next evening but suggested he might like to call Karen, and a romance ensued.

Karen had an extremely good job at the United Nations, and by the time she retired, she was among the highest-ranked women with the rank of D1. After retirement, she went to Somalia for a year on a UN contract, which was dramatic and involved wearing a bulletproof vest most of the time. While she was working at the UN, she married William Dreher, who had a house on Egypt Lane and an apartment on Park Avenue. After their wedding reception at the Maidstone Club, they chartered a plane to fly to Washington for their honeymoon, and on their return, gave three housewarming cocktail parties on three consecutive evenings, dividing their friends alphabetically, so we went on the third night. The marriage ended in divorce, and Karen lives in an upscale retirement community near Savannah. Her only daughter, Elizabeth, lives with her husband, John, in San Francisco, and Karen dotes on her granddaughter Isabel. It is thanks to Karen that I still have my New York apartment.

In the late fall of 1969, I visited my former roommate June Dickinson with her husband and three small children in Conway, New Hampshire. I traveled to Montreal, wondering about getting a job there. I could stay in Canada for the rest of my life if I wished, as a landed immigrant since 1964, but I did not want to live there again on my own. The US had a strong pull, even though at this time I knew it would be well-nigh impossible to get another green card.

Susan Stanwood came back into my life, and in January 1970, I attended her New York wedding to Howard Kaminsky. After dinner at Orso's, I went back to their apartment to feed the cat. Howard was working at Random House in charge of subsidiary rights. After a very successful stint at Warner Books, he returned some years later to Random House as president of their trade books division. Bob Bernstein described him as having a "first-rate editorial mind." He published Donald Trump's *The Art of the Deal* as well as many best-selling authors, such as Norman Mailer, Andrew Greeley, and Nelson DeMille. He published Xaviera Hollander's *The Happy Hooker* and Judith Krantz's *Scruples*. His greatest coup was when six weeks after Nixon resigned, his company paid $2.5 million for the former president's memoirs.

He and Susan, who raised a daughter, Jessica, collaborated on five novels, writing three of them under the pseudonym Brooks Stanwood, a combination of her family name and Howard's cousin, Mel Brooks. *The Glow, Seventh Child*, and *The Twelve* still grace my bookshelves. Until 2008, when Susan died, we used to socialize in the city, attend their book signings, and occasionally spend weekends together at their country house upstate or at ours in East Hampton. Susan was fiercely loyal to her old friends, Sallie Warden and myself, but I sensed that Howard, the iconoclast, found the Wardens and Rittenours a bit too conventional and stuffy. Howard died in 2017 at the age of seventy-seven.

A week before my six-month tourist visa was due to expire in March, I knew I was not going to risk becoming an illegal immigrant. An acquaintance had just been deported because his dumped girlfriend turned him in to the immigration department, and although I had not rejected any boyfriends or made any enemies intent on revenge, I did not want to take any chances. Once again, I got lucky. I was asked to give a ride to a couple in New York invited to the same party in Greenwich because my date had a car. As luck would have it, the husband was the number-two man at the Irish export board, which was part of the Irish consulate, and a week later, I had a job in their New York office with a State Department A-2 visa, which was given to foreign nationals working in foreign government offices such as embassies and consulates.

Soon afterward, I met my future husband, Charles Rittenour, at a dinner party in New York. He had grown up in West Palm Beach, son of Missourians. His father's family owned a small bank, which was unable to provide adequate incomes for all the family members, so Austin Rittenour left Brookfield for Florida with his wife, Elizabeth, being fond of golf and desiring to live in a warm climate. We were introduced by a friend of Charles's and his family, William Told, who also grew up in Palm Beach and persuaded Charles to relocate to New York and find a job there. He had been flying small planes around South Florida and working as bookkeeper for a wealthy landowner, Baron Collier. Bill was working for Manufacturers Hanover Trust at the time, and I had met him with a group of friends who often played bridge together. Bill invited me to the dinner party where I met Charles in April 1970. Charles was working for Peat Marwick as a consultant. Shortly after our marriage, he was let go and was soon hired by Chase Manhattan Bank, where he stayed for the rest of his career. Peat Marwick had hired him for his putative connections to prospective Palm Beach clients through his father, but he did not deliver, not being a "rainmaker" or possessing a salesman personality.

I left the Irish government for the British one in 1972, specifically the consumer division of the Trade Development Office. Charles, a devout Anglophile, loved the perks: cheap booze from the consulate every month and being able to import an MGB sports car duty free from England. It took nearly two years to persuade him to apply for my green card, a first for the immigration department officials who had never met a native-born American who had ever waited so long to file for a foreign spouse. I had by this time disabused one cynical girlfriend that I was marrying primarily for the coveted green card, which was actually blue by the seventies.

Charles, ever the Anglophile, had no interest in my becoming an American citizen and did not think that my being disenfranchised on both sides of the Atlantic was a big deal. In the nineties, there was a flurry among non-US friends to become citizens to avoid estate tax levied on foreign spouses, but we were not rich enough to worry about that.

In the late nineties, I sent for the application forms and started to fill them out anyway. The requirement to list all the business and pleasure trips taken outside the US with dates and locations during the twenty-five years since I got my 1972 green card was too daunting, so I put it off for a few years.

After I accepted an early retirement offer from the Quebec government in 2000, I decided to tackle the process again. Andrée Dean was a paddle tennis and bridge friend, and her son Howard hoped to be the Democratic nominee for president, so I wanted to vote for him. I pored over three expired passports. Many of the foreign country entry and departure stamps were illegible. I contacted friends asking for dates when we had been together in India, trekking the Everest trail in Nepal, hiking in the Jebel Sahro in Morocco, or traveling together elsewhere on the planet. The list of overseas trips ran to several pages and was still incomplete. I completed the filing, hoping that I might become a citizen in time to vote for Howard Dean. He never got the nomination, but I got called for the interview.

A gentleman of Latinx origin was my interlocutor. He was having a bad hair day or disliked me on sight. I did not fit the profile, huddled masses and all that. Although I was of course polite, it riled him that I seemed so entitled, with a house in East Hampton, an apartment on the Upper East Side, financially and socially secure, simply not needy enough. Then he pounced. Where was the death certificate for my first husband? I replied that there never was one because the bodies were not found where he and his friend drowned in the icebound Arctic in 1967, but there was a document from the Supreme Court of Canada pronouncing them legally dead. As I wrote earlier, the young lawyer had persuaded the Court to change the law requiring the usual seven-year waiting period when no bodies are found, given the extreme Arctic climate, the water temperature of the Back River, and the certainty that they had perished from hypothermia. He went on to have an extremely distinguished law career. I pointed out that I could not have gotten a marriage license or green card without this document, even though I no longer had a copy. Once more, my unusual situation was too much for him, so he banished me to another waiting room while he went in search of a superior. A bad two hours ensued. I was unable to concentrate on reading the *New Yorker*. However, I was finally summoned by another official and told everything was in order and that I would be called for my citizenship ceremony within a few weeks.

It was the coldest day recorded for a hundred years, that January morning in 2004. I took the subway very early, not wanting to risk a taxi breaking down. Charles was not interested in accompanying me so he stayed warm in bed for another couple of hours. When I reached the Broadway federal office, everyone else was surrounded by family members taking photos. We were given another form to fill out. The people sitting on either side of me looked extremely alarmed. They could hardly read English and had had assistance with their paperwork up until this moment. I explained that they were being asked if their status had changed since their recent interviews, for example if they had got married, widowed, or divorced within the past few weeks.

We shuffled along, hundreds of us, through a series of rooms, no one looking very happy. On my way out that morning, Ray, our Albanian doorman, had told me horror stories of people being pulled out of the line and deported for some recently discovered infraction of the law. A group of Russians were complaining among themselves, so a large guard who was herding us, exclaimed, "Why are you's guys giving me attitude!" A line I will never, ever forget.

Then, finally, the certificates were given out like diplomas, accompanied by a scratchy rendition of "God Bless America" played on a tape recorder, but I mentally congratulated the woman calling us to collect our documents for pronouncing all our names correctly. We were then dismissed and advised to head to the nearest post office to apply for US passports. *Exeunt* a bunch of new Americans. A glamorous and uplifting occasion, sadly, it was not. I had expected drumrolls, flags waving, and congratulations, having read about more inspiring ceremonies, so I was very disappointed. Soon afterward, on an icy-cold Saturday evening, we gave a party in East Hampton to which friends, to my surprise, brought presents. Charles may have been indifferent, but I was proud to become an American.

This chronicle returns to April 1970 when I met Charles Rittenour at that dinner party in April. The man I was dating at the time, who drove me and the Irish government couple to the party in Greenwich that changed my life, announced the evening after the dinner party that he was too old for me and I should find a younger man, canceling our plans for the weekend. I am sure he had met someone else and simply wanted to dump me. Apart from wondering how I would now spend the weekend, I do not remember being particularly devastated. I have always thought I took rejection well, probably because I am resilient and adaptable. On Saturday morning, Charles called. He had such a deep, sexy voice, and asked if I remembered meeting him the previous Thursday and if I would like to go to a museum. We started at the Metropolitan, went to the Whitney, and then the Museum of Modern Art. After dinner, we returned to my sublet apartment on East 69th Street. That was the first and last time in my life that I ever went to those three museums on the same day.

A happy summer followed, going back and forth across Central Park between my temporary place on Second Avenue and his apartment in a brownstone on West 70th Street. His had a lot more charm, situated in an attractive block off Central Park West, with an exposed brick living room wall, but the kitchen, entered via the bathroom, left much to be desired.

During the summer, a stepcousin, Peggy Anderson, visited us in New York on weekends. After earning her PhD in London, she came to work at Cold Spring Harbor for the illustrious Dr. Thomas Watson, Nobel laureate, on DNA and RNA research. One Sunday visiting her at the laboratory, we passed the famous scientist on a foot path, small child riding on his shoulders. Years later, we used to see Peggy in Scotland, usually with Mary Niven in Edinburgh, and I still keep in touch with her through annual Christmas cards. She also became a keen botanist and studied rare plants in China, including at high altitudes in Tibet.

Our first weekend together was over the Memorial Day holiday, 1970. We took the train to Montauk and stayed at the Sands Motel. I still loved to bask on the beach. Charles, who grew up in sunny Florida, to my surprise, got a terrible sunburn. For the July Fourth weekend, we went to Rhode Island and Block Island, but it rained, so we watched Wimbledon tennis matches on TV. At some point, we became engaged. I had met Charles's sister and brother-in-law, Carolyn and Gary Lind, but did not meet his mother until September. She came up to New York for a sad reason. Her daughter Carolyn (Con) had a very serious nervous breakdown over Labor Day weekend and was hospitalized for several weeks. This was probably caused by a combination of undiagnosed postpartum depression and legally prescribed amphetamines because of Con's obsession with her weight. She was diagnosed with anorexia later.

Slightly sheepishly, Elizabeth Rittenour showed me a diamond pin. She had given up on Charles ever getting married but offered to have it remade into a ring. I much preferred another one with small diamonds set in onyx and accepted that instead. Some years later, when I was working for the Government of Quebec, accompanying my boss to an event at Lord & Taylor, I bent down to pick up his briefcase and the ring caught in the escalator, the stones shearing off, which was lucky because I might have lost a finger.

Elizabeth Rittenour stage-managed her daughter Carolyn. This was done with love but had unfortunate consequences. She believed that one could not be too thin or too rich. Con was a pretty girl and an excellent tennis player. In fact, she married a moderately rich man, Gary Lind, whose family owned a successful financial printing business. During her hospitalization in the fall of 1970, her mother and husband visited Con every evening, so Charles and I babysat the two little girls, Elizabeth and Alexandra, aged three and one at the time. A wonderful nanny housekeeper, Nellie, from Trinidad, came to the rescue and stayed with the children throughout their childhood and took care of the household. I agreed with Charles that some of Con's problems came from growing up in Palm Beach.

Austin Rittenour was a well-respected trust officer at the Atlantic Bank and a founding member of the Everglades Club. He and his wife were socially impeccable, but they lived on his salary. Their children were surrounded by trust-fund babies, a rather unhealthy situation, because it drove Elizabeth to push her daughter too much. Charles did not escape entirely, because he developed champagne tastes on a beer income and seldom encountered a new gadget that he did not love, too easily acquired with plastic. After the first week of marriage, we never shared a credit card. Nor did we ever have a joint bank account, which for us worked very well throughout our marriage.

On November 21, 1970, Charles and I were married by Father von Meysenbug, a friend of the Rittenours, at the Catholic Church, Saint Jean Baptiste, on Lexington Avenue and 78th Street, New York. We had considered St. Ignatius, but because it was to be a small wedding, we were relegated to the crypt. My boss, Donal Scully, head of the Irish Export Board, had old-fashioned ideas about widows, even young ones, remarrying. He did not approve and only gave me a couple of days off, although he liked Charles very much. My beloved stepfather, Robert Niven, came from England and was well entertained afterward by my godmother Una and her husband, John Kernan, now living in New Haven. Una was my matron of honor. Their son Sean and daughter Brigid also attended, as did Charles's parents, sister, and brother-in-law, plus assorted friends of ours. Bill Told, who had introduced us, was Charles's best man. It was a happy group of about fifty celebrants. I met most of the Rittenours' friends, who had generously sent wedding presents, the following Christmas in Palm Beach.

John Kernan's good friend Dana Smith kindly lent us his beautiful apartment in the Pulitzer House on Fifth Avenue at 11 East 73rd Street for our reception. The main living room had been transported from a chateau in France. After the reception, we dined at the Plaza Hotel and went back to my sublet on 69th Street as Charles's childhood friend, David Morrish, and his first wife were borrowing our Manhattan apartment, where I am still renting fifty-one years later.

We spent our first Christmas and most of the next thirty-nine in Palm Beach. We stayed with the Rittenours in their house on Dyer Road, where Charles and Con had grown up. There was some culture shock for this supposedly sophisticated, well-traveled Thursday's child. It is a beautiful place where man has definitely improved on nature, gorgeous houses and clubs facing the ocean or the Inland Waterway.

After our frugal childhood Christmases, where we hung a stocking at the foot of our bed, which on Christmas morning contained some candy, trinkets, and usually a tangerine in the toe, followed by a few modest gifts under the tree, I was agog to see a whole roomful of presents for Gary and Con's little daughters, Liz and Alex. There were many Christmas and New Year parties in friends' houses, the Everglades Club, and the Bath & Tennis Club. We always enjoyed the tennis and beach life.

Charles was very happy growing up on Dyer Road, and for our entire married life, we drove or flew to Palm Beach for Christmas and a spring holiday almost every year.

The Palm Beach friends were important to us. Charles's parents' generation had all been friends, as were many of their children who grew up together, like David Morrish and Charles (we introduced David to his second wife, my dear friend Kacey Conway Walthieu), Judy and Lindley Hoffman, and of course, Bill Told. Rosemary Killen and her brother Tim grew up there, and although their parents were friends with the Rittenours, they were younger than Charles. Rosemary is a successful landscape gardener, and we spend time together in East Hampton. Other friends came to Palm Beach for the winters, bringing spouses and children, including Phyllis and Michael Dennis, a successful plastic surgeon who in recent years has been instrumental in improving the health system in the area.

We always enjoyed spending time with Mercedes and Jack Cassidy. Mercedes's father had run a Cuban airline before Fidel Castro drove a large exodus of emigrants to South Florida. Jack had served with Alexander Haig in the military and when he made a bid for the presidency, the Cassidys did not want to fly up to New York for the evening and sent us instead to the dinner at the Waldorf Astoria.

When Austin and Elizabeth died in the same year, 1981, they were buried in Brookfield, Missouri, where they had both grown up before moving to Florida. After Austin's funeral in January, Charles and I were designated to accompany his coffin by plane to Kansas City where his nephews, Charles's cousins Jim and John Murphy, met us. They and their wives, Alice and Sherrill, looked after us well during the burial and its aftermath. Having heard so many stories of people losing their luggage while changing planes in Atlanta, I worried unnecessarily because the funeral home assured us that the right coffin reached Brookfield.

During the summer of that year, Elizabeth became very sick with cancer, and Charles often flew to Palm Beach to visit her. One of her closest friends, Elio Reeves, used to meet his plane and help Charles during these trips. Elio's daughter Eleanor Petersen had grown up with Charles, and we have kept in touch over the years and spent weekends in each other's houses. Eleanor is well traveled and enjoys dry fly fishing. We had found a wonderful Irish caregiver called Bridie who looked after Elizabeth until she died on October 15. The following year we sold their house. After a few years of shared vacation rentals, Con and Gary Lind bought a house on Via Palma, where he still lives.

We had so many wonderful friends in Palm Beach, but none as special as Dotsy and Gavin Letts. Dotsy's parents, Buck and Dorothy Wood, were friends with the Rittenours. Originally from Kentucky, they settled in Palm Beach and raised Dotsy and her brother Marshall there. Father and son were both lawyers. Dotsy met Gavin Graham Kenyon Letts in Edinburgh, Scotland, where he was a solicitor. They moved back to Palm Beach in 1955, and Gavin received his law degree from Washington and Lee University. He became a judge and was an expert on matrimonial law but attained perhaps his greatest fame on a dissenting opinion about civil rights, which led the Florida Supreme Court to strike down random bus searches in 1989, later reversed by the US Supreme Court. In 1982, he competed with his friend Judge Alan Schwartz for a seat on the Florida Supreme Court, but it went to a third candidate. Gavin was a sportsman who loved golf and tennis and was known for his wit. Quoting from an obituary in August 1993, after his death, "To him, the only thing worse than being boring was being dishonest."

Charles and I spent many Christmas and Easter vacations with Dotsy and Gavin, their daughter Sophy, and foster daughter Debbie, and after Gavin's death with Dotsy and Sophy. There were perennial Christmas traditions, such as eggnog in the morning after opening presents. A beautifully decorated tree stood in the bay window of the living room. We would usually go to a movie in the afternoon and several friends sat down to a feast in the evening. I was allowed to make the brandy butter (hard sauce to Americans) for the Christmas pudding. There were always parties before and after Christmas and a big dinner dance on New Year's Eve. I remember when the Iraq War broke out, I was dancing with another judge, Owen McGivern, (whose widow and daughter, both called Joan, are still friends of mine), who told me it reminded him of the dance in *Vanity Fair* before the Battle of Waterloo. Sophy became a lawyer, and I am sure Gavin is looking down on her from heaven with pride.

In the summer of 1971, we rented our first East Hampton place, belonging to the family who owned the local funeral parlor, a one-room cottage nestled in a nursery garden within walking distance of the railroad station. We did not own or need a car, took the train on Fridays and Sundays, and used our bicycles to go to the beach. The following year, we shared a house with a friend who was going through an anti-men phase, having divorced her alcoholic husband just before he came into a large inheritance. She took out her frustrations for the bad timing on Charles. That fall, he insisted we look around for a place of our own, so we bought a half-acre lot in Clearwater Beach, in the hamlet of Springs in the town of East Hampton. We built a house, which was completed in late summer of 1973 and was more or less completed in time for Robert's visit. It was a one-of-a-kind, a very modern wooden house across the road from Hog Creek, a saltwater inlet that flows into Gardiners Bay, facing the privately owned Gardiners Island, possible site of the hidden Captain Kidd pirate treasure (dubious, but a good story for children) and an annual sailing race around the island. Houses like ours were satirized in a *New Yorker* cartoon as "arrogant and freaky." During the ensuing decades, Charles organized improvements and additions to 151 Waterhole Road. Our architect was Carl Hribar, who became a friend until he died of COVID-19 in 2020.

We were so pleased when our friends Sally and Jimmy Warden, who had returned from London to live in Philadelphia, spent two weeks with their little boys James and Andrew in our house every summer for several years until they bought their own house in Settlers Landing. When we drove out from New York on Friday evenings for the weekend, they always had supper waiting for us and left thoughtful and generous gifts at the end of their stay.

Life in East Hampton was never dull because we had many friends, most of whom, like us, worked in New York and came out on weekends. Among these were Anne and John Oliver, who both worked in advertising. We spent afternoons on their beach at the end of Whalers Lane in Amagansett as well as enjoying many dinners in each other's houses—also with Barbara and Lee Peltz, Henriette (my erstwhile literary agent) and Dick Neatrour, Sue Seidman, a "character" devoted to cats, Karen O'Brien, and many others. Summer weekends extended into year-round weekends, with dinner parties in front of roaring log fires. To this day, I am grateful to Robert Wick. When he and his wife, Deborah, came for a winter Saturday dinner, he taught me how to set a perfect fire. In the summer, we frequented ocean beaches, played tennis, and in 1976 joined Devon Yacht Club where for a few years we sailed our sunfish. I enjoyed crewing for Tom and Cathy Peacock on Swan's Way during summer afternoon races and once joined them for the Round Gardiner's Island Race. For one season, I crewed for Rosalie Arkell on her Alerion. However, the Alerion races were very competitive, and she needed more talented and aggressive support from Kevin Fallon and other expert sailors. His parents, John and Mary, bought our sunfish for their boys growing up and kept it for many years.

East Hampton was and still is replete with celebrities: artists, writers, movie and TV stars, moguls, etc. One summer weekend, we were mystified by four black-and-white cows' heads, which were washed up on the beach off Kings Point Road. Was this a nefarious experiment by the secretive animal-disease government laboratory on Plum Island? It turned out to be our local celebrity chefs who had a house there, Craig Claiborne and Pierre Franey, who were apparently trying to prepare a veal dish, tête de veau, which involved skinning the heads, but they must have changed their minds or had extra heads so they dropped them down onto the beach, expecting the tide to wash them out to sea.

Another culinary story from our early days in East Hampton concerned a very good friend, Virginia Powell, who is now married to Warren Schwerin, lives mostly in Florida, and is a bridge Life Master. Ginny was an attractive red-haired divorcée at the time, and one of the many men who asked her out was a notoriously cheap elderly gentleman who disconcerted his opponents on the tennis courts because he kept containers of heart tablets in his shorts pockets, which rattled so much, they feared Leonard might go into cardiac arrest at any moment. He called her to say he had found a dead pheasant by the side of the road and he would cook it for dinner if she would come to his beachfront house. Ginny politely declined, whereupon he asked indignantly, "What's wrong with you! Do you prefer girls?"

Charles, being such an Anglophile, loved meeting my family in England. In the fall of 1971, we visited many members of my family as well as old friends, staying with my stepfather and his sister Mary Niven at Stratton End. I remember my godmother, Blanche Hanbury-Tracy, saying about Charles that my mother had picked him for me from Up There. My mother once said to me, knowing she was dying, that I should go back to America and with luck marry an American, because she heard they were kinder to their wives than Europeans. There was no kinder or more devoted husband than Charles.

When we visited Coolavin, I was nervous, because my aunt Felicity claimed that she did not like Americans, although she had never been there. I had warned Charles, and they were both on their best behavior, which was touching but rather a strain.

On being shown the family tree, Charles asked why my parents were listed by name but I was merely "issue" plus birth date. Felicity replied with a certain hauteur, "Daughters of daughters don't count."

Well, maybe not, but now is the time to tell our very own Romeo and Juliet story, which, like so much Irish history, is a mixture of truth and fiction.

Una was the great-granddaughter of the last king, Rory. Her father, Brian Og MacDermot, was recognized as chief of the clan, and while no longer living on the Rock, he was still a powerful man. In good fairy-tale style, she was of fair complexion with long blonde hair, apparently a beauty, and doted upon by her father.

Tomás Láidir was a gallant, brave warrior from the neighboring Costello clan, reputedly the strongest and most valiant in

Ireland, a true champion. Unfortunately, the MacDermots and Costellos were not the best of friends. Indeed, there are accounts in the *Annals of Loch Cé* of many skirmishes and battles between the two feuding families and between Brian Og and Jordan Boy Costello in the years preceding this tale. Eventually Jordan Boy was killed in battle by the Burkes, who were allies through marriage with Brian Og. Tomás, son of Jordan Boy, while fighting against Cromwellian forces with his prodigious strength, saved the life of Turlough Og MacDermot, Brian Og's son and heir. They brought him back to Castle Island where he met Úna Bhán, and like Romeo and Juliet, they fell in love.

When Brian Og learned of this, he strictly forbade any relationship, as Tomás was the son of his enemy and also a poor man, while the MacDermots at the time were rich. Brian Og sought a more suitable match, so he arranged a bounteous feast to which he invited all the eligible bachelors of the province, including Tomás Láidir. When dinner was finished, Brian Og rose and instructed his daughter to stand up and drink to the health of the wealthy man he had chosen as her consort. However, she rose and toasted Tomás Láidir Costello. Her father was so angry that he struck her hard with the palm of his hand to the side of her face. She did not want the guests to see her tears, so she took a pinch of snuff to cover up her pain. Tomás left the room.

After that, she took to her bed, lovesick and suffering from her father's blow. Her father, despairing of her condition, allowed her to send for Tomás. When he arrived, he was taken to her chamber. The joy in her soul did her so much good that she fell into a deep and peaceful sleep, the first for a very long time. Tomás sat by her bedside holding her hand for a long time. However, realizing she would not soon wake up and not wishing to overstay his welcome, he loosened his grip, went downstairs, and told his servant to saddle his horse. He waited outside for many hours, hoping that a MacDermot messenger would come to bring him back to Úna, but none came, and eventually his servant convinced him that the MacDermots were humbugging and tricking him. He took an oath and swore by God and Mary that he would never again turn back or speak another word to Úna, his love, unless the MacDermots sent him a message before he crossed the little river, the Donogue. He remained in mid-river for half an hour, hoping against hope, until finally at the insistence of his servant he crossed the river to the other side, sealing his decision forever.

No sooner had he crossed the river when a messenger came running to the riverbank to tell him that Úna had woken up and wanted him to return, but he would not. When Tomás did not come back to her, she fell into despair and melancholy, withering away and dying of grief. She was buried on Trinity Island in Lough Key.

Thomas was grief-stricken that he had taken his servant's advice. Night after night he would swim out to the island and throw himself on Úna's grave. Some years later, he too died of a broken heart, having left instructions that he be buried next to his beloved Úna.

It is said that two noble ash trees grew from their graves, leaning toward each other as they grew so that their branches intermingled and the tops of the two trees bent upon one another in the middle of the graveyard.

# Chapter Fourteen

C harles was very fond of my cousin Brian Hugh, son of Frank MacDermot. He came to New York quite often to see friends and relatives. He accompanied us one evening in 1983 to celebrate the Centennial of the Brooklyn Bridge and watch a firework display. Unable to find a cab, we headed for the subway only to discover Brian Hugh had never been on it in his life, but he survived the experience.

He was not yet married when we first stayed at his London house in Rutland Gate. He had been born in Paris in 1930, went to Downside (Catholic boys' school) and New College, Oxford. In 1955, he left the Irish Guards and had a successful career in finance before starting the Mathaf Gallery in Knightsbridge. He was also master of the Worshipful Company of Bowyers, one of the London guilds dating back to the Middle Ages. It gave Charles great pleasure to arrive at his house after a night flight from New York to be served breakfast by the housekeeper, with the *Times*, ironed, beside his plate. On one visit, he rushed to Knightsbridge after breakfast to buy himself a new Burberry raincoat, having forgotten his as we left for the airport, which I did not believe. Charles always had good taste, and he particularly liked Brian Hugh's French breakfast china, by Gien, a flower pattern with peacocks.

Charles was annoyed at being excluded from a meeting I was having with a friend from Palm Beach, an Anglo-Argentinian, Louis Pryor, who had worked for Dupont in several countries. His lovely English wife, Joanna, had been at school with Charles. Louis took me to meet a friend of his at the Bank of Boston to set up a bank account in the Channel Islands after I inherited the only funds my wicked stepmother could not inherit from my father's estate, a trust known as a marriage settlement set up in 1935 at the time of my parents' marriage, which had appreciated considerably in more than forty years. Only the surviving children of the couple named in a marriage settlement could inherit after their parents died. When we met later for lunch with our old friend Tessa Greig, who had returned to England and married an Englishman at the Park Lane Hotel, Charles dropped a receipt onto the table, which he said I was paying for: a complete set of Gien china.

We visited Brian Hugh once when his father was staying with him at the Clock House during his last days, having outlived Elaine and given up their elegant Paris apartment. On the evening we were invited to dinner, we were told that the cook had been rushed to hospital with a serious medical condition and we would have to go to a restaurant. "Very inconvenient of her," said Uncle Frank. Charles was highly amused. On his deathbed, Frank told Brian Hugh that he was very proud of his only son, who had done so well in life, but his only regret was that he hoped he might have become prime minister.

The Mathaf Gallery specialized in Orientalist paintings, nineteenth-century depictions of the Arab world, Jean-Léon Gérôme being one of the best known, which were bought mostly by wealthy Arabs. One day, an old friend with whom he had served in the Irish Guards asked Brian Hugh if he could help find a job in a London gallery for his daughter Gina Gallwey. Brian Hugh needed an assistant, so he hired her himself. During a selling trip to Saudi Arabia, he proposed, and I went to their wedding in Ireland in 1985. Gina, although twenty-five years younger than her husband, and a very beautiful young woman, wasted no time pensioning off the housekeeper and telling him there were too many photographs of the royal family around the house. He had accompanied Prince Michael to the Sahel and written a book, *Cult of the Sacred Spear*, about the Nuer tribe in Ethiopia. Gina and Brian Hugh were very happy and raised two children. They used to exhibit at international art shows in New York and Palm Beach, and we always enjoyed seeing them.

On a couple of visits to London, we also stayed with Sallie and Jimmy Warden, living in a charming flat in Tennyson Mansions, also in Chelsea. We also spent some happy Thanksgiving holidays with them in their house on Eastern Avenue in Philadelphia.

During a subsequent visit to England and Scotland, we dined with my uncle and aunt, John and Bridget Christie-Miller, at the Army and Navy Club (known as the Rag) in Pall Mall. At this time, John was high sheriff of Cheshire. Also present were their youngest daughter, Charlotte, and her fiancé, Jack Beatson.

Their careers have been very impressive. They met in 1970 while studying law at Oxford. Charlotte was at Somerville College (Margaret Thatcher's alma mater, also Charlotte's mother's, my aunt Bridget's, from 1936 to 1939). Jack was at Brasenose College. After graduation, Charlotte studied for the

Bar in London and qualified as a barrister in 1972. At the time, it was difficult for women to make a career at the Bar, and she was more interested in working in industry. However, as companies were not hiring newly qualified barristers, she became a legal editor for a law publisher, Sweet & Maxwell, now part of Thomson Reuters.

Jack completed his graduate degree in 1872 and taught law at Bristol University for a year before being appointed the law fellow at Merton College Oxford. They married in 1973, lived in a college house in Oxford, and then bought their own home in 1977.

Charlotte became a legal advisor in the Oxford City Magistrates Court. In those days, she was called a "court clerk." Magistrates require legal advisors to sit with them in court to advise them on the law. She was the first woman and the first barrister to be appointed, and she encountered fairly rampant sexism from the younger male court clerks until they realized she was no threat to them, many of whom went on to become local judges.

Their son, Sam, was born in 1976 and their daughter, Hannah, less than three years later. Jack took a year's sabbatical, and they greatly enjoyed their time at the University of Virginia after a semester at Osgood Hall in Toronto, much enjoyed by Charlotte and the children too.

Back in Oxford, Charlotte did some freelance work for Oxford University Press, then was appointed appeal secretary at Somerville College, where she was successful in raising a large sum of money. In 1987, she joined the university's central administration and became a European research grants officer, negotiating and managing contracts between Oxford researchers and those from other European countries, funded by the European Union. She described the job as an eye-opener to the amazing scientific research going on in Oxford and to the idiosyncrasies of European bureaucracy.

In 1989, Jack was appointed for a five-year term to the law commission in London, after which he accepted the Rouse Ball Chair of English Law at Cambridge. Their son, Sam, was diagnosed with a brain tumor, so Charlotte was able to work part time as legal chairman for a tribunal set up by the government to hear appeals about children with special education needs, while she cared for Sam, who had severe bouts of ill health. She continued to work as a senior tribunal judge, leading it through a merger of separate tribunals under the Ministry of Justice after Sam's tragic death in 2004.

In 2003, Jack had been appointed a high court judge. This was very unusual because, unlike in the US, there was no tradition of academics being appointed to higher courts. He worked half the year in London and the other half out "on circuit," coming home on weekends. Myths tend to romanticize the grandeur of life for judges on circuit. In fact, their lodgings are often rundown and uncomfortable, and there is no longer the pomp and circumstance of being driven to court in robes with police outriders. This was abolished at the height of the IRA threat when judges were required to keep a low profile. Their cases, largely dealing with rapes and murders, were grueling. However, Charlotte and Jack enjoyed the continuing tradition of entertaining and being entertained by the local high sheriff (her father, my uncle, had been high sheriff for Cheshire) all over the country.

They moved back to Oxford in 2011, and two years later, he was appointed to the court of appeal in London. Charlotte was appointed to the social security and child support tribunal in Oxford. She retired from both in 2015 and became trustee for a local charity, Home-Start Oxford, which supports disadvantaged families with young children. Following in her father's footsteps, she became governor, and later vice chairman of governors, of Stockport Grammar School until 2013. She refers to being vice president of the Stockport Lads' Club, following in her father's and our grandfather's footsteps, as her "remaining link with the past," adding that it was a purely honorary role and she was probably kept on as "something of a relic and the last survivor of the dynasty."

Jack retired from the court of appeal in 2018. Since then, he has been appointed to the Astana International Financial Centre Court in Kazakhstan and sits on the court of appeal of the Cayman Islands as an arbitrator, which has produced some interesting work.

Their daughter, Hannah, now lives near her parents with her husband, Bill, and two daughters, who at the time of writing are attending my alma mater, Rye Saint Anthony School. Jack received a knighthood, so they are now Sir Jack and Lady Beatson.

My stepfather, Robert Niven, and his sister, Mary, arranged a trip in 1974 to Scotland. We traveled to Edinburgh by train from London. Mary loved that city and, after her beloved brother's death, made it her home until she died. We explored the highlights and dined well. We photographed each other on Christie-Miller Avenue and beside the Craigentinny Marbles, described earlier. Then we visited various relatives in Aberdeenshire, where the Nivens came from, and were treated to a scenic tour of the famous golf courses and the highlands, where years earlier Ian and I had skied before there were any kinds of ski lifts.

The following year, Robert and Mary visited us in East Hampton and New York. By then, he had been diagnosed with an inoperable brain tumor, and he died on February 6, 1976, at the age of sixty-four. I flew over and rushed to the Royal

Hampshire County Hospital in Winchester to say goodbye to him, but he was already in a coma.

The writer of his obituary in the *British Medical Journal* stated: "To his students at Millbank he was an inspiring teacher. As counsellor and guide he was unremitting in his efforts to further careers and encourage academic excellence. Two characteristics stood out: his urbane and debonair demeanor and his mordant wit; the latter rapier-like in its precision may occasionally have disturbed his listeners, but it was never unkindly intended for he bore malice against no one.

"The kindliness of his character was best seen in his home life; at his charming period cottage near Winchester he and his wife were the most generous of hosts. The harmony of their life together transmitted a sense of warmth and welcome to all who knew them."

I enjoyed my four years with the British Trade Development Office in New York working on store promotions, trade fairs, and missions. Those were the days of British Weeks at Neiman Marcus, Bloomingdale's, and other major department stores, as well as smaller specialty stores. Leading up to 1976 Bicentennial celebrations, Marvin Traub, president of Bloomingdale's, asked my UK-based boss Alan Titchener, head of consumer affairs, to organize a British menswear promotion. Alan promised a "minor royal" for the celebration. To our surprise, Mr. Traub took himself to London and arranged through the royal household for Her Majesty the Queen herself to come to Bloomingdale's to open the promotion.

There were festivities aboard the Royal Yacht *Britannia* followed by an event at City Hall. Some time that afternoon, Her Majesty appeared in Bloomingdale's basement menswear department. She seemed a little uncomfortable in such a confined space and must have been exhausted by all the activities inflicted on her by her former colony. Bloomingdale's was extremely happy, and the general merchandise manager offered me a job by way of thanks for my help in arranging the royal visit. He showed me a pile of resumes for would-be employees and said I could jump the line and join the executive training program. When he told me more about the exigencies of the job, I respectfully declined. We had recently built our house in East Hampton, and I was not going to work on Saturdays, even for such a prestigious store as Bloomingdale's was at that time.

Years later while staying in Edinburgh, we visited the *Britannia*, this time docked a few miles away as a museum and tourist attraction. I was surprised how small and relatively unpretentious the staterooms and accommodations were.

My position in the consumer section was not stressful, and after a while, I knew I needed to move on because promotion for local staff was limited. Colleagues were an interesting mix of local hires like myself and more senior staff who were UK-based and were usually transferred to another overseas posting or back to London after three years. They were our bosses, but we provided the local contacts and knowledge of the tri-state area market. There were a great many enjoyable social events because entertaining prospective American buyers of British goods and services was part of the job. There was no bottom line to worry about. We introduced buyers and agents during trade shows, missions, or individual visits, then it was up to the British firm to make the sale.

We had a local staff association, so I used to visit the British embassy in Washington to negotiate pensions, which did not exist for locally engaged staff. There were still long-time employees of the embassy who remembered working with our notorious spies when they were stationed there, Kim Philby and Donald Maclean. Kim Philby was an intelligence officer and double agent of the Soviet Union, and Donald Maclean was a British diplomat. Both were members of the traitorous "Cambridge Five."

We had a selection of props for store promotions. I kept the closet keys and provided items on request, such as Union Jack flags, cardboard Beefeaters, mugs, tote bags, and other British paraphernalia. To this day, I keep logs beside my fireplace in a wooden whiskey keg, a thank-you present for items sent to a British war brides group many years ago. Another memento is a runaway ivy plant. After years in a pot in my office, I planted it in our East Hampton garden. It now covers the trunks and branches of many trees, including those of my next-door neighbor, who never complained.

Early on the morning of the Bicentennial celebrations, I had gone to my office and typed my resignation, having accepted the position of market officer for the Hong Kong Trade Development Office at Rockefeller Center, which offered more money and more responsibility.

My duties were similar and my retail and wholesale contacts worked for Hong Kong businesspeople, much as they had for the British. I was in charge of groups in trade shows and arranged for US buyers to visit Hong Kong. At that time, many US companies were manufacturing in Hong Kong, so we found them suitable factories.

Charles flew out to Hong Kong during my first business trip. After marathon days of visiting factories, it was difficult to summon the energy and enthusiasm for evenings out with him, though we enjoyed dinners with old friends of my mother and stepfather, Doctors Philip and Barbara Mao, who introduced Charles to more cultural than commercial aspects of life in Hong

Kong. There were endless business banquets for Hong Kong businesspeople on both sides of the Pacific, and the Chinese food was always superlative.

Most marketing and promotion was done in New York by the American companies, the majority of Hong Kong companies being content with the profits from manufacturing. One exception was an Indian firm based in Hong Kong, Murjani, who advertised heavily and put on a lavish show at Studio 54 with Gloria Vanderbilt, who was spokesperson for their jeans. We arranged for Ms. Vanderbilt to travel to Hong Kong as our guest for our big ready-to-wear show. She insisted on bringing her toy poodle, and somehow we arranged that too.

Young Hong Kong fashion designers wanted to become known by name, and the Council spared no expense flying out US fashion company representatives and journalists first class. When one of the invited fashion writers canceled, I was assigned her first-class seat. Returning to New York was another story. As staff, I was lucky to get the last available seat in coach on the last flight out before Chinese New Year and found myself sitting next to the president of Tiffany's. I was surprised he was not traveling first class, but he explained that he chose to accompany one of his jewelry designers who was seated with her husband a few rows ahead of us. I had not expected her to be manufacturing in Hong Kong, and Tiffany's kept that rather quiet too. Although the fashion spectacular was luxurious, and guests including Gloria Vanderbilt and her little dog were well entertained, the mission was not accomplished. Hong Kong was not destined to become a fashion center like Paris, London, or Milan. Talented home-grown designers went to one of those fashion hubs as soon as they could.

While employed by the Hong Kong Trade Development Council and subsequently by the Province of Quebec, we worked with New York State government as well as the US federal government and gave seminars on how to help small businesses export goods and service. The concept of hands-on assistance from the Departments of Commerce to US companies did not come naturally. Government was perceived as a regulator and collector of taxes, not as friend and advisor to small business. New York State found our seminars very helpful. Staff of US companies were often surprised by my phone calls as a government representative calling on behalf of our exporters interested in doing business with them. We must have been somewhat successful, judging by the letters of appreciation I received from the Association of Chinese MBA at Columbia, or at trade shows sponsored by us, where exhibitors found agents or made direct sales. We got write-ups in the trade press covering our group participation in trade shows and industry missions incoming to the US or hosted by us in Hong Kong or Canada, from journalists as well as manufacturers.

Going through old letters and testimonials was very satisfying and made me feel appreciated and sometimes amused. I found a cartoon of a giant canine surrounded by tiny vehicles, drawn by a member of a US utilities group whom we took on a mission to Quebec. At the last minute, one executive canceled, saying he had missed the plane due to traffic held up by "a dead dog on the road," so one of his competitors drew the picture. Manufacturers thanked me for helping to find them agents and for introducing them to purchasing and procurement managers. I did not deserve the enthusiastic thanks of a wooden birdhouse manufacturer who did very well selling in New York State. I had done little more than give the small company a list of nurseries.

My colleagues and I could open doors, but it was up to the individual companies to follow up and work hard to secure orders. It was a sales job with no bottom line for us, no quotas, a win-win.

Much of my work for Hong Kong and Quebec involved the clothing industries. We offered showroom space in the Canadian consulate in New York for our companies to show their lines to potential buyers and agents. Although a memo used to circulate at the Quebec delegation before Christmas reminding us that as government employees we should not accept gifts, it was hard sometimes to refuse a thank-you gift. Also, Quebec fashion designers like us to wear their clothes, so we often bought wholesale, like true New York "garmentos." I always refused offers to wear designer jewelry for some business or social event, even though it was insured.

After four years of doing my job well, I was fired for the first and only time in my career. Years later, I ran into my Canadian counterpart, to whom the same thing had happened; although at the time I was told she married a rich doctor and did not want to work any longer, and she was told that I had also left voluntarily for another job. In fact, we were both guilty of inadvertently causing our Chinese bosses to lose face by having too much visibility and credibility among our business contacts and for the sin of being white women. I had an extra strike against me being British, because the Hong Kong Chinese understandably resented their colonial status at that time.

Once again, a store promotion was planned, this one with Jordan Marsh in Boston, and one of my duties was to pay the models, some of whom were internationally famous, who had agreed to work "off the books." Charles was horrified that I was expected to carry large amounts of cash late at night, so he wrote to my boss saying that he hoped a security guard would be provided. That was all the ammunition they needed. I was given three months' severance (but was rehired before it ran out) and replaced by a Chinese male colleague from the Dallas office.

Another aspect of my life during the seventies and the decades following was volunteer work. My mother-in-law was very happy when I joined the Junior League of New York, because her daughter Carolyn had no interest. She was also delighted that Charles and I were in the *Social Register*, thanks to a glowing letter written by John Kernan outlining our antecedents and suitability. To me, the point of volunteering is to make oneself useful to a worthy cause, not as a leg-up for entry into some exclusive country club or for personal gratification. The Junior League fit that social category, but I wanted to be involved in gutsy or at any rate meaningful projects.

I chaired a committee to help the then small and struggling American Folk Art Museum when it was on West 52nd Street. We provided volunteer docents, league members, which enabled the museum to stay open for longer hours each week. Two gutsier committees involved the New York Police Department and the court system. The rape committee raised money through the advertising council to place posters in the subway cars encouraging women to report rape. We had a photograph taken depicting women of all races and ages with the slogan "Rapists Don't Discriminate," also to promote the idea that it was a crime of violence rather than sexuality, so women should not feel shame as victims. We received an award from Mayor Abe Beame. Charles would not allow me to be in the photograph along with the other committee members, such was his paranoia that someone might recognize me, so I did coffee and snacks.

The second "gutsy" program was short lived. One night a week, I and another volunteer worked at the main courthouse downtown for several hours. Our job was to try to contact family members when someone was arrested and arraigned. We would telephone and ask a relative to come downtown to bail out the offender. One night, we were present at the arraignment of the murderer made famous by the movie *Looking for Mr. Goodbar.* I remember him as a rather seedy, pale young man demanding his next dose of Corazine. During our breaks, we went to Chinatown for food. Charles used to drive downtown around midnight to collect us in our red MGB.

Another volunteer group I joined while working for the Hong Kong Trade Development Council was the New York branch of the Fashion Group, an international professional association of women executives, representing every phase of fashion: manufacturing, marketing, retail, communications, and education. There were more than five thousand members in thirty-four regional groups in the US, Australia, Canada, England, France, Mexico, Korea, and Japan. A nonprofit organization, it served as an international clearinghouse for the exchange of information on tastes, trends, and development. In my time, the New York membership consisted of women from the fashion press, the Fashion Institute of Technology, the Costume Institute at the Metropolitan Museum, major New York department and specialty stores, textile companies, buying offices, and many talented designers.

Besides speaking at a career day for students of fashion organized by the Boston Fashion Group in 1979, my main contribution was to co-chair the Adrian Retrospective fashion show at the Waldorf Astoria in December 1980. Joseph S. Simms, a teacher of cinema and history at Cheltenham High School in Wyncote, PA, put the collection together over many years, starting with Janet Gaynor, who had been Adrian's wife. Adrian designed clothes for many Hollywood stars besides his wife, including Joan Crawford, Greta Garbo, Norma Shearer, Jean Harlow, Jeanette MacDonald, Katharine Hepburn, Rosalind Russell, and Greer Garson. Before his death in 1959, he was commissioned to create the costumes for *Camelot* on Broadway, where, as a gifted neophyte, he had begun his career as a designer for Irving Berlin.

A very different volunteer job landed in my lap in 1978 while I was working for Hong Kong. Harking back to school days, my admiration for Mother Bridget as teacher of English, headmistress, and favorite nun never left me. I was contacted by Kenneth Wagg, who was formerly married to the movie star Margaret Sullivan, who had also been married to Henry Fonda and Leyland Hayward; so he was stepfather to Brooke Hayward, author of *Haywire*, a book he hated, now married to a St. Mary's Ascot fellow alumna. How could I say no when he told me Mother Bridget sent him to me? He asked me to be president of the American Friends of Westminster Cathedral. This charity was hardly compelling in the US, which made fundraising very difficult. However, the Duke and Duchess of Norfolk helped us raise funds in the early years, having the considerable cachet of their titles. Miles was earl marshal of England and its premier Catholic duke. Also, some donors mistakenly thought they were supporting Westminster Abbey or a Protestant cathedral.

I am indebted to Bill Told, who was at the time an officer at Manufacturers Hanover Trust and did most of the preparatory work of organizing fundraising lunches and dinners in New York while I was on a business trip to Hong Kong. The English-Speaking Union gave a dinner on May 23 at their headquarters on 69th Street, at which the duke said, "No other family can boast of having two ancestors beheaded by Henry VIII, Anne Boleyn, and Catherine Howard." However, at a dinner the following evening hosted by the Pilgrims Society, its president complained that the duke was not ducal (pompous?) enough. In fact, Miles Fitzalan-Howard, who inherited the dukedom from his cousin Bernard, had been a very modest family man, serving in the army. I accompanied him and his wife, Anne, while they shopped at Macy's, where they found the sheets and towels to be much better and cheaper than English ones. They could be described as cozy, and the following year invited us with a major donor to lunch at Arundel Castle in Sussex, where they did not reside full time. He and Charles found it amusing that the white wine had frozen.

Some years later visiting London, when we accompanied John Grant to stay with his son, Geoffrey; his wife, Annette; and their children, I attended Miles's funeral. John, waiting with a car and driver to take us to lunch, was impressed when Her Majesty the Queen exited Westminster Cathedral ahead of the rest of the mourners.

We tried to keep things going and held modest benefits in New York. Basil Cardinal Hume's visit in 1980 was a success and raised some money for the cathedral. The duke's thank-you note to me is signed, "All love to you and Charles." After the Norfolks were no longer involved with fundraising, though of course he remained England's premier Catholic duke, it became much more difficult. We American board members attended a charity auction and dinner at Guildhall in London in September 1981, where Bob Hope was master of ceremonies, and hanging in my dining room is a painting by the duchess of a rural scene in Kenya, which I bought. I handed over the presidency to Una Chang but remained on the board for a few more years.

In March 2007, we were rewarded for our perseverance. Una Chang, Henry Lievre, and I flew over to London for a reception at 10 Downing Street followed by dinner for about sixty people at the Ritz, hosted by the Swiss bank, Banque Piguet & Cie. Cherie Blair was a most gracious hostess, and it was a huge thrill to be at Number Ten. She and I were the only ladies wearing skirts; the Swiss bank wives and others all wore black silk pants. This was a truly memorable evening, following lunch with Peter Cannon-Brookes; his son, Stephen; and daughter-in-law, Olga, at the Athenaeum, and a walk across St. James's Park on an exceptionally warm un-English March day.

There were always Washington connections from 1972 until 2000. I loved that city. On more than one occasion, I visited the Folger Shakespeare Library and received flattering attention as a former Christie-Miller. Their collection included purchases from the Britwell Library, and not only did I see the First and Third Folios on display (from 1632 and 1685, respectively), I was shown many more treasures behind the scenes, notably Elizabethan manuscripts, which came from the family collection that was auctioned by Sotheby's between 1910 and 1927. The Folger has the world's largest collection of Shakespeare editions, as well as books, manuscripts, and prints from Renaissance Europe. Henry Clay Folger and his wife, Emily, started amassing the collection in 1889 and opened the library in 1932. Charles and I joined the Friends of the Folger and attended at least one black-tie event.

When Martin Morland was counselor and head of chancery at the British embassy from 1979 to 1982, I dined with him and Jenny during business visits to the nation's capital. I had not seen them since their wedding in 1964. By this time, they had three children. After serving as British ambassador to Burma (mentioned earlier), his final post was UK permanent representative at the United Nations in Geneva. The last time I saw the Morlands was when they visited Charles and me in East Hampton just after

9/11. Jenny's mother, Blanche, my godmother, had died in Spain in 1993 at the age of eighty-five. Jenny wrote me all about her funeral in the Arundel family chapel at Wardour Castle, where Jenny and Martin were married. She added that undoubtedly our mothers were having a fine old time, reunited in Heaven. She visualized Blanche, whiskey in one hand, cigarette in the other, telling God what He needed to do. Jenny died in 2018, two years before her husband. According to my cousin, Alan MacDermot, Brian's eldest son—who is secretary to the Wardour Chapel Trust, which owns the chapel and the primary school attended by his sisters Lucy and Jacinta, and where he has also been a governor and teacher—Jenny occupies the last space in the crypt below the chapel, and Martin's ashes will be interred there too.

Charles and I used to visit Richard Crowson, who was the special Hong Kong representative attached to the embassy. I was working for their Trade Development Council in New York, but we were a registered foreign agency without diplomatic privileges, whose mission was to promote trade and commerce. Because Hong Kong was still a British colony, legislative matters were handled by the embassy in Washington. Richard, who was divorced, had brought his daughter to East Hampton for a visit. In the '80s, we stayed with him and his second wife, Judy, whom he had met and married in Washington, when they were stationed at the British embassy in Berne, Switzerland.

Listening to the eulogies and earlier interviews for Ruth Bader Ginsburg following her death on September 20, 2020, I noted that she mentioned being invited to become the first woman member of Washington's famous Cosmos Club. I was a guest there for dinner once and was impressed by its hallowed status.

# Chapter Fifteen

In December 1980, I went to work for the Association of the Nonwoven Fabrics Industry (INDA), as manager of meetings and conventions, located at 1700 Broadway. INDA was a marketing association consisting of many major corporations involved in manufacturing film, fiber, geotextiles, fabrics that were neither knitted nor woven, and machinery that was also used in paper manufacturing. The industry was a sort of inverted pyramid, many different products purchased by a few huge corporate end users in diapers and hospital disposables, such as Kimberly-Clark, geotextiles, and so on.

My job was to coordinate technical and sales meetings for members (Scott Paper, Johnson & Johnson, DuPont, the Oxford Industries division of The Hartford Corporation, Rohm and Haas, Chicopee, and others) in addition to managing our major international trade show and conference in a US city every two years. Travel was involved to select suitable locations for meetings, known as "fam trips," as in familiarization. Because INDA represented so many important corporations, cities and resorts competed for our business, which meant I was royally treated and often stayed free in presidential suites in high-end hotels. On one embarrassing occasion, I received luxurious accommodation for a sales meeting while our illustrious six-foot-plus chairman had a rather small room situated over the hotel nightclub, a situation that was soon rectified. Charles sometimes accompanied me to a resort meeting, paying his fare and the room supplement for a second person. He came to California and Arizona and to the Breakers in Palm Beach, where he could visit family and friends while I ran our meetings.

My first visit to our European association was in Amsterdam in early 1981. It transpired that our president, John Mead, did not own a passport and was rather leery about foreign travel, so he sent me in his place. This was not appreciated by the Europeans, so we both went to the next European show in Geneva, where Charles joined me for a short vacation afterward. Mary Niven flew out from Scotland to spend a few days with us in Geneva, and we took a trip to Chamonix. Charles and I rode the cable car to the top of the mountain, part of the Massif du Mont-Blanc, where we could look down at the Aosta Valley of Italy, the Rhône-Alpes of France, and Switzerland's Valais. On the way up, it lurched rather violently, and a gentleman sitting beside me clutched me in a moment of fright. After apologizing to Charles and me, we three joined Mary for lunch when we descended. He told us he was in Switzerland on business for the Getty Museum, but when we saw him later in the week dining in a restaurant, he ignored us. We could not help wondering if there was some nefarious art deal being transacted and he needed to conceal the identity of his employer.

The international trade shows I managed in Philadelphia and Baltimore were very hard work, but I was ably assisted by the cities' marketing and promotion departments and the hotel staffs where our exhibitors, speakers, and participants stayed, because they all appreciated the business we were bringing to their cities. Exhibition companies, restaurants, taxi companies, and others benefited from the influx of business visitors from all over the US and Europe attending IDEA 84, the International Conference and Exhibition at the Baltimore Convention Center. The city was enjoying a period of renewal, developing their Inner Harbor, so our show was important to them.

The three days of the show were intense, and once again I thank my forebears for those good genes. Although already in my forties, I had the energy to run on three or four hours' sleep, preparing for early morning speakers, monitoring the show all day, making sure exhibitors and speakers had everything they needed, attending evening receptions and dinners, and winding up in hospitality suites until the wee hours of the morning.

IDEA 84 brought in hugely increased revenues from additional exhibitors (I had personally persuaded some printing companies to exhibit for the first time, which proved profitable for them and the association). I really had no plans to leave, but I had been approached by the government of the province of Quebec's New York delegation to apply for the post of commercial attaché, which I was offered after a couple of interviews. When I asked John Mead if he could match the salary, he declined, so I agreed to work for Quebec. I had some mixed feelings, having greatly enjoyed my time at INDA, my colleagues, the travel, and liked many of the members very much. However, once again I got lucky, because soon after I left, INDA moved its offices to Raleigh, North Carolina, a transfer Charles and I would never have been able to accept. He could not have given up his job at Chase Manhattan Bank in New York, and we would have missed our friends and our beloved house in East Hampton too much.

While I was still working at INDA, in 1983 Charles and I visited my father at Crawfordsburn Hospital, Helen's Bay, near Belfast. He was very crippled and suffering from Parkinson's disease. During a few short days we became reconciled, and after we returned to New York, he dictated letters to his nurses for me because he could not write himself. He hugely appreciated our visit and was charmed by Charles. He wrote that we brought him great happiness. I asked him to tell me about his war experiences and I am including the most interesting stories.

In June 1944, a British gunboat took him, two Greek officers in exile, and a few Greek soldiers from Bari, Italy, to Kalamata, Greece. The British Military Mission to Greece was planning to take over the government as soon as the Germans pulled out. They joined forces with a Communist general, Ares Velociosas, who had built up an army and attacked the Germans from his hideout in the mountains. My father described him as having a beard down to his waist and three pistols in his belt. He wanted to take over the country when the Germans left and fight the British if necessary. At Corinth, they met up with the British army who were supporting the Communists. The latter were delighted when Clement Attlee defeated Churchill, mistakenly thinking the Socialists and Communists shared the same beliefs. While my father was escorting General Velociosas, he described a rather charming incident when the soldiers milked a flock of sheep to provide welcome liquid refreshment on a hot afternoon. General Velociosas attacked Athens, but after several months of hostilities, the Communists pulled out. He was captured by the Greek Royalists and beheaded.

In 1945, my father left Greece for Algiers, where he was commandant of a prisoner of war camp at Cap Matifou containing nine thousand Italian soldiers. Field Marshal Graziani was his most important prisoner. The prisoners lived in tents, but he had "a very pleasant cottage overlooking the Mediterranean." The British found a good chef among the prisoners of war to cook for the officers' mess. Graziani told my father that he was a good governor and offered to write a testimonial, which he declined, because he could not accept one from a prisoner of war. The Jewish doctor from London who hated Fascists and Nazis thought my father was too kind to Graziani and said that if he gave any trouble, he would cut his wine ration, but he never carried out the threat. When my father received orders to prepare to move Graziani to Italy, he tried to bundle him quietly into a car to drive out of the camp, but a parade of about five thousand Italian prisoners gave him the Fascist salute as he waved from the back seat, denying that he had ordered this send-off. He was tried by the Italians but died of natural cause before the sentence could be carried out.

My father wrote that his worst war experience was while walking down Regent Street in London. He saw a German buzz bomb start to descend. He dived into an entranceway with three glass walls, but luckily the bomb landed on the bank of the Thames and no one was hurt. His army battery was deployed on the Tyne, and there were air raids every night.

My father's letters, written by kind nurses, stopped in 1984 when his Parkinson's disease grew worse. I discovered that he had been awarded several medals, including the Greek Distinguished Service Medal, the Italy Star Defense Medal, and the War Medal and General Service Medal "with clasp Palestine 1945-48," and was mentioned in dispatches in 1945.

I saw him once more before he died in 1988 at the age of seventy-eight. While visiting Bunty Simonds in Dublin, we drove to the north one day so she could check on the Whyte family home at Loughbrickland and I could visit my father in the Ulster Volunteer Force Hospital in Belfast. Driving back near the border between Northern Ireland and the Republic, we found ourselves caught between two British military vehicles whose occupants were shooting at members of the IRA running across a field. I was sure we would be killed in the crossfire, but somehow we made it back safely to Wellington Road. I was still shaking when Charles telephoned from New York, because he had forbidden me to go to the north, so I never told him; I just said my teeth were chattering because the phone was in a chilly place.

In one of his last letters, my father wrote, "I have your photograph on the table at the end of my bed. The pair of you I see last thing at night and first thing in the morning." At the end of his life, it was as though twenty-eight years of estrangement had never happened.

In 1985, I went to work for the Quebec delegation at Rockefeller Center and stayed there for fifteen years. Our third-floor offices overlooked the skating rink, but later we moved up to the twenty-fifth floor of 17 West 50th Street. The delegation was almost an embassy incorporating besides our trade section, the tourism department, and a visa section. Quebec was permitted to prescreen immigrants to Canada from francophone countries, but the Canadian federal government issued the actual visas. It was a delicate time, politically. The Separatist movement was alive and well in Quebec, which often raised tensions in our work with the Canadian consulate in New York and the embassy in Washington. Our mission, whether federal or provincial, was to assist Canadian businesspeople commercially in the United

States. I was doing the same sort of work as I had done for the Irish and British governments and for Hong Kong, and with a certain lack of modesty, I can say that by now my contacts were pretty substantial, which was the reason I was hired.

I really loved my job and my clients in both countries. I had the womenswear dossier, and many small but successful high-end companies who used mostly European fabrics and designs were located in Quebec and found a niche market amongst the US specialty stores. We used to hold a Canadian fashion week at the RIHGA Royal Hotel in New York, which was very successful for our companies, many of whom made good sales or found US agents.

Montreal furriers put on a show on the Rockefeller Center ice rink when wearing fur was still acceptable. For once, we got some publicity (alas, Canadian fashion like Hong Kong was not newsworthy), because PETA supporters protested by skating through our show naked.

I was also given some industrial dossiers in the defense, building materials, utilities, and transportation industries, plus the United Nations, which consisted mostly of placing consulting firms with expertise needed in francophone countries—for example, specialists in Napoleonic law who could serve the UN in Cambodia. My Quebec colleagues liked me to arrange meetings with different UN staff, and I remember meeting Ellen Johnson Sirleaf at the UN, years before she became prime minister of her own country, Liberia. A Quebec company won a major railroad contract administered by the UN in one of the former French colonies in Africa. I like to think I played a small part by taking the UNOPS representative to lunch frequently on my expense account and listening sympathetically to his troubles, personal and work-related, while he downed several martinis and I toyed with a glass of wine.

An unfortunate attempt by senior Quebec officials to discuss a Montreal satellite office for which I had to make appointments with assistant secretaries general caused ire and consternation when the Canadian federal government heard about it. We tried to mitigate the faux pas with a lavish lunch at Le Bernardin for officials involved.

Helping defense industry companies, many of whom were subsidiaries of and suppliers to Bombardier, involved trips to the Canadian embassy and various trade shows in Washington, where we developed useful contacts with the Department of Defense and the military establishment. Because of the friction between some Quebec colleagues and the Canadian government, as a non-Canadian neutral employee I could open doors for our companies. As an extremely ethical person, I was shocked one day when a lobbyist, encountered briefly at an embassy reception, arrived in my New York office with a proposition for one of our companies to lowball a contract with all the illegal shenanigans that could have entailed and offering me a cut.

Staff of a small but highly specialized Quebec electronics firm whom I introduced to a US prime contractor in defense electronics negotiated for many months. It transpired that Westinghouse Electric was shaking up its original supplier, who had gotten sloppy or too expensive or both by threatening to hire another company. (Canadian companies were entitled to US defense business thanks to offsets, because Canada bought US fighter planes.) General Electric got the message and did not lose the business. However, the Quebecers felt rightly that they had been exploited at considerable expense flying engineers down for meetings in Baltimore. I was asked what went wrong, was it that I refused to sleep with the Westinghouse procurement manager? This was long before the Me Too movement, and I found it rather amusing. I told this story to a couple of young women recently. They were shocked by such rampant sexism, but times have changed.

As I mentioned, we brought a US utilities trade mission to James Bay to visit the famous hydroelectric plant, which provided electricity all the way south through Quebec and the northeastern US. Hydro-Québec operates about sixty hydroelectric plants in the province of Quebec and produces about a quarter of the world's hydroelectricity. We flew to James Bay on the Premier's private plane.

Senior Quebec government officials asked me to arrange a trip to Brookhaven National Laboratory by helicopter, the US government's premier institution for fundamental research in nuclear and particle physics. This was arranged by Mary Fallon, who was at time in charge of the science and technology department of New York State, having formerly been East Hampton town supervisor. I escorted a mission of construction industry executives to the province to encourage them to purchase Quebec building supplies. As it was November and out of season, we stayed at the Château Frontenac at government expense. Our good friend, Sam Lester, who had completed renovations on our house in East Hampton and was rebuilding one for our friends John and Susan Jaxheimer, came on the mission and made my life easier. We always had a drink in front of a roaring fire at the hotel before going out to a much-too-long dinner. Culturally, these long lunches and dinners did not sit well with the US businessmen.

The delegate general who hired me was Leo Paré, a very courtly Quebecois. He was succeeded by a dynamic woman,

Rita Dionne Marsolais. Two Anglophones followed, Reed Scowen and Kevin Drummond, who was married to Mary, Galt MacDermot's sister. They lived in a fine apartment in Museum Tower next to the Museum of Modern Art owned by the Quebec government.

Soon after I went to work for Quebec, there was a vacancy for another commercial attaché. Alden Prouty, a Smith College graduate, applied for the job. My boss, Andre Migneault, asked me to have an initial meeting with her. He accepted my strong recommendation and hired her after his more formal interview. She had an excellent background, and her limited knowledge of French could be improved with an intensive course in Quebec. She was a divorced mother of three, Brooks, Honor, and Nicholas, and over the years we have all become very close friends. I refer to them as my adoptive American family.

Alden accompanied me to Ireland where we first stayed with Veronica Sanderson, my goddaughter in Dublin. We drove to her charming house on the Long Walk in Galway, with a stop at Coolavin for lunch. Alden, who has impeccable manners, said as we sat down at the historic mahogany dining room table, "Something smells delicious." My aunt Felicity replied, "How do you know? You haven't tasted it yet." I was slightly embarrassed of course, but Alden took it well. She was intrigued by Coolavin, especially the oratory, which I described earlier. Another year we visited Scotland and stayed in Mary Niven's guest suite. Mary and Alden got along extremely well and kept in touch until Mary died. We spent a long weekend in Edinburgh and took the train to Glasgow where we visited Peggy Anderson and some of the famous Cameron Mackintosh buildings.

In 1987, Charles and I visited Wanda and John Rix at Wodehouse, their Hampshire home, which I had known and loved since my return from Canada in 1967. It was an extremely comfortable house, unpretentious, surrounded by five acres of beautiful gardens, lawns, trees, a field where horses grazed, and a magnificent gypsy caravan. As we know from *My Fair Lady*, hurricanes hardly ever happen in Hampshire, but in the middle of the night on October 15, one hit hard, known as the Great Storm of 1987, which caused massive destruction at historic Kew Gardens, killing eighteen people in the UK and causing over two billion pounds sterling in damage. Eighty-six-miles-per-hour winds raged with gusts up to 134. Next morning, people were wandering around in a daze saying the devastation and debris everywhere reminded them of the blitz during World War II. By some incredible luck, none of the Rix's buildings, some containing a collection of antique cars, were hit by falling trees. The power went out for three weeks, but they had an AGA stove so were able to cook delicious meals for ourselves, friends, and neighbors, eating up lots of fresh salmon and strawberries before the contents of everyone's freezers melted and spoiled.

There was just one chainsaw between several families, but we managed to clear the driveways to the roads. Not many miles away at their riverfront house on the Thames at Henley, untouched by the hurricane, David and Joan Christie-Miller gave a family lunch for us two days later, cooked and served by their daughter Diana. We spent the weekend with John and Bridget in their beautiful Cotswolds home.

My hair still smelled of wood smoke from the tree limbs we had burned on bonfires at the Rixes' when we arrived in Venice on the Monday. Watching Italian TV from our hotel bedroom after dinner, listening to voluble and excited commentary, neither of us understood Italian, but when numbers flashed on the screen, we realized the markets had plunged and it was Black

Monday, October 17. The next morning, many American tourists seemed to be wandering round St. Mark's Square in a state of shock, but we decided to enjoy the rest of our vacation. Our broker, Tony Cowen of Cowen and Company, had been trying to reach us unsuccessfully by phone. This was many years before the arrival of the internet to simplify or complicate our lives.

# Chapter Sixteen

**W**anda Rix persuaded me to accompany her on a trek. She had already shown me her photographs of Everest and Annapurna treks in Nepal, so I agreed to accompany her to Sikkim.

Sikkim, also called Nye-Mal-Ale—which means "heaven" according to its original inhabitants, the Lepchas—was, with Bhutan, one of the lost kingdoms of the Himalayas, connected more with Tibet than India. It came under British protection in the nineteenth century to protect it from the Nepalese, and in 1950, Indian protection was accepted. In the 1970s, the king became increasingly unpopular, particularly after his second marriage to an American; and in 1975, Sikkim became the twenty-second state of India.

Our trek was organized by Exodus, and we flew from London to New Delhi in late April of 1992. Excerpts from my diary follow:

Writing in air-conditioned comfort in my room in the Hotel Siddarth, an oasis from the heat and morning bustle of two hours' drive from the airport. Emission control standards appear to be non-existent: mopeds, small cars, three wheelers, buses, bicycles and sacred cows clog the streets. Our guide, B.K. Gupta, claimed "bus drivers not nice people at all" (apparently they all come from some area he despises). Our driver nearly ran down a bevy of little girls in their blue school uniforms, overtaking one of those "nasty buses." We were seven: two unrelated couples named Brown, Donald, a retired headmaster of a comprehensive school in Somerset, and his wife Barbara, Andrew and Elizabeth who farm nine hundred acres in Kircudbright, Scotland, Alan Dunkley, a semi-retired doctor, Wanda, and myself.

We were jet-lagged tourists cramming as many sights as possible into a short time: the Minar Mosque, a large modern Hindu temple, the Red Fort, the Gandhi Memorial, impressive government buildings dating from 1911 when the British founded the city, and the India Gate, memorializing the British and Indian regiments who fought in World War One, my favorite being Skinner's Horse.

In the wee hours of Tuesday, April 28, after four hours' sleep, we drove to the Indira Gandhi domestic airport and boarded an Air India 747 for Bagdogra. We ate a second breakfast of excellent curried vegetables, fruit and coffee as we flew over the plains, glimpsing snow-covered Himalayas in the distance. We drove in a little bus from Siliguri uphill for three hours, stopping only once for tea and cheese pagoras, round hairpin bends past poor villages clinging to the steep hillsides, cattle and goats, less skeletal than their New Delhi counterparts, graceful sari-clad women balancing loads on their heads, tiny shops everywhere, and school children in English style uniforms. Fearless buses and a few cars passed us and each other on the steep narrow road with much hooting of horns, which was scary.

The Windermere Hotel in Darjeeling was a period piece. We lunched in an oval windowed room, like the prow of a liner, clouds descending. After a walk through the town with its steep narrow streets, limbless beggars, haggling shopkeepers, an ethnic mix predominantly Nepalese and Tibetan, we returned to the Windermere for tea, a relic of the Raj complete with three-piece string orchestra. Darjeeling is as popular a hill station for Indian families escaping the heat of Calcutta as it was for the British administrators and their memsahibs. A sign in my bathroom states, "The chain-action water-closet in this room has been in dependable service since 1912."

We visited the Darjeeling Zoo which has a snow leopard breeding center, several ferocious looking Siberian tigers and a somnolent black bear or two. We also saw Tenzing Norgay's tomb and monument. He had been Sir Edmund Hillary's Sherpa during his triumphant ascent of Mount Everest on May 29, 1953, although it was not announced until the day of Queen Elizabeth's coronation.

The Himalayan Institute is unique as a museum of mountaineering, also fauna and flora: birds, butterflies, bats, flying foxes and squirrels. There were displays of equipment from famous expeditions. One wonders how they managed to climb wearing all that heavy leather and canvas. One pair of boots belonged to a Swiss climber who must have lost all his toes to frostbite, the foot was so short. We watched Tibetans carding wool, using bicycle wheels to spin it, and in another room mostly older women with few teeth, flat, handsome faces and radiant smiles, weaving carpets on handlooms.

Once again we rose at 3.30 a.m. for a sunrise excursion. We piled into two 1952 vintage jeeps held together with assorted spare parts and drove with hundreds of other jeeps to Tower Hill. Ours stopped once so that one driver was able to give the other a paltry pint or less of gas.

The sun was already over the Eastern horizon, silhouetted against clouds, willow pattern trees and green terraced hills. Hundreds of colorfully dressed women with their husbands and children, mostly from Calcutta (Kolkata) were getting out of jeeps, trucks and cars. The majestic Kachenjunga range, which means five treasures of the eternal snows because of its five magnificent peaks, was briefly visible above the clouds. Most of the time the mountains are shrouded in heavy mist which prompted one of our group to christen Sikkim "cloud cuckoo land." In fact our dogged uphill walking was often accompanied by the sounds of cuckoos and dzo-bells.

Unfortunately next day I came down with a severe case of the Darjeeling equivalent of Montezuma's revenge and took to my bed, visited frequently by Elizabeth, Barbara and Wanda who when I told her I had a temperature of a hundred and two, said I was silly to take it. She had a point because sick or not we would leave early next day, May Day.

We drove beside the Teesta River and entered Sikkim, stopping at two passport checkpoints and spent the night at the Pandin Hotel before starting our trek through mud and rain and encountering leeches in the rain forest, along with many plants such as arisaema (the snake plant), zephyranthes (pink crocus), carinata, curcuma aromatica (wild turmeric), cardamom, the cash crop of Sikkim, and ainsliae which were little star shaped white flowers. Sikkim is home to more than six hundred species of orchids and forty of rhododendrons. Man has improved on nature in the cultivation of rhododendrons in western countries. Some were about sixty feet tall and grew on steep slopes. Their insipid blooms which were rather sparse and straggly looked like soggy kleenex in the constant rain, which was disappointing, although in dryer weather colors were more visible, mostly yellow, but some pink, mauve and even red.

In Pemayangtse we visited the second oldest monastery in Sikkim, the next day at Yoksum, the former capital of Sikkim, we climbed in the rain to the Dubtek monastery. We visited many temples and monasteries but unless one is a serious student of Tibetan Buddhism, all those garish and gilded religious frescoes, the miles of prayer flags on bamboo poles and prayer wheels on the temple walls tend to blur in one's memory, except perhaps for the modern, teaching monastery at Rumtek where the monks meditate around the clock to select an important lama, a two-year-old boy living somewhere in Sikkim waiting to be discovered. Apparently they never make a mistake, for the chosen child-lama always answered their spiritual questions with unfailing, mystical accuracy.

When we embarked on our trek from Yoksum through the rain forests we encountered leeches as they dropped onto us from the branches. If Pasang, B.K.'s assistant who had served with a Gurkha regiment in Borneo, was within range he despatched the nasty creatures with his lighted cigarette but at night we would find soggy leech corpses inside our hiking boots when we peeled off our socks.

As we ascended there were stops at tea houses and simple huts for refreshments. After climbing all day through cold rain it felt good to sit in front of an open fire and drink thumba, a local alcoholic brew. I saw an enormous bloated leech wriggling across the floor and wanted to throw it on the fire but one of the porters stopped me, and good Buddhist that he was reverently carried it outside.

Our packs were carried by dzos (cow mother, yak father) and dris (yak mother, bull father) who wore bells like Swiss cowbells. One had to be careful when overtaking them on trails, lest they turn suddenly and strike with one of their heavy horns. Our ten dzos, dris and yaks were cared for by three porters. Our group consisted of fifteen people, including BeeBee, a Sikkimese paramilitary officer. At some point we were joined by two particularly mangy dogs christened Scabby Dog and Loppylugs by

Andrew who never left us until we descended Kachenjunga.

On the lower slopes we slept in primitive lodges, in our sleeping bags on hard wooden boards, but as we climbed higher we slept in tents. Our cook, Nur Muhammed from Kashmir, and his assistant performed miracles in primitive conditions though every campsite had a kitchen hut. Four course dinners would appear, soups, curried vegetables, chicken, meat, the predominant flavor being cardamom, puddings, oranges, bananas etc. washed down with endless cups of tea. At 6 a.m. every morning a cup of tea was brought to our tent followed by water to wash with. Before going to bed at night our water bottles were filled with hot water which at the bottom of our sleeping bags kept us warm and became the following day's drinking water while trekking.

At one overnight stop at Thangsing, in a freezing stone hut basically two rooms and a kitchen, but with a magnificent view of Kachenjunga, the third highest mountain in the world, we listened to the State Opening of Parliament on Donald's transistor radio. Near the Prek River in which a year earlier a dozen people had died during a flash flood after a glacier collapsed into a lake upstream, indeed its white boulders are quite formidable, we encountered a young man wearing wellingtons and a jacket made out of old sacking. He had a healthy looking herd including three baby dris. When I tried to photograph a black one, he kept popping under his mother for a drink of milk. A dzo can carry as much as a hundred kilograms on its back if properly balanced.

We arrived at the holy lake Samiti, its waters a glacial turquoise. We pitched our tents and walked to some Buddhist chortens, memorials to dead lamas. On the way up we passed piles of mani prayer stones as well as ubiquitous colorful prayer flags. Green signifies cultivation, blue water, red blood, white purity and black demons. Buddhists must walk clockwise round these, some of which show the face of Buddha with eleven lines above his eyes, representing his teachings.

On the night of May 8, Elizabeth and I shared a tent because poor Andrew was suffering from altitude sickness and had gone back to Dzongri with one of the porters. We passed a rather sleepless night knowing we had to get up at 4.30 to trek to the Goecha La Pass, our triumphant highest point at just over seventeen thousand feet.

We enjoyed our descent except for one snowstorm. Monday, May 11 was our last day of trekking and we were served bed-tea at 5 a.m. We

saw a wonderful yellow-beaked, long tailed mag-
pie, a red tailed kestrel (cuckoos having been the
most ubiquitous bird), and heard woodpeckers.
We watched a group of elderly American very
serious bird-watchers head uphill. Apparently
one had to be carried up the night before on a
yak. We stopped to wade or dunk in mountain
torrents, ate a cooked lunch near a suspension
bridge, and stopped at a tiny lean-to tea house,
where a tiny Nepalese man rinsed metal beakers
with ash and water, while we sat on his bed
watching his three cows and a calf. The tea when
finally brewed was delicious, apparently with tea
leaves all the way from Darjeeling. We picked
delicious wild yellow raspberries after a swim.

Before they left us, we divided up our surplus
clothing and other gear for the porters, sav-
ing better stuff for the cook and his assistant.
Farewell speeches were translated by B.K. I gave
the cook my spare watch and Pasang a pedom-
eter and compass/thermometer. Although we
only trekked about forty miles, and climbed
more than ten thousand feet, we felt a sense of
achievement, having coped with rugged terrain,
altitude, snow, sleet, hail and rain.

A bus picked us up and drove us to Tashiding
where we were entertained by a blind man
playing "Frère Jacques" and Nepali folk songs.
Some signs viewed from the bus amused us: "use

dipper at night," "slow drive long life," "hitch-hike—save fuel," "creep is better than cripple," "speed is thrilling but also killing," and hotel names, Dolph Inn and Calamity Inn. Andrew invented the best one: "slow—leeches crossing." We watched school boys playing soccer in bare feet, although their coach had one shoe on one foot! We were surrounded by terraced hillsides growing maize, rice and barley. Herds of goats abounded and stray dogs slept on steps, one in a flower bed. We spent a night in Gangtok, visited more monasteries (my readers like Andrew will probably yawn and say "spare us" so I will) on a daily basis. After Kalimpong, which used to be a wool trading center for Tibet, we left Sikkim driving through rain and thunder to a quaint, old world hill station, arriving in time for tea at the Himalayan.

Our charming hostess Mrs. Williams (her in-laws from Inverness had built the house in 1905) spoke perfect English and introduced us to her English retriever dogs Tom and John and two adorable eight-week-old Lhasa apso puppies, Shin Tu, little lion, and Doma, little lady. Proudly, she showed us family photos and some of the King of Bhutan who had stayed at the age of sixteen with his mother and sisters and of his coronation. Next morning Elizabeth woke us to admire a spectacular sunrise over the Himalayan range looking towards Tibet.

We arrived at Bagdogra Airport to find a group whose flight to New Delhi the previous day had been canceled, still waiting patiently which was not auspicious. However, we passed about five hours further delay playing card games, eating, drinking, and buying books from an extraordinarily well-stocked shop. We landed in New Delhi at about 9 p.m. in 116-degree heat and headed for the Hotel Siddarth where my first bath in weeks was sheer heaven.

After some more sightseeing we had an unforgettable last dinner in India to thank B.K. for looking after us so well. His charming wife Manjulika, an artist, joined us. She, like the Inuit carvers, "sees" her subjects in pieces of wood and carves around them. She and B.K., whose families come from Lucknow, have no children but forty-eight nieces and nephews, his eldest brother being twenty-eight years older than he is. They spoke fondly of their camp in Manali, where apparently English settlers who intermarried with local Indians introduced trout fishing. B.K. driving away on his turquoise blue motor scooter, Manjulika riding behind him clutching a bunch of flowers, her gray-blue sari floating gracefully, was an unforgettable sight.

Our flight to London was diverted through Bombay which for me involved a mad dash to Terminal 4 at Heathrow for the last flight to

New York. There was a group of Japanese tourists on the same inter-terminal bus who pointed at my hiking boots, giggling madly. I remembered that a Japanese lady climber had just summited Everest, a word they understood, and supplied her name. Maybe they thought I had accompanied her, at least partway up the mountain.

My darling husband Charles had been waiting patiently for five hours at JFK. Air India had told British Airways that I would be on the last flight, as indeed I was thirty hours and nine and a half times zones after leaving New Delhi.

Briefly, I believe we enjoyed what is mostly lost in twenty-first-century first world life, a respect for the power and vastness of nature, a rediscovery of our planet's grandeur, and for ourselves a sense of achievement when even the mundane act of breathing required effort at high altitudes.

# Chapter Seventeen

I took two more treks with Exodus.

On October 15, 1993, I flew to London and took the bus to Woking, where Wanda met me and we had a happy reunion at Wodehouse with her family and friends. Elizabeth and Andrew Brown joined us from Scotland, and we reviewed our photos of our Sikkim trek.

We flew to Marrakesh via Casablanca and spent the night at the Hotel Foucauld. Next morning, we drove in two mini-buses over the High Atlas Mountains via Ouarzazate (where the *Indiana Jones* and other movies were made) through the Draa Valley to Nkob in the Jbel Saghro, passing olive groves, fruit trees, and date palms, sellers of amethyst, cobalt, and topaz, as well as colorful pottery and small fortified villages whose houses were built of red beaten earth and often contained interior courtyards. As we entered the Draa Valley via the Tizi n'Tichka pass over the mountains, the landscape grew bleaker, picturesque rocky ridges alternating with undulating sandstone slopes. The Berbers in their long roses, herding sheep and goats, looked positively biblical. We could have been in the Dakotas, a perfect setting for westerns except for the beau geste–style French Foreign Legion old forts and the Berbers. Actually, it was hard to distinguish between the dried ruins and the fairly modern buildings in villages. The walled villages had turrets on each building, and every village had a mosque.

At Nkob, we unloaded our gear in a dusty courtyard, took off our shoes, and drank mint tea sitting on a carpet in a room off the courtyard. We spread our sleeping bags on the roof and had a magnificent view of the surrounding mountains lit by stars, the Milky Way, and a crescent moon. We were woken early by the sounds of cocks crowing and mules braying. Our muleteers also looked biblical, wearing djellabas over trousers, red leather shoulder bags, and curved silver knives on their hips.

On our first day of trekking, we covered twelve miles, heading northwest on a well-marked track over a stony plain in hot sun under a cloudless sky. Nomad children herding goats and the occasional passerby hailed us with the usual *"salaam alaikum."* During our two-hour lunch stop, I observed that one of the mules must have drunk at least four gallons of water. We passed through the Oued Hanedour Valley and spent the night at Igi. We marveled at the skill with which our Berber muleteers pitched our tents in stony ground, and we admired a passing Berber woman herding brown goats, carrying a baby in front and huge bundles of sagebrush on her back. After supper, we went to bed early, listening to the howling of many dogs answering each other from one side of the valley to the other. Jbel Saghro dogs are wild, rabid, and dangerous.

Next day, we trekked to Berkou, where Omar, one of our muleteers, lived, and camped in what used to be a small garden.

Another, Zaid, a tailor by trade, gave us ladies a henna treatment on our right hands. Water was becoming scarce, barely visible at the bottom of the well. The following day, we climbed almost nine thousand feet up Jbel Amlal, seeing sheep on craggy mountaintops, bottlebrush palms, and ubiquitous "barbed wire" plants—wild thyme emitting a pleasant aroma. Rocks perched on other rocks at the summit, each rock signifying the sacrifice of a sheep. Lunch regularly consisted of sardines, onions, peppers, tomatoes, olives, cheese, and local almonds. Dinner was usually tajine and honeydew melon for dessert. Zaid made us Berber coffee, consisting of coffee beans, pepper, coriander, cumin, and mint—a veritable witches' gunpowder brew. We had to put chlorine in our water bottles, which tasted like drinking from a swimming pool but was an essential safety measure. Omar's mother had made a superb rope out of plaited sheep and goat hair for letting the bucket down the wells.

We walked past interesting rock formations, notably Er Flon, or Camel's Head. During a break on a sunny plateau, we watched our Berbers playing Frisbee in extreme heat. We passed many stagnant frog ponds where we saw primeval, coelacanth-like fish. Supper was late and everyone was weary from walking for ten hours in the heat, but it was well worth waiting for: soup, couscous, and more green melon. At last we had a chance to wash ourselves, our hair, and our underwear, in a limited amount of water. Six ladies were stripped to the waist when a Berber and three mules came by to borrow two of our plastic basins to give the mules a drink. He was quite unfazed.

At Tadout n'Tablah, we were walking through a valley encircled by extraordinary rock formations when we saw our first Berber goat hair tent, inhabited by two women and three small children. Their dogs rushed out snarling and baring their fangs, until one of our group hurled a rock at them and they slunk away. I photographed a baby camel suckling its mother's milk. After crossing the Tizi n'Taggourt River, we walked to scenic Bab n'Ali (Gates of God). Our lunch-carrying mule became restless and tried to throw her load, galloping in circles with 150 kilos on her back before Omar caught her as part of it fell off, Zaid rushing to help. A mule can carry up to 200 kilos and a camel 250 to 300. The scene was watched by a young Berber woman wearing a yellow-tasseled headdress and carrying an infant on her back. We were amused to learn that they wear woolly trousers or leggings, sometimes red or purple, under their robes all year round despite the heat.

Next day, we walked to the village of Zit, where we bought scarves, djellabas, Cokes, and Fantas, then on to Sito and Tissilit, through a fertile valley with modern buildings and some old fortified castellated ones, past salt and magnesium deposits on a cliff face, a sandstone overhang above the dry falls like a band shell.

The nights were beautiful: moonlight and masses of stars with Orion moving cross the night sky, no pollution, city lights, or planes overhead, no noise except for the dogs that barked all night.

Oleander grows wild, and its pods are poisonous. Small-leaved mint, twiggy fig trees, olives, oranges, carrots, cumin, coriander, bright patches of red and green peppers, and almonds are grown despite the dry climate. High up on our climb to Jbel Amlal, we saw twisted juniper growing at crazy angles, their trunks almost horizontal.

We learned about the Battle of Bon Gaffer, which took place in 1933. The Berbers did not want to be colonized by the French, so six thousand Ait Atlas Berbers assembled at Bon Gaffer. The war against the French lasted forty-five days until the Berber chief Aso Baslam surrendered to General Bournasy after four thousand Berbers had been killed and two thousand Frenchmen died fighting. Many French and Berbers were buried on the mountainside. The French had vastly superior weaponry, whereas the Berbers fought with rocks and hunting rifles. Many Berber women were killed fetching water from a well, which we saw. Several pieces of shells and bombs were lying around, and in fact, I photographed Mohammed standing beside an unexploded shell. His grandfather had fought in the battle and survived.

We spent two nights at Bon Gaffer, and the second evening there was excitement about having a whole sheep for supper. After about two hours in a pressure cooker, it was quite edible, although obviously they had hacked the beast to pieces and thrown them into the pot with herbs. Later that night, many dogs appeared to finish off the bones. On our last night, the muleteers joined us for dinner. During our trek, they always ate by themselves. Omar, Zaid, and Mohammed prepared tajine for twenty-six of us. Grinning, they tried to teach us a few Berber words. We ate heartily with our fingers, extracting the meat from under the vegetables. The Berbers picked choice pieces of mutton off the bone for us. We finished the meal with caramel pudding, which they did not care for, and green tea; then everyone sang Berber and English songs, a muleteer played the Berber flute called the lassau, and everyone shook hands. We gave them two large plastic bags of our clothes with which they seemed very happy. We danced a little and sang "Auld Lang Syne."

There was one more day of climbing when the first rains came. Then we boarded minibuses, did not see much of Ouarzazate in the teeming rain, and spent the night at Aït Benhaddou, sleeping where we had had supper on the restaurant seat cushions. The next day, from the bank of a torrential river, we saw what had been the movie sets of *Lawrence of Arabia*, *Indiana Jones*, and *Secrets of the Nile*. We retraced our route across the Atlas Mountains to Marrakech and again to the Hotel Foucauld. Even a tepid bath was welcome.

Paul Bowles described the Anti-Atlas as "the Badlands of South Dakota writ on a grand scale." This is equally applicable to the Jbel Saghro, with its outcroppings of igneous lava, red, rose-tinted terra-cotta, and ocher. There was not much wild fauna: Barbary squirrels, with black and white stripes and bushy tails, small hoopoes, kestrels, and partridges. Too many flies were less repulsive than Sikkim's leeches. We all agreed it had been a once-in-a-lifetime experience.

We found Marrakech to be a very interesting city. We visited the Koran School, built in the fourteenth century, which lasted until 1960. Magnificent, intricate carvings were made from Italian marble. The builders used to swap a pound of salt for a pound of marble. Our guide, Sharif, told us there had been no rain in Marrakech for a long time until today. Touring the souk and the main square, we observed sellers of spices, fish, everything imaginable; snake charmers; and dentists at work. The alleys of the souk were dark and crowded, but we made a few stops. The herbalist produced anti-wrinkle cream, aphrodisiacs for men and women, anti-herpes balm, green lipstick that turned pink, amber, musk, saffron, and pumice "pour la cellulite" wrapped in colored string.

Then we repaired to the carpet shop, where we were ceremoniously seated and given the usual mint tea. The proprietor instructed his minions to spread several carpets and rugs, old and new, for our inspection. Folk tales are woven into patterns, as there is no written Berber language. He pointed out the signatures of the weavers, a single forehead tattoo for virgins, forehead and chin for married women. He explained the natural dyes: eggplant, saffron, poppy, indigo, olive, and various plants, flowers, and shrubs, and pointed out the intricate knotting of wools and silks. I bought a small silk Tuareg rug for Charles and carried it home in my backpack.

We enjoyed our final dinner of excessive food and wine and our last night in the hotel. We flew to London via Casablanca, and I continued on home to New York. We were sorry to leave, but at least we had brought the longed-for rains.

A postscript to this trek was a reunion the following spring in the Lake District. Charles came with me, and we stayed with Andrew and Elizabeth Brown at their beautiful sheep farm in Kirkcudbright, Scotland. Elizabeth met our train from Edinburgh, where we had been visiting Mary Niven. On the way to their large farm, we stopped at the cemetery, which commemorated the Lockerbie air disaster of December 21, 1988, where many of the victims were buried. Readers will remember Pan Am Flight 103, which exploded over Scotland, killing the entire crew and passengers, as well as thirty-eight people on the ground thirty-eight minutes after leaving London, where two Libyan terrorists had planted a bomb. I had known Jack Schultz, former general merchandise manager of Bloomingdale's, when Her Majesty Queen Elizabeth visited during the Bicentennial. He and his wife lost their son Thomas Britten Schultz, one of the many University of Syracuse students on the fatal flight, memorialized at Lockerbie. They also tragically lost their other son while looking at a house to buy in Greenwich. The boy picked up an object in the basement, which turned out to be a live grenade that exploded and killed him.

After a couple of days with the Browns, we joined the alumnae of the Morocco trek and spent a happy weekend in the Lake

District hiking, eating, and drinking. My tentmate, Barbara, a retired teacher from Birmingham, and I were planning a trek to Tibet the following fall. She complained of a backache caused, she thought, by lifting a heavy suitcase, and kindly drove Charles around sightseeing during the days when the rest of us were climbing. Tragically, a few months later, she died of lung cancer, having never smoked a cigarette in her life. Birmingham had been a very polluted city.

My third and final trek with Exodus, called Everest Panorama, started on October 9, 1994. I booked this after the tragic death of Barbara and cancellation of our Tibet trek. We flew Bangladesh Airlines from London, changing planes in Dhaka. The plane was full of Bangladeshi families, many with noisy children, and beautifully dressed women wearing much gold jewelry. My seatmate was returning to fetch his bride of three months. Before boarding our flight to Kathmandu, I noticed a sign in the airport: "Visitors from India must go through plague desk." This resonates today.

Nepal's capital city, Kathmandu, to me could have been any major city in India, with its seedy buildings, dusty, dirty, ubiquitous pi-dogs, beggars, ramshackle vehicles spewing out diesel fumes, noise, and crowds everywhere. The goats looked slightly better fed than their Indian counterparts, being incongruously led on pieces of string. We dutifully did the pre-trek sightseeing: the inevitable Buddhist and Hindu temples, funeral pyres burning by the Bagmati River, the old and new palaces (we saw the king emerge from the latter), and monkeys everywhere. (The brother of one of my schoolmates had been tutor to the then king of Nepal.) Our visit coincided with a week of major festivals, including the Festival of New Clothes and New Resolutions, though we did not actually observe any animal sacrifices. People smeared their foreheads with tika, feasted, and exchanged presents.

Having described my first Himalayan trek in detail, I will only mention highlights, or low points, such as our Russian helicopter ride to Lukla, which was hair-raising as we flew so close to mountainsides. This proved too much for a couple of young Englishmen who had overindulged the night before, but unfortunately airsick bags had not been provided.

On our first night of camping, it was pleasant to fall asleep once again to the sound of dzo bells. Having crossed the Dudh Kosi River with spectacular views of the Everest range, we had a tough climb, entering the Everest National Forest at Jorsalle. We visited the Kunde Hospital, which is part of Sir Edmund Hillary's Himalayan Trust (which also runs schools, infrastructure, and an Austrian hydro bringing electricity to the region). Medical personnel teach basic hygiene and walk miles to assist in childbirth. Operating facilities are limited, and they augment their medical supplies with surplus medications donated by expeditions like ours. They treat tuberculosis, impetigo, measles, and other formerly lethal ailments. Fifty percent of all children used to die before the age of five. Although Nepal is one of the poorest countries in the world, tourism brought relative prosperity to the region. We were told by a New Zealand doctor that of approximately ten thousand annual visitors, one in a thousand dies of altitude sickness.

As we climbed, we had magnificent daily views of the peaks surrounding Everest: Kusum Kanguru, Ama Dablam, Thamserku, Khumbila, Imja Tse, Lobuche, Cholatse, and Lhotse Shar. Unfortunately, we encountered yak traffic jams on the narrow trail, as well as too many trekkers, American, German, Canadian, Japanese, British, Dutch, Italian, and Spanish. For me, the most memorable event was encountering two Scottish doctors and their Sherpas who had summited Everest. We were the first people they met as they descended, and they—Charlie H (indecipherable) and Roddy Kirkwood—signed my diary: "British Mount Everest Medical Expedition, Very best wishes, Summit 12.00 October 11, 1994." There were seventy-five medical researchers at base camp.

Our "summit" was rather tame, by comparison, at the Sri Dewa or Sunrise Lodge, altitude 14,471 feet.

And so we descended in easy stages to Lukla. Our flight by Twin Otter took off safely from a short runway ending at the edge of a mountain with a perpendicular drop off. We did some more sightseeing in and around Kathmandu, and while waiting for our London flight had a layover long enough for a tour of Dhaka. The city seemed to consist of more water than land and buildings. Then we flew home via Dubai, Frankfurt.

A friend of my teenage years in Farnham, Surrey, Susan Pugh, married to her second husband, Keith Webb, having been widowed young, persuaded me to join her on a Jules Verne tour of the Royal Cities of Rajasthan over Easter 1997. Neither of our husbands fancied the trip. Charles instead accompanied our friend Dotsy Letts on an English-Speaking Union cruise in the Caribbean. Later I disappointed her when I said I was not jealous, even though Charles, in a cheaper cabin, was summoned to her more luxurious one to do up zippers before dinner. Theirs was a very special friendship.

Sue and I greatly enjoyed traveling together and reminiscing about our youth during long bus rides, to the amusement of the others in our group. We spent two days in Delhi. This time we took a rickshaw ride through the Chandni Chowk market. I revisited the Red Fort, and again I was deeply moved by the India

Gate Memorial, Lutyens' Viceregal Lodge where the governors lived in days of empire, the Minar Mosque, and other famous places in the city.

From Delhi, it was an eight-hour drive through Haryana into Rajasthan. We spent the night in the Castle Mandawa, a fort turned into a comfortable hotel, and the next night at the Royal Castle in Khimsar, after a refreshing swim and a sighting of the Hale-Bopp comet before dinner and Rajasthani dancing. On the way to Jaisalmer via Osian, we spotted jackals and kudu deer, also round thatched houses made of cow dung. We had an Easter welcome at the Heritage Hotel with garlands of African marigolds then walked to the Hindu cremation grounds across from a huge fort, the Golden City. In Jaisalmer, we admired the ornately carved lattice work of the havelis, which allowed wind but not sandstorms to pass through.

The highlight of the trip for me was our camel safari in the Thar Desert. I was given the leader of the pack, Lanu, owned by Amar and led by Dal Pat, aged eight. His camel was called Michael Jackson. Amar explained that the streak of red paint on his nose meant that he was engaged and would marry within the year. We rode across dunes, which was exhilarating. At sunset, the camels knelt down, and we leaned back and watched the sun disappear over the desert horizon. Driving back to the hotel, we had another spectacular sighting of the Hale-Bopp comet, often visible in the northern hemisphere that year, but I had never seen it until I arrived in India. After washing off the sand, we dined, listened to musicians, and watched a pretty young dancer in a yellow sari and bangles dance on knives and upturned glasses. That evening over dinner, I told the group my camel's name. There was a silence followed by raucous laughter; several other camels in the pack were called Michael Jackson. It transpired that there was one television set in the camel herders' village and they had all watched a Michael Jackson concert in Mumbai.

In Jodhpur, home of the Rathore rulers of the princely state of Rajasthan, we toured the magnificent Mehrangarh Fort, founded in 1459, and the Jain temple at Ranakpur, dating from the fifteenth century, with eighty domes and more than fourteen hundred carved pillars, after a lunch stop in the orchard at Maharani Bagh.

To reach Udaipur, we drove over wooded hills, leaving the desert scenery behind us on switchback roads past farms where bullocks driven by children who worked the wells. We stayed at Heritage Resort on Lake Bagela in Nagda with wonderful views of Jain temples on the far shore of the lake, watching herons and egrets, as well as peacocks. Udaipur, surrounded by the Aravalli hills, was founded by the royal house of Mewar. The city palace overlooking Lake Pichola was the home of Maharana Pratap, who lost the Battle of Haldighati against the Mughals. My favorite miniature in the museum was of Chetak, his horse who, having ferried his mortally wounded master across a ravine, gazes at him with utter devotion as he dies. We took a boat ride to Jagmandir, past the luxurious Island Palace Hotel on its own island. It was originally built for Shah Jahan. Women and children were sequestered there during the Indian Mutiny.

Adji, our driver, explained that the old shoe that hung from the front of our bus, as well as being painted on the registration plate, was to ward off the evil eye. I enjoyed collecting amusing road signs in India: "hang loose designer shorts," "bookings available, take unfair advantage," "the cleanest sound you can see," "bum chum" (men's underwear), "Tress Passers will be prosecuted."

Goats in Rajasthan have very silky coats. A box in a temple was labeled "Donations for Cows," because old ones must not be allowed to starve when they no longer give milk.

After Ajmer, which we could not get away from fast enough (hustlers, noise, crowds, filth), we drove to Pushkar, a small town sacred to Hindus where Lord Brahma reputedly killed a dragon with a lotus, and lakes appeared where the petals fell. It's also the site of the famous annual camel fair. A very bumpy road led to Jaipur, the Pink City, where we checked into Hotel Clarks. I have a cherished photo standing beside the life-size stuffed tiger in the lobby. The open-air observatory built in the eighteenth century contained outsized astronomical instruments, including a giant sundial. Another city palace, also a museum, contained a royal wardrobe, musical instruments, some gruesome weaponry, chandeliers, carpets, ornate ceilings, and the largest silver pieces in the world, over five feet high and capable of holding 1,800 gallons of liquid. Reputedly, Madho Singh took them to the coronation of King Edward VII filled with Ganges water. We visited Jaigarh Fort on a hilltop, containing the world's largest cannon and tanks big enough to hold sufficient water to withstand a six-month siege. We saw a mongoose and many monkeys, some with babies. Elephants bore us up to the Amber Fort, four persons per elephant. One member of our group dropped and smashed her video camera, which was picked up by one of the elephants. Her husband swore at her loudly but later was embarrassed and bought her an expensive carpet to make up. We entered through the Ganesh gate, past carved marble lattice-work screens, which allowed ladies of the harem to watch what was going on without being seen. The zenana (harem) contained separate apartments for each of Man Singh's twelve wives.

Fatehpur Sikri was the home of Akbar, who sequestered his pregnant wife in this sandstone fort. We were shown a stone ring where his favorite elephant was tethered. It was also his judge. A plaintiff had three chances with the elephant and if not trampled to death was presumed innocent. Later, we visited its grave. More than five thousand women had stayed in the zenana over fifteen years, many of them courtiers' wives and concubines.

On the way to Agra, we were rather put off by shaggy brown-black dancing bears on chains with their handlers, but apparently the government was trying to abolish this cruel practice.

Our stay at the Mughal Sheraton in Agra was delightful for me because it was also home to the "Puppy Love" kennels on the hotel grounds. Two Indian kennel staff members gave me a tour to greet four Alsatians, one mothering her puppies, four retrievers, and a Boxer.

I expected to find the Taj Mahal a sort of cliché, but in fact, the real thing is breathtaking. We walked there from our hotel at sunrise as the morning haze was rising off the Yamuna River, with the Red Fort in the distance. We toured India's most famous monument built by Shah Jahan in memory of his wife, Mumtaz Mahal, who died giving birth to their fourteenth child in 1631. He was so heartbroken that he stayed in his room for a week and supposedly emerged gray-haired. Twenty thousand people worked on the building between 1631 and 1653. Another story, which may be apocryphal, is that as he grew old and blind, he gazed at the reflection of the Taj Mahal in the Koh-i-Noor diamond.

An inOf course we all posed for photographs sitting on Princess Diana's bench in front of the Taj, a fitting place to end my account of this unforgettable journey.

# Chapter Eighteen

I n May 1990, there was a family tragedy. I have mentioned
Dorothy Whyte's son, John, Ursula's brother, my cousin. He
had become a distinguished professor of politics, most recently
at Queen's University, Belfast, and University College Dublin. He
had been a research fellow at the Center for International Affairs
at Harvard and also a fellow in residence at the Netherlands
Institute for Advanced Studies. He was en route from Dublin
to Washington for a conference on Anglo-Irish Relations and
Northern Ireland, organized by the prestigious Woodrow Wilson
International for Scholars at the Smithsonian Institution, which
was to take place at the Airlie House in Virginia, comprising
delegates from the UK, Ireland, and the US.

He was quoted as "having given so freely of his time during
his years in Belfast to create a space for empathy and sanity." He
was truly an expert on the complicated political and religious
situation between the North and the Republic, the relationship
with the UK, and the viability of changes and possible solutions.

Pessimistically, he summed it up as follows, comparing Northern Ireland's situation to Cyprus, Lebanon, and Sudan at the time: "They hold on to what advantages they have, lest in the course of bargaining they are forced to lose even more than they have lost already."

Changing planes at JFK in New York, John collapsed and was taken to Jamaica Hospital. He never regained consciousness and died a few days later. His wife, Jean, flew over from Dublin. Dorothy's stepcousin Carl Tiedemann and his wife, Mary, were enormously helpful, arranging a simple service attended by some former Harvard colleagues and dealing with the complications of shipping the body back to Ireland. The Tiedemanns, Charles, and I looked after Jean for a few days in East Hampton. We became friends, and when Ursula, John Whyte's sister, visited us, Carl entertained us in the house he built in Georgica, incorporating into the roof the beams he had bought years earlier from Hever Castle in England and which had lain in a nearby field for years.

In 1991, Charles and I went to England for the wedding of Emma Cannon-Brookes to Andrew Coker at Caroline and Peter's family home Thrupp in a tent on the lawn. Among many family members present was Stephen Cannon-Brookes, Emma's brother. Stephen also visited us in New York and East Hampton when he became a museum lighting expert, his first job in New York being at the Frick Collection on Fifth Avenue. Later, he renovated the lighting of the Isabella Stewart Gardner Museum in Boston, as well as illuminating the collections of many wealthy private individuals. He used to come to East Hampton from New York for visits. I would drive him to the Orient Point–New London ferry where he took the train to Boston. We used to stop for lunch at the American Hotel in Sag Harbor. By this time, Stephen was part owner of two wine bars in London and an expert oenophile. He was very impressed with their wine list. Stephen married Olga Gaikovich, who is Russian and a fine artist and illustrator. They live with their son Edward in London. They have both worked for the Hermitage in St. Petersburg.

In 1995, Charles and I celebrated twenty-five years of happy marriage. Bill Told, our best man and dear friend, had given fifth and tenth anniversary dinners, and he gave another in his apartment on East 57th Street, at which Charles presented me with a sapphire-and-diamond ring, which I cherish. In the fall, we flew to London and saw the usual friends and family members, including Caroline and Peter Cannon-Brookes who, because of their connections in Prague, its art world, and the many tours she had escorted for Martin Randall as guide and lecturer, provided a to-do list for that city, which we reached by train after a few days in Berlin, a city Charles had always wanted to visit. Staying at the Ritz in Berlin, I encountered a young man in the unisex baths who invited us to join his opera group from New York for a modern performance of *Orpheus and Eurydice*, in which the underworld was a twentieth-century subway.

Prague, situated on the Charles River, is a beautiful, historic city filled with photogenic palaces and quaint streets, always full of tourists, and at that time average restaurant food. What I enjoyed most was dropping into churches to find a free concert in progress playing classical music.

Vienna was freezing and very expensive, but we toured the Schönbrunn Palace and other must-see places. We found a McDonald's for cheaper breakfasts than the hotel's but, inconsistently, paid the concierge a small fortune for seats at the opera plus twenty-five dollars each for a small glass of champagne at intermission. It was a thrill to hear "The Magic Flute" in the completely restored opera house on a special anniversary. It had been bombed during World War II by the Americans, as our guides kept telling during a tour of the city earlier that day. We went from Austria to Scotland to visit Mary Niven. British Airways lost our luggage between Vienna and Edinburgh, but it caught up with us the next day, which I regarded as another example of so much good luck in my life, being the only time I have ever lost my luggage!

In 1998, I flew to Ireland for a long weekend for the wedding of Niall and Jan's daughter Siobhan, brother of Rory. A convivial pre-wedding supper was held at Coolavin where I stayed the night. I slept in my old childhood room next to Felicity's master bedroom. Sometime during the night—I was oblivious from jet lag and much red wine—she moved the heater from my room, which was attached to a long cable on an industrial-size wooden roller, to her room. I awoke freezing and was happy to spend the next night luxuriously at Markree Castle after the wedding reception.

Siobhan was the first MacDermot bride to be married from Coolavin. The ceremony took place in the parish church, St. Aidan's, in Monasteraden where the MacDermots and their consorts are buried in a private outdoor mausoleum. A plaque in front of the family front row pew in the church commemorates Uncle Hugh, killed at Gallipoli: "Greater Love No Man Hath That He Laid Down His Life for His Friends."

On July 31, 1998, we flew to Johannesburg for what Charles claimed was the best trip of his life, organized by our dear friend Patti McGrath. Our safari group consisted of Patti and her husband, Jack; friends of theirs, Michael and Sue Maney; and Jake and Betsy Underhill. We flew from New York to Johannesburg where we stayed at the Courtyard Hotel at Bruma Lake outside the city. At that time, it was a war zone downtown, cars being hijacked and people living in gated communities.

We flew to Bulawayo, where Dave, our guide, met our plane and drove us by minivan for about four hours through ranching country, well-fed cattle, and small granite hills called kopjes; and in the evening, we arrived at the Lodge at the Ancient City, a splendid hostelry with some rooms incorporating the rocks as walls. We stayed there to visit Great Zimbabwe, the site of thirteenth-century fortifications, where we explored the ruins with Moses, our Shona guide. Little mole-like creatures, hyrax, or dassies, scampered over the ruins, delighting us.

Dave and Linda, his wife, drove us to Amalinda, a wonderful safari lodge built into a cliffside. On our first game drive, we saw five giraffes, four white rhinos, many baboons, and more hyrax. Bird life abounded: sun birds, a black eagle, Egyptian geese, spur-winged geese, shrikes, lilac-breasted rollers, yellow-billed hornbills, jacana, and grey herons, plus ubiquitous guinea fowl. We enjoyed two game drives every day and went for elephant rides. On subsequent drives, we saw Plains-Burchell's giraffes, hippos, wildebeest, impalas, klipspringers, waterbuck, springbuck, and steenboks. It was cool in the early mornings, and Charles always sat in front of the Land Rover next to our very attractive leader, Linda. Later, we learned that he had discovered the heater and teased him mercilessly.

There was a large community of local very poor people. We visited a medical clinic and a school. Some children wore uniforms, others ragged clothing and were barefoot. They lacked textbooks and writing implements but sang and danced for us.

Linda and her sister Sharon's father owned 25,000 acres in the Matobo Hills and were trying to preserve it as a game reserve. The Matobo caves contained prehistoric paintings. Patti and Jack had one in their bedroom at Amalinda. One day, we climbed up to World's View, a monument to Cecil Rhodes, and visited his grave.

On August 7, we were supposed to fly from Harare to Victoria Falls, but President Mugabe had commandeered all the planes for a summit meeting of other African dictators, including President Kabila of the Congo, so we drove there in time for lunch at the Elephant Hills Hotel, the presidential motorcade passing us en route. After visiting the famous falls, we went to our tented camp at Kindehar beside the Zambezi River. An unforgettable sight was a lone elephant crossing in shallow water, silhouetted in the sunset. After visiting a crocodile farm and shopping in Victoria Falls, we flew to Botswana.

We stayed in a houseboat called *Big Boy* on manmade Lake Kariba, which I remember mostly for the bird life, especially the marabou storks that somewhat resembled old ladies bundled up in gray fur coats. Other birds were wattled plovers, kingfishers, fish eagles, hoopoes, cormorants, lily trotters (jacana), goliath herons, oxpeckers on buffaloes, and egrets around elephants. We saw anthills, which, like icebergs, only show their tips; as well as kudus, impalas, and waterbuck. We saw the spoor of a black rhino but never the beast itself. Near Maun in Botswana, we stayed at Camp Okuti on the Okavango Delta, in the Moremi Game Reserve. One did not wander unescorted back to one's tent after dinner. Crocodiles crept up from the water's edge, and serious wildlife such as lions, elephants, or hippos might be lurking not far from the campfire. The scariest happening was one evening when returning from a game drive, we watched a pride of lions feasting on a putrefying elephant carcass, as well as a pair of mating lions. He bit her neck before mounting her, repeated several times, oblivious to the surrounding Land Rovers full of gawkers. After observing a leopard devouring her prey in a tree, we found ourselves in the middle of a herd of elephants, angry that our two Land Rovers had split them, but luckily we got back to the lodge without incident.

By the end of our safari, we had seen all of the Big Five: elephant, rhino, lion, leopard, and cape buffalo. Leaving Camp Okuti by small plane, the runway had first to be cleared of a herd of elephants with babies, a fitting end to an amazing wildlife experience.

We took two more European trips before the turn of the century. After staying with Sallie and Jimmy Warden in their charming mews flat in Tennyson Mansions, Chelsea, we spent a long weekend in Paris. Of course we visited museums and ate and drank in sidewalk cafes, bistros, and occasionally, by mistake, an overpriced restaurant catering to tourists. Personally, I loved staying in the quaint, old L'Hotel, where Oscar Wilde lived during his last years and died on November 30, 1900, though the other three did not like it as much as I did.

Charles and I spent a happy week in 1999 driving round Portugal, staying at the Ritz in Lisbon, that country's beautiful capital city on the Tagus River, and visiting historic places whence their famous explorers departed to discover the world in the fifteenth and sixteenth centuries. We drove through forests where the trees' bark is harvested for cork, and towns with Roman ruins, walking along the ramparts of castle walls. At Évora we stayed in a pousada (the name given to Portuguese historic hotels situated in palaces, castles, and former monasteries) beside the ruins of a Roman temple attributed to the god Jupiter, goddess Diana, or Emperor Augustus. We drove to Cabo da Roca, the westernmost point in Europe, wild and scenic, ending our stay in Sintra and Cascais at the Albatroz Hotel, one of my favorites. At that time, I was fortunate to be taken on as a client by Henriette Neatrour, a literary agent who represented some popular novelists at the time and believed she could find a publisher for my spy stories—one inspired by this Portuguese trip, another based on my experiences with the US defense industries. She came very close with a major trade books publisher. She had chosen me, which was very flattering considering how hard it has always been for an unknown author to find an agent. Tragically, she died of lung cancer a couple of years later.

After I retired from the Quebec government in 2000, I was hired as a part-time contributor to *Fashion International*, news and views of the international fashion world published by a famous New York fashion maven Ruth Finley, who owned and published *The Fashion Calendar*. She wielded enormous power in the New York fashion world because she controlled when and where designers showed their spring and fall collections. All important New York fashion events were listed in her *Fashion Calendar*.

In the fall of 2000, I covered several young designers' spring shows. Some became well known and others did not, but the fun part was reporting in a variety of unusual, mostly downtown, venues. As Four showed in the Chinatown YMCA, Akiko Elizabeth Maie at the Angel Orensanz Foundation, James Coviello at the Soldiers' and Sailors' Club, Arend Basile in a landmark former bank acquired by Cipriani's, and People Used to Dream About the Future in two suites of the Chelsea Hotel, where the audience reclined on king-size beds as models wandered through various rooms.

The following spring, I wrote again about young designers' fall collections. The auto industry featured prominently: ChanPaul in the Mercedes-Benz tents, Thomas Steinbrueck in the BMW showroom, and Rubin & Chapelle in a taxi repair garage. Ford promoted their new Focus model at a group show comprising ten designers, including my niece by marriage, Alexandra Lind, at Cipriani's on 42nd Street.

My final reporting was for shows that took place on the evening of September 10, 2001: presentations of their collections by Sarafpour, Rubin & Chapelle, Pierrot, and Coviello. On the eleventh, my morning was free because I had covered the evening shows. I was making our bed and heard a shriek from Charles in the living room, so I immediately thought Thurber, our Labrador, had done something bad. It was the attack on the Twin Towers, and the rest of Fashion Week was canceled.

We all remember how we spent that day in shock, disbelief, and grief. We lined up at Doctors Hospital on East End Avenue (now a luxury high-rise apartment building) to give blood, which, alas, was not needed. We wandered up and down the East River talking to strangers, watching the smoke in the distance. When we could no longer bear to sit in our apartment in front of the TV, we took a (free) bus to our favorite pub on Third Avenue, JG Melon, for supper and more TV. That day and for several days afterward, friends and family called from all over the world to make sure we were safe and to sympathize with the American people.

In the fall of 2000, we had planned a trip to Fiji and the South Island of New Zealand where our dear friend Judy Hyde lived when she retired from British Information Services in New York. Charles, during a routine medical checkup, was told he needed a stress test, which he failed, then had an angiogram to find out what was wrong with his heart. During a follow-up visit, his cardiologist informed him that he needed valve repair and a double bypass. When he mentioned that we were due to leave the next week, Dr. Franklin replied that he hoped Charles had bought a one-way ticket, because he would likely return in a box. Dr. Wayne Isom successfully operated the next week, and Charles lived for another ten years. When we rushed home to call Judy with the bad news, we found a message from her telling us not to come because her sister had been killed in a car crash.

We rescheduled the trip for the following year, substituting Australia for Fiji. It was just after 9/11, and everyone we met in Australia and New Zealand wanted to know where we were when the towers came down. We loved Sydney, its opera house, botanical gardens, fine restaurants, and its famous magnificent bridge over the harbor. Buildings dating from Victorian times stood beside modern skyscrapers. Our hotel, a converted warehouse on the waterfront, had magnificent views of the bridge and the harbor. A P&O cruise ship sailed right past our bedroom window, so close one could almost see into the cabins.

Ayers Rock is the largest rock monolith in the world and is reputed to be 550 million years old. It is composed of basalt, granite, magnesium, and iron and turns blackish after rain, though it is usually reddish. At the Sails in the Desert Resort in the Red Centre, we were subjected to touristic hype, which is not all bad, a sprinkling of aboriginal culture, and men carving their musical instruments from mulga wood and playing the didgeridoo, which has a haunting sound. We dined while watching the setting sun behind the domes of Kata Tjuta (the Olgas) on barramundi, emu, crocodile, and bush salads. Oddly enough, we never saw a single kangaroo during our entire stay in Australia. We did some stargazing but did not see the Southern Cross till early next morning.

We watched the sunrise over Uluru (or Ayers Rock, named after Henry Ayers, premier of Southern Australia) and learned more about aboriginal tribes, particularly the local Anangu, supposedly the oldest inhabitants on Earth, dating back 35,000 years. The blades of their spears are tied with sinew from kangaroo legs. We listened to folk legends about lizard man, bird man, and stolen emus. Some of us walked up a canyon through the Olgas (named curiously for Olga, Queen of Württemberg) and were rewarded with magnificent views.

My favorite time in Australia was our trip to Heron Island on the Great Barrier Reef. We flew up the Gold Coast from Sydney to the port of Gladstone where we took a helicopter to Heron Island, which we shared with Andrea Paulson, granddaughter of the original owner of the island who disappeared one night in the thirties in his dinghy. Heron Island actually sits on coral. We could walk from the beach to the edge of the reef where the waters were teeming with life.

The island contains a research station for the University of Queensland and a sort of Club Med resort for visitors. The wildlife was amazing. Noddy terns nested outside our veranda, their smelly, messy nests seemed too close together, their pale gray faces atop black bodies bore solemn expressions. We saw egrets, three kinds of plover, kingfishers, pied oystercatchers, ubiquitous gulls, and some almost extinct cormorants. Most interesting were the mutton birds, whose eerie nocturnal noises sometimes sounded like cats fighting, while other times, they keened like lost souls or moaned with happiness at being reunited again with their mates-for-life after flying thousands of miles apart over the Pacific. They build their nests underground, and after fifty days of incubation, their chicks are born. However, they do not emerge for many days and only learn to fly after their parents are long gone.

When the tide went out, the Reef was clearly delineated, the sea appearing turquoise near the shore, deep blue on the other side. We snorkeled and rode a "semi-sub" through the coral, small mounds of which are called bommies, sadly observing the dead places caused by global warming. We saw turtles, eagle rays, potato cod, damsel fish, angel fish, one shark, and the most colorful parrot fish, sea stars, sea cucumbers, and sea urchins.

One evening, we watched turtles coming up from the beach to lay their eggs, digging deep into the sand several hundred yards inland, above the high-tide mark. For loggerheads, the nesting process can take up to two hours, and for the green turtles up to three. They first scrape out a broad body pit using all four flippers. The egg chamber is scooped out using only the hind flippers, and on average, each lay 120 eggs. When finished, she covers the nest using all four flippers and returns to the sea. Heron Island has two distinct turtle populations: residents and those who migrate from feeding grounds as far away as Indonesia or New Caledonia. Turtles can swim up to seventy kilometers a day during migration. Although I was fascinated, Charles announced that he had seen similar activity in Florida and did not need to come all the way to Australia to watch turtles laying their eggs.

After a three-hour flight from Sydney to Christchurch in New Zealand's South Island, we were met by our friend Judy Hyde who lived in Akaroa, on the Canterbury Peninsula, the only original French settlement in New Zealand dating from 1840, a beautiful small coastal town on the Banks Peninsula. We were there for their Spring Garden Festival. We visited a lavender farm on our way to a boat ride on the *Canterbury Cat*, where we saw Hector's dolphins, the world's smallest of the breed, as well as the little blue penguin whom we saw swimming all alone.

Judy's garden was amazing. Her plantings included strawberries, lettuces, peaches, pears, kiwi fruit, David Austin and other roses, freesia, lavender, bearded iris, Chatham Island forget-me-nots, hosta, snapdragons, euphorbia, larkspur, mertensia asiatica (succulent, blue flowers), delphiniums, granny's bonnets, day-lilies, geraniums, moses-in-the-bullrushes, heuchera (like coral bells), phlomis, catnip, carnations, and native grasses.

Judy's sister, Gay Menzies, invited us for the weekend on their two-thousand-acre farm where they bred Merino and Romney sheep and Angus and Hereford cattle at Menzies Bay. As we were driven along a scenic route with a steep drop to the Pacific from the hillside, we noticed that Gay and her husband, Rick, undid their seatbelts "in case we have to jump out in a hurry." Gay was also a keen gardener, growing roses, succulents, perennials, and shrubs. Her red-fleshed peaches were particularly delicious. She served butterfish Thai curry for dinner. Rick had caught the fish, having built his own thirty-five-foot yacht. Walking along the shoreline, we saw paradise ducks and oystercatchers and gathered pana (abalone) shells.

Judy arranged a magnificent scenic tour for us, driving across the Southern Alps, passing Mount Cook, over twelve thousand feet high; many cattle, sheep, deer, and alpaca farms; Lake Tekapo; Lake Pukaki; Lindis Pass; and Lake Wakatipu, arriving at Queenstown in the evening.

The next day, we donned long black waterproof coats and life jackets and boarded a jet boat on the Dart River, a most exhilarating ride upstream, bumpier and scarier coming down across shallow rapids, surrounded by snow-covered mountains in greenstone country. The Maoris used the nephrite for tools. We walked through red and silver birch, as well as lance trees in Mount Aspiring National Park. Millions of years ago, New Zealand was part of Gondwanaland, which explains why there are no large mammals or predators, hence the survival of flightless birds. The South Island is famous for its majestic royal spoonbills.

From Queenstown, we drove along the edge of Lake Wakatipu beneath the rugged Remarkables to Fiordland National Park, through the Eglinton Valley, known for its ancient beech forest, stunning waterfalls, and famous mirror lakes, descending to Milford Sound, where we were duly dazzled by Mitre Peak, rock walls scarred by glaciers, and waterfalls from hanging valleys tumbling into the Sound.

On our fourth day, we traveled along the shores of Lake Wānaka and Hāwea, to the Haast Pass, through the treeless grasslands of Central Otago where the majestic peaks of the Southern Alps dominate the landscape to the Fox and Franz Josef glaciers. The latter is more than seven thousand years old. We spent our thirty-seventh wedding anniversary at the Hotel Franz Josef Glacier. New Zealand and Chile are the only places in the world where glaciers are so close to rainforests.

Before returning to New York, Charles, Judy, and I spent some time in Christchurch, a charming city with a fine cathedral, the "Chalice," a large modern sculpture, and many handsome buildings. Punts on the Avon River were reminiscent of Cambridge, and we enjoyed walking in the beautiful Botanic Gardens. Tragically, the 2011 earthquake, which killed almost two hundred people, destroyed the cathedral and many other iconic buildings.

Of course, with my passion for polar places I enjoyed visiting the Antarctic Centre. Since I worked at the Scott Polar Research Institute in 1968, for SCAR (Scientific Committee on Antarctic Research) nations. At that time, only twelve nations belonged; now there are forty-three.

A footnote: everywhere we wined and dined in the antipodes, we were never disappointed and enjoyed high culinary standards and the best domestic vintages.

# Chapter Nineteen

Charles retired from Chase Manhattan Bank (now JPMorgan Chase) in 1995, and at last we were able to adopt our first dog, a yellow Labrador called Thurber. Charles proved to be an avid dog lover. While taking a cooking course somewhere in downtown Manhattan, he often rushed home by expensive cab to take the puppy out. Charles did not actually do much cooking, but he acquired many esoteric culinary accoutrements, some of which still languish in a closet off our rather small East Hampton kitchen. Similarly, his interest in dry fly fishing was somewhat short-lived, and an excuse to buy the gear and equipment and take a course with Orvis in New Hampshire. There was ham radio for a while, and he took a course at the Museum of Natural History to grind the lens for a telescope, which we occasionally dragged onto the back lawn in East Hampton to examine the craters of the moon. His longest love affair with a hobby and its equipment was photography, and when we built our East Hampton house in 1973, he arranged for a dark room to be constructed in the basement. After his death, I donated the equipment to the International Center of Photography, which still taught courses on film and developing pictures even in the digital age. Then of course there was gardening, and our old shed is still full of tools and gadgets. His love of stuff included presents to me, clothing, jewelry, and handbags, more expensive than I would have bought myself and some still cherished today. He had superb taste and loved furnishing our East Hampton home. When my stepfather died, Charles encouraged me to have some fine antique pieces of furniture shipped from England, which his sister Mary did not want. They remain in the New York apartment out of reach of marauding dogs.

Until I retired in 2000 from the Quebec government, Charles liked to stay in East Hampton, driving me to an early-morning Hampton Jitney on Mondays, coming to Manhattan with Thurber midweek for a couple of nights, and meeting me at the station when I took the Friday afternoon "Cannonball" train out from the city. After retirement, I worked part time at Decorum, an antique and decorative arts store in Amagansett, and part time for John Grant in his textile company. John's business was in decline because the T-shirt business had gone mass market. Many of his original customers at brand-name companies had retired, though we still made sales trips to L.L. Bean. His Mexican factory was barely breaking even, but he liked my company, especially in his New York showroom where he claimed I brightened things up a bit with his two rather grouchy salesmen. John always liked company for lunch or dinner. He, Charles, and I dined together often in New York and East Hampton after he and his wife separated. I never earned any commission on non-existent sales, though not for want of trying, but he kindly gave me a check in appreciation of long hours spent with his company.

Then I took a full-time job as executive director of the East Hampton Historical Society, whose mission is "serving residents of and visitors to East Hampton by collecting, preserving, presenting and interpreting the material, cultural and economic heritage of the town and its surroundings."

According to an *East Hampton Star* article by Stephen Longmire on September 11, 2003, local museum directors played musical chairs, except for yours truly. John Eilertson took over the Bridgehampton Historical Society, having been executive director of the Hallockville Museum Farm and Folk Arts Center in Riverhead, the former director Geoffrey Fleming having left to take over the Southold Historical Society. William McNaught, formerly in charge of the American Museum in Bath, England, took over the Oysterponds Historical Society in Orient on the North Fork. Zachary Studenroth, who once led the Huntington Historical Society, and had worked for the Society for the Protection of Long Island Antiquities, became director of the Sag Harbor Whaling & Historical Museum.

With no formal museum directing credentials (I mentioned my early career at Christie's during interviews), I was hired thanks to the encouragement of Isabel Furlaud, who was president at the time, and the late Billy Rayner, who was on the board of trustees. Isabel's successor as president, Michael Braverman, also endorsed me. My job turned out to be a management one, basically taking the Society from the red into the black, which, with the assistance of a very capable assistant, Carrie McMillan, we succeeded in doing. Special thanks are due to a board member, Robert Plancher, a financial professional who gave me valuable assistance. Given my lack of knowledge in that area, I was fortunate to have expert part-timers to take care of curatorial matters. Other trustees and volunteers made my life easier: for example, Mary Clarke was always hands-on with practical assistance and advice, as were Frank Newbold and the late Jim Oxnam. To this day, members and visitors have benefited from Barbara Borsack's creation of a winter lecture series free to the public on the last Friday of every month. Hugh King's lantern tours were extremely popular. Special part-timers were Barbara and Jack Driver, parents of eight children and several grandchildren. She was a wonderful docent at the Marine Museum, and he was then and still is in charge of maintenance, nowadays a full-time job.

The historical society at that time operated five small museums with collections of approximately twelve thousand artifacts: Mulford Farm (the house dates from 1680 and the barn from 1721); Clinton Academy built in 1784, the first teaching academy to be chartered by the New York State Board of Regents; the Town House built in 1731; and the Osborn-Jackson House, the Society's headquarters as well as a museum, which is owned by the Village of East Hampton, having been generously donated to the by my friend Susie Cartier's father, Lionel Jackson. The fifth property, the Marine Museum on Bluff Road in Amagansett, was originally created as a naval barracks in 1940 and consists of three floors of exhibits. In my time, it consisted of a diorama of the fishing village at Fort Pond Bay in Montauk in 1916, which was obliterated by the 1938 hurricane; displays on shore whaling and the fisherman-farmer; artifacts including harpoons and a whale skull; an exhibit on shipwrecks, the Finest Kind Gallery containing remarkable photographs of baymen taken in connection with the late Peter Matthiessen's *Men's Lives*; and several boats of historic interest. During this time, the East End Classic Boat Society started a workshop at the Marine Museum.

The board of directors was informally split into two groups: those who supported the East Hampton Village museums and those who favored the Marine Museum. We actually looked into the possibility of splitting them, but the costs and complicated New York State regulations for museums made this impractical, so we continued to muddle along. Our budget was very slender, and fundraising was difficult. Donors usually prioritized their philanthropic gift-giving to their alma maters or disease of choice before donating to the arts. Also, our wealthier members and trustees were mostly from the city and they wanted to relax over the weekend, having a surfeit of benefits to attend in New York during the week. We held antique shows at Mulford and cocktail parties as fundraisers, but we always tried to keep things local with other simpler, cheaper, or free events. Local actors put on plays in the summer at Mulford Farm, and there were historic reenactments.

Having installed an effective security system, my nights were often plagued by alarm calls. My devoted husband, Charles, would also get up with me in the middle of the night, sometimes meeting a representative of the village at Mulford or Clinton Academy or Osborn-Jackson House. The culprit setting off the alarm was usually a raccoon or a squirrel or mice.

By the end of 2005, I decided I no longer needed such a demanding full-time job and wanted to do more traveling with Charles and share the dog care. We now had two energetic dogs, having acquired a black Labrador, Sophie, in 2000. Fortunately for the Society, Richard Barons, who was head of the Southampton Historical Museum and an excellent mentor to me, told me that he would love the East Hampton position, nearer home, and was actually a bigger and more challenging position than his present one. He took over early in 2006. His long tenure was an enormous success and he brought the EHHS to a new level. He always gave me credit for leaving it in good shape and financially healthy. Having been executive director, I rated a small entry in *Who's Who in America 2006*, 60th Edition, a source of pride to Charles and myself.

When I stopped working full time, I took on more volunteer projects. Because of my love of dogs, and because she had been a mentor to me running my first and only nonprofit organization, when Sara Davison, executive director of Animal Rescue Fund of the Hamptons (ARF), asked me to volunteer, of course I accepted eagerly. I am still an enthusiastic volunteer and have adopted two rescue dogs from ARF, Scott in 2010 and Shawn in 2015. During that time, Polly Bruckmann was president of ARF and we have become friends. She is a dog lover, philanthropist, world traveler, and first-rate wildlife photographer.

I also became a member of the Garden Club of East Hampton and am still very active in this important community group. A highlight was being one of the representatives at the annual National Affairs Legislation (NAL) Conference in Washington, DC. We stayed with the late Jacquie Quillen in her lovely Georgetown house where she gave a dinner party for all Garden Club of America (GCA) representatives. There were many interesting lectures on conservation, climate change, and the environment. We toured the Supreme Court and had a meeting with New York Senator Kirsten Gillibrand in her office. Since 2009, I have served excellent Garden Club presidents, including Mary Clarke, who died in January 2021 and will be greatly missed in the community. At the present time, Julie Sakellariadis is a wonderful president, ably steering the organization through the challenges of the pandemic.

In New York, I volunteered one morning a week for the American Cancer Society's Hope Lodge, and for about nine years, I spent two afternoons a week as a volunteer in the executive offices of the Metropolitan Museum of Art. Thomas P. Campbell was director and Emily Rafferty was president at the time. We also assisted the development office.

In 2006, Charles and I went on our first Swan Hellenic cruise, best known originally for their tours of famous Mediterranean antiquities sites. We boarded *Minerva* in Cyprus, exploring the ruins of Curium. From there, we sailed to Knossos, in Crete, then Thera on the island of Santorini, Methoni Castle on Pelos, sailing on to Delos—the birthplace of Apollo, Olympia, Mycenae, and Epidaurus in Nafplio—before disembarking in Athens. After exploring the Acropolis, the National Archaeological Museum, and other places in Greece's capital, we sailed on to Turkey. We visited the Library of Celsus in Ephesus, Miletus and then sailed through the Dardanelles past the Gallipoli Memorial where I remembered my uncle Hugh, who was killed in battle. We finished our tour in Istanbul, touring Hagia Sophia, the Topkapi Palace, and all the famous sites.

The next year we took another Swan cruise, which started in Barcelona, visited the Alhambra, sailed to Malta, and then Libya, where we docked in Benghazi and Tripoli. While docked in Libyan ports, the bars were ordered to be closed, no alcohol allowed in that Muslim country. However, *Minerva*'s enterprising staff made sure that bottles were available for the passengers by hiding them in utility closets and producing them when immigration officials went ashore in the evening.

Unfortunately, Muammar Gaddafi, who was still in power, did not allow Americans to disembark in Libya that year, but luckily I still had a British passport. I explored the amazing mosaics at Sabratha and the famous ruins of Leptis Magna, prominent city of the Carthaginian empire abandoned in the seventh century, with its outstanding Arch of Septimius Severus. We made a special pilgrimage to the Imperial War Graves, and an Anglican minister traveling with us led a short prayer service. We were particularly moved while studying the graves by how young the soldiers were and how many former empire and commonwealth countries' servicemen of all faiths also gave their lives for Britain during World War II.

Before leaving Libya for Tunisia and more ruins, we were being driven back to the ramshackle harbor of Benghazi with its half-submerged ships during rush hour when we saw one of the funniest sights I have ever seen: three camels seated in the back of a rather small pickup truck.

In Tunisia, we visited the ruins of Carthage near Tunis, the Phoenician settlement founded in the ninth century and destroyed by the Romans during the Punic Wars (264–146 BCE). Our final port of call was Madeira—hilly, picturesque, but not particularly interesting.

Charles's last trip to Scotland and England was in 2009. We stayed with Mary Niven, but poor Charles suffered from a violent nosebleed the day we arrived, so instead of taking Peggy Anderson out for dinner, she drove us to the emergency room (A&E) of an Edinburgh hospital. From there he was transferred to a hospital about forty miles away where he received excellent treatment, including painstaking translation of his American medications into Scottish ones. Fortunately, another MacDermot cousin, Henry, one of Brian and Mary's nine children living in Edinburgh, was able to drive me to visit him, and two days later to collect him after paying the bill for three days, which amounted to less than $1,000. We flew south, having canceled some visits in London and elsewhere, and spent our remaining time with the Cannon-Brookes family before returning to the US.

Charles was taking blood thinners and other medication to prevent strokes and for his heart condition. He was losing energy and sleeping a lot but still enjoying life enormously. We spent one last Christmas with Dotsy Letts and all our old friends, flying to and from Palm Beach rather than driving as usual, enjoying the season's social whirl.

The year 2010 started off well, dividing our life between New York and East Hampton, mostly the latter. Charles loved spending time with his friends, especially Jack McGrath. They spent many happy hours with their fishponds. We had many friends at Devon Yacht Club, where I played tennis and we both played duplicate bridge and enjoyed excellent dining and special evenings. Charles was slowing down, and there were some trips to the emergency room of Southampton Hospital. On the morning of Tuesday, August 10, he woke up feeling terrible and asked if I would cancel a movie date and a bridge game for that evening and the next one. He loved to dance, and we had been dancing at Devon the previous Saturday evening. I called the ambulance, and I remember that Rob Anthony was on duty that morning, as he had been for several of Charles's previous trips, and he helped carry him downstairs. I followed soon after by car with the two dogs, Sophie and Scott.

After examining him and doing various tests, while trying to contact his cardiologist in New York, it was decided to admit him as soon as a room became available. At that point, I realized it would make sense to board Scott and Sophie with Robin Foster at Edge of Pond Kennels overnight to be able to spend more time with Charles at the hospital. During the afternoon, he complained of terrible pain and suddenly sirens went off and I was banished from his room. A few minutes later, a nurse came out to ask if he had a living will. I said it was at home forty-five minutes away and I did not want to leave. Not long after, I was told that he had died. I spent some time with him until I could bear it no more and assured everyone that I could safely drive home, where there was a reception committee of friends and neighbors. The medical examiner did not recommend an autopsy, and his death certificate listed the cause of death as a massive internal hemorrhage.

His funeral at Most Holy Trinity, our Catholic church in East Hampton, was well attended by so many people who knew Charles, even though it was the middle of the working week. David Morrish and Jack McGrath gave heartwarming obituaries. Jack gave me permission to reproduce some of his:

> Charles was one of my best friends. He was a wonderful man and a good friend to all of us. He was a perfect Palm Beach, East Hampton gentleman. On a safari in Africa twelve years ago, Charles, being his usual self-sacrificing self, always offered to sit in the low Land Rover seat next to the driver on our chilly morning game drives. On our last day, my wife, Patti, went out with a guide on a reconnaissance trip to look for a leopard and discovered that the seat which Charles always occupied had a heater. While we froze, "sacrificing Charles" was warm as toast!

> Charles and I greatly enjoyed our fishponds, which contained fish, lotuses, water lilies, and frogs. Charles had an amazing bullfrog. At one of the Rittenours' great parties, everyone

thought it was a fake frog sitting on a rock. As a guest drew closer, it jumped into the pond.

Everyone loved Thurber, their beautiful yellow Lab. Thurber and Charles grew older together and became more and more alike. In their later years, they would spend their days sitting on the couch together. When we lost Thurber earlier this year, it was a sad day for Charles and all of us. He and Charles were a perfect example of men and dogs being close. They even looked alike.

We will all miss Charles terribly. I think he is probably looking down at us now, sipping a scotch and soda and smiling, with Thurber at his side.

Our parish priest invited everyone to take Communion after the funeral Mass. This was unusual in the Catholic Church, and it was appreciated by the non-Catholics who attended the service. A festive reception was held during the afternoon at Devon Yacht Club, and I received many beautiful flower arrangements, gifts of food and wine, letters, and heartfelt sympathy messages.

Alden drove Valerie Kaempf and Tricia Sayad (a Palm Beach family friend) from New York to Charles's funeral along with her son, Brooks. Her other son, Nicholas, came from Greenwich, and all three of her children wrote tributes to Charles. I quote from her daughter Honor's letter, "Easter will never be as fun: Charles had a gift for lighting up the room. I was always so happy to see him and listen to his wonderful observations and stories. He just brought such a sense of occasion to things, plus he had an ease about him that had a contagious effect. Most importantly, he was madly in love with you, which made him even more of a gentleman. We all love you so much and welcome you even closer to our family." Once again, lucky me. My cousin Jan, Niall MacDermot's wife, wrote that he seemed very cuddly and she loved his gravelly Southern drawl. Recently, rereading more than two hundred cards and letters, I noted there were repeated comments about his wit, his sense of fun, our happy marriage, and many allusions to his deep voice, my favorite being, "Charles, the cheerful curmudgeon with the voice of a bullfrog."

I went to grief counseling organized by the East End Hospice with two other widows for about six months and found it helpful, and I also read many books on bereavement.

The following year, I started boarding dogs. My card reads, "Your Dog's Home Away from Home," offering overnight stays and much longer visits when clients take business or pleasure trips. I would also walk dogs during the day. It has been such a rewarding micro-entrepreneurial business, but one must really and truly love dogs. They do not keep office hours and of course there are "accidents," but they all get along and enjoy each other's company. I have had some wonderful clients who have become friends over the years. Ian Irving, formerly in charge of Sotheby's silver department and now a private international consultant and dealer, and his partner, Mia Spence, hired me to look after their Wheaten Terrier CousCous, Pookie. She had come from the pet shop on Lexington Avenue many years ago, and in 2019, Ian's daughters Olympia and Ariadne flew their dog Pepito to New York from London via Paris so he could meet the dog they had grown up with. Pookie had a great life and lived to be sixteen.

I am on some second dogs now—for example, Seamus has been succeeded by Pablo, belonging to a very generous couple, Michael and Barbara Press, who before the coronavirus pandemic used to take me to dinner at Nick and Tony's. They sent a huge box of edibles in 2019 while I was in rehab, which I shared with the nursing staff because inmates ("residents") had to open gift boxes at the nursing station. I wonder what they suspected us of smuggling into our rooms. Michael and Barbara continue to send me annual gifts of Florida oranges.

There are too many wonderful owners past and present to mention them all, but I am especially fond of Baxter, a large white Labrador, now thirteen, who has boarded with me for many years. His owners, Nancy and Bill James, live in one of the oldest houses in East Hampton. For many years I boarded Lilo, a gentle Boykin Spaniel with the softest brown coat, who belonged to Curt and Angel Schade. Debbie and Henry Druker continue to board their sweet Bailey with me. Pam and John Mallory board Rocky and Happy. Jack, belonging to Lilee, the lovely flower lady, is a favorite, even though he does not like men sometimes and tried to attack John Mallory, thinking he was protecting me. Debbie Haab's Lance is always such a good boy. Annette and Jacques Franey's Gigi has always been an angelic little boarder. Since the pandemic started, new daycare pups are brought to my house on weekday mornings, whose owners work remotely during the day, and they have a wonderful time. Boriana's Junox, the young Weimaraner, plays all day with Stephanie's Cavachon Skippy, and recently Sari and Erica's Vinnie, a Bernedoodle. Ellen White's endearing Robin, a Cavalier King Charles puppy, is spending the winter in Key West, but the pups and I look forward to his return. He will be very grown up. Sarah and Scott Marden's English Setter, Gunner, is another favorite. Scott, our Labrador Retriever mix rescue, whom we adopted in January 2010 from ARF, is now thirteen and feeling his age, slowing down but putting up with the lively dogs that come and go exuberantly and invade his space.

My next two journeys to India were after Charles died, the first in December 2012. My travel companion was a retired Belgian diplomat, Arlette Laurent, whose final posting had been *charge d'affaires* for the European Union. She decided to live in New York and became a US resident. She and I had mutual friends and some career connections. We shared a love of the subcontinent and of Swan Hellenic's *Minerva*.

We flew to Dubai, she in business class, me in steerage, and enjoyed a few days in that fascinating city with its unparalleled tourist amenities. However, I soon understood that in this United Arab Emirate, the Emirati come first and foreigners are merely tolerated. A charming Princeton lawyer, friend of the late Warren Dix (Dotsy Letts's significant other, an excellent bridge player, who self-published a spy novel in his early nineties), and his Indian wife, Steve and Renata Matthews collected us in his Maserati and entertained us in their house before dining in a restaurant. Foreign businessmen in Dubai are required to have an Emirati partner who is not actually expected to do any work, only to lend his name expensively. The Emirati enjoy an extremely benevolent situation thanks to the oil revenues, at the time mostly provided by Abu Dhabi. Education is free all the way through graduate school, and every male receives a new car when he gets married. There is a mosque every five hundred yards or so, in order that the faithful will not have to walk far in the extreme heat.

We explored the sites, historic and modern, from forts, museums, palaces, and mosques to the world's only seven-star, sail-shaped hotel, the Burj Al Arab (friends from East Hampton, Beverly and Michael Kazickas and their two children, stayed there one Christmas), the artificial palm-shaped island, and the Burj Khalifa, the world's tallest building. One evening, we took a supper cruise on the Dubai Creek surrounded by picturesque dhows.

We boarded Swan's *Minerva* in Dubai, which was berthed next to the original *Queen Elizabeth*, and sailed to the port of Khasab, the capital of Musandam in the northernmost part of the Sultanate of Oman. We visited the seventeenth-century Fort of Khasab, built by the Portuguese seeking dominion over the Strait of Hormuz, then drove to a Bedouin village. We drove on steep roads into the mountains in four-by-fours until we reached the summit of Jebel Harim and explored ancient prehistoric sites.

As we sailed past the coast of Pakistan, it is worth mentioning the Nawab of Junagadh, who acceded his territory to Pakistan in 1947, later tragically disputed and now part of India. He was a lover of dogs who held dog weddings marked by state holidays, and he saved the Asiatic lions of Girnar.

Piracy in these waters was a real threat, so we had a pirate drill on board *Minerva*, although to date, no cruise ship has ever been captured, pirates considering them too complicated, too many people, not enough loot. There were military security officers on board, only recognizable because these fit-looking men were younger than regular passengers. Unlike the standard lifeboat drill, it was not necessary to muster in designated areas. When the siren went off, you stepped out of your cabin, closed the door, and stood to one side in the corridor, so that if the pirates boarded through your cabin window, you would not be shot in the back. Several grandparents announced that their grandchildren would be fascinated by the possibility of being boarded by pirates.

Porbandar was only memorable as the birthplace of Gandhi and an expedition led by our on-board naturalist to a swampy area redolent of chemical aromas, which surprisingly attracted a number of exotic birds.

Bombay, which I left as an infant, is now Mumbai, a great city immortalized in many novels, my favorite being *Shantaram* by Gregory David Roberts. I will not compete with Mr. Roberts's literary descriptions. Of course, we also visited Elephanta Island, Marine Drive, the Gateway of India, Dhobi Ghat's immense open-air laundry, and the Victorian Chhatrapati Shivaji railway terminus.

From Mumbai, we sailed along the coast of Kerala, passing Cape Comorin, where three seas meet and where Gandhi's ashes were scattered, to Tamil Nadu, going ashore in Mangalore and Kochi, a highlight being an Alleppey Backwaters Cruise through picturesque canals and wide lakes, and visited Palayamkottai, Tirunelveli, and Madurai before sailing to Sri Lanka.

It had been more than fifty years since I was in Colombo, which was then the capital of Ceylon, now Sri Lanka, a port of call on my way to Singapore and Indonesia back in 1955 and 1956. This time, my favorite expedition was to the Pinnawala Elephant Orphanage. Before the arrival of the British in 1815, an estimated thirty thousand elephants lived on the island. By the 1960s, they were close to extinction, prompting the government to found an orphanage in 1975 for elephants that had been separated from their mothers or their herds. Among the elephants at Pinnawala was one that had lost a leg when it stepped on a mine and another that was blind. Employees feed them with leaves from palm trees, and twice a day they make the journey to the river to bathe.

The following December I returned to Colombo, this time to sail with *Voyager* (Voyages of Discovery being the sister company of Swan Hellenic) up the east coast of India. Before leaving Sri Lanka again, I needed to revisit the elephants. Even though our jeeps got bogged down in mud and we had to clamber out of them, the pachyderms in Udawalawe National Park did not disappoint.

Docking in Chennai, we explored the rock carvings and monolithic sculptures of Mahabalipuram, the only surviving pagoda of the seventh-century Dravidian Shore Temple. Our final shore visit in India was to Kanchipuram, City of One Thousand Temples, one of the seven holiest cities in India.

On arrival in Yangon, Myanmar, we visited the Shwedagon Pagoda, built more than 2,500 years ago. A great testament to the faith of the Burmese, the pagoda is covered in gold, and for the last century, a new layer of gold has been added every ten years. The top of the stupa is encrusted with 4,531 diamonds, the largest being a seventy-six-carat solitaire.

Some of us flew to Bagan (formerly Pagan), arriving at sunset and staying overnight at the Hotel at Tharabar Gate. Before dinner, we ladies were given beautiful multicolor Burmese sarongs, which I still wear as a long skirt on festive summer occasions. Bagan is one of the richest archaeological sites in Asia. Approximately two thousand monumental stupas dot the dusty plains in this extraordinary lost city, which was once one of the most remarkable religious capitals in the world.

I used to brag that I would never set foot as a tourist anywhere in Asia where I had lived in embassies or with my parents, but once again, I ate my words as a tourist in Thailand. I found myself thoroughly enjoying the resort town of Phuket and sharing an elephant ride with a gentleman who had been my seatmate flying to and from Bagan, a retired senior intelligence officer who had served under six presidents of the United States. He claimed to have the dirt on all of them. His other claim was rejecting the marriage proposal of a woman who was worth hundreds of millions. For a while after the cruise, he used to send me emails about dogs. He admitted that our cruise was not up to the level of luxury he and the couple he was traveling with were used to. The cruise ended, luxuriously enough for me, in Malaysia. As we left the ship at Penang, much had changed since our honeymoon visit in 1962. We flew back to London from the capital, Kuala Lumpur, which also claims the world's tallest building.

# Chapter Twenty

I had always been fascinated by Madagascar and regretted that Charles and I had not visited Richard Crowson when he was British ambassador to that island country off the west coast of Africa, so unique in its fauna and flora. Reaching Mauritius from the US, popular with wealthy Europeans escaping winter climates, required an overnight flight to Paris, a layover at Charles de Gaulle Airport, and another overnight flight on Air Mauritius to Port Louis, where I joined Voyages of Discovery's *Voyager* for a two-week cruise.

Mauritius is known as the sugarcane island of the Indian Ocean. Discovered by the Portuguese in 1507, the French assumed control in 1715 and brought slaves to work the plantations. It is densely populated by descendants of Indians who worked after the abolition of slavery, many Chinese and a number of Creoles descended from French colonists, also Africans and Malagasy people. The island's most glittering moments were in the nineteenth century, when Joseph Conrad and Mark Twain both dropped by. Baudelaire visited for three weeks, and Darwin could not resist this naturalists' paradise, so the HMS *Beagle* put in there on her famous voyage. The British claimed the island officially at the Treaty of Paris in 1814. Mauritius only became an independent republic in 1992.

Interestingly, it was home to the dodo. Endemic to the island, the unfortunate creature was reputedly too nice to survive. This flightless bird was so tame that it was child's play to shoot it. Soldiers and sailors gleefully used it as target practice. Wanton killing for the sake of killing, man quite deliberately exterminated it. Today, we are left with a few reconstructed specimens in museums. However, the dodo lives on in memories, on stamps, coats of arms, and in common parlance meaning something totally extinct. In Port Louis, we only had time to visit the Pamplemousses Botanic Garden and admired the giant water lilies (as big as the ones I last saw in Bogor, Indonesia, more than fifty years ago).

We sailed five hundred miles to Réunion, a French overseas département and the westernmost Mascarene island, which rises out of a bed of volcanic lava. Scenic coastal forests border a mountainous interior, where three immense volcanic craters have formed lush valley basins. I was reminded of Switzerland as we ascended through pastures where cattle grazed on our way to the volcano, Piton de la Fournaise, which was boringly quiet that day shrouded in clouds. Two weeks after the cruise, I heard on the radio that it had once again erupted in a spectacular fashion.

At one time, most of Réunion's population was slaves from Madagascar and Africa working the coffee and sugar plantations. The island is a meeting point for many cultures. However, it is popular with retirees and visitors from France, and its atmosphere is as French as croissants and café au lait.

On our way to the east coast of Africa, we stopped for an afternoon to go ashore on the tiny Island of Mozambique, once the capital of Mozambique. In blistering heat, we explored the Palace of São Paulo and the São Sebastião, the old Portuguese ruined fort built by thousands of slaves over four hundred years ago, with four hundred cannons still pointing out to sea. We saw the ruins of the prison from which slaves were shipped mostly by Arab traders to the west.

We docked at Dar es Salaam in Tanzania. One side of the port was teeming with African life and shanty buildings, the other side with sterile modern office buildings. Six of us enjoyed a short safari at Tsavo East in Kenya. We were greeted at the airport by a young Muslim African woman and a young man in uniform. We guessed wrongly that he was the pilot. She flew us via Nairobi to the small airstrip close to the lodge. This brought back happy memories of our 1998 safari with its wonderful game drives. Though we did not see any lions or leopards, just elephants, giraffes, zebras, antelopes, and hartebeests, to the disappointment of our guide, there were many birds at the watering holes mingling with the animals, including bustards. Most fascinating were the white storks, magnificent birds with wingspans of approximately six feet that live as long as thirty-five years. They had flown eight thousand miles south from northern Europe, most likely Poland, to enjoy warmer winter weather.

We stayed in a very comfortable international lodge at the Selous Game Reserve. Many Kenyans were enjoying Christmas holidays with their families. In the buffet line, a Kenyan told me that the US had given little aid to his country, but after the terrorist attack at a shopping mall in Nairobi, more money was forthcoming.

Tanzania's name came from the former British colony of Tanganyika and its island of Zanzibar. The Omanis came, saw, and conquered the island, and the sultan made Zanzibar his capital, introducing clove cultivation and encouraging the slave trade, making his jewel of a city into the most prosperous port on the east coast of Africa. Many magnificent buildings remain from the sultan's days.

One of our passengers had been working as a secretary in the House of Commons when the British government drew up the new constitution for Tanzania. She typed the document and was thrilled so many years later to visit the tomb of the revered first head of state, Joseph Nyerere, whom she had met in 1961 just before the country's peaceful transition to independence.

Second only to visiting Antarctica, my greatest bucket list wish was to visit Madagascar, to see the lemurs. The fourth largest island in the world after Greenland, New Guinea, and Boneo, it was populated more than fifteen centuries ago by Indonesian settlers, and later by people from East Africa. The magnificent, terraced paddy fields have the same serenity as those of Java, and the slender outrigger canoes of its fishermen were surely inspired by the Bugis sea gypsies, those infamous pirates who still haunt the seas and archipelagos of the Philippines, Indonesia, and Malaysia. The Portuguese, Dutch, and French tried to colonize Madagascar, which was ruled by a succession of Malagasy kingdoms. It finally became an independent republic in 1960.

Because of its geographical isolation, the island is home to thousands of unique plants and exceptional fauna. The most extraordinary plant is a curious carnivore, the nepenthes, whose long, twisted stem ends in a pitcher with a lid to protect it from rain. Flies, mosquitoes, butterflies, dragonflies, and even small reptiles fall into the pitcher and drown in a lethal liquid. As their remains dissolve, the plant absorbs the nutrients.

There are still several species of lemur despite deforestation, which has led to massive extinction, the ring-tailed being the most common and the only ones we saw. Six varieties of baobab tree grow in Madagascar, whereas the African continent has only one kind. There are at least one thousand species of orchid. Madagascar exports a quarter of the world's production of vanilla.

We first went ashore at Tuléar, a picturesque little port sheltered by flame trees and tamarinds. We were happy tourists for the day, visiting the Ifaty and Spiny Forest, admiring baobabs (which can hold up to 120,000 liters of water) and winsome ring-tailed lemurs, enthusiastically photographing both. At one point, several of us held hands as we encircled an enormous baobab trunk.

My other connection with Tuléar is a small white dog. The Coton de Tuléar, recently recognized as a breed by the American Kennel Club, is a highly prized, extremely expensive canine, closely related to the bichon, which is not surprising because Portuguese sailors in the fifteenth century and French sailors from the seventeenth century onward brought bichons on their ships and left them on the island, where they came to be regarded as indigenous. A breeder of Cotons in New England told me that often the sailors could not swim when their ships were sunk in battles or storms, but the little dogs made it to shore. Marlene Schroeder, owner of Willy, an English sheepdog who has stayed with me often, has just acquired an adorable pup, Dante, from the above-mentioned breeder. We went ashore again in the north at Nosy Be, a very scenic area for walking and swimming, which was most welcome after the confines of the ship, and explored the bays of Antsiranana, Sugar Loaf Mountain, and the fishing village of Ramena Bay.

When I returned to the US, I railed once again at exploitation of third-world countries by greedy first-world importers and marketers. Madagascar is one of the poorest countries in the world. The locals have not benefited from the exportation of Cotons or vanilla. Bred in the US, the former sell for thousands of dollars a pup, and have you priced vanilla gelato in your supermarket lately?

My last Swan *Minerva* cruise was with my good friends Susie and John Cartier. Although beloved for decades by their British customers and some from other countries, they were offering too much for too little and were caught up in a global glut of larger ships whose passengers did not care about the high academic quality of the lecturers on board. Speakers' spouses also traveled free and were expected to look after the ships' libraries.

We boarded *Minerva* in Lima, Peru, on January 18, 2016, and disembarked at Valparaíso, Chile, on February 1. The waters between Callao and Valparaíso have seen an extraordinary history of maritime exploration, military action, and lucrative trade. Spanish conquistadors began to subdue and colonize the west coast of South America in the sixteenth century. Also in the sixteenth century, Francis Drake passed through Valparaíso, Arica, and Lima, seeking Spanish treasure, making himself rich and famous, and enhancing England's maritime power. Magellan's epic circumnavigation took him through Chilean waters, and the Spanish who found subsequent riches in Peru established ports up the coastline, creating the colony of Chile. After Spain was conquered by Napoleon, her domination of South America weakened, and independence movements gained momentum. Charles Darwin joined the second voyage of HMS *Beagle* between 1831 and 1836 as naturalist and botanist for the survey of the coastline of South America.

Captain Thomas Lord Cochrane of the royal navy, nick-named the "sea wolf," in Valparaíso in 1818 took command of the Chilean navy, routing the Spanish navy and ensuring victory to the freedom fighters of Chile and Peru.

Peru is known for its extraordinary legacies of ancient civilizations and natural beauty. The coast is famous for bird, marine mammal, and fish life abounding in its waters. After touring Lima, we landed at the port named after General San Martin, where we boarded small boats to sail to the uninhabited Ballestas Islands. There we saw many birds, including the Guanay cormorant, Peruvian boobies, pelicans, and Inca terns.

Chile, defined by Pablo Neruda as "a long petal of sea," has always fascinated me since befriending expatriate Chileans in Spain back in 1964. Going ashore, we visited Arica and the Atacama Desert, the driest place in the world, and saw the strange Diaz Fleming sculptures in the Azapa Valley. We then sailed on to Iquique, Coquimbo, and La Serena. At La Serena, we saw eight-thousand-year-old mummies in the architectural museum. In the evening, we drove through the Elqui Valley to the Alpha Adea amateur observatory for some spectacular stargazing. We went ashore on Robinson Crusoe Island, where the Scottish navigator Alexander Selkirk was stranded for more than four months in 1704, which inspired Daniel Defoe to write *Robinson Crusoe*. The cruise ended at Viña del Mar and Valparaíso.

On the way to the capital, Santiago, from Valparaíso, John arranged for us to visit a winery and do some tasting of wines, mostly exported to exclusive customers in the San Francisco area. After a brief sightseeing tour of Santiago, I left the Cartiers, who wanted to spend more time in the capital, and flew back to

New York. We had fun traveling together and spent many happy evening cocktail hours in their suite drinking excellent cheap wine bought ashore, and then drank more expensive wine over dinner. As always, there were excellent lecturers as well as evening entertainers with singing and dancing.

In June of 2017, I once again visited Scandinavia. I had been to Denmark, sailing with my father from Kiel in Germany in the early fifties. I flew to Stockholm to meet Alden Prouty and spent a happy weekend in that fine city, dining with her son Nicholas's stepson, Ian, whose father is Swedish. We went to Oslo by train and spent a night there before taking another scenic rail trip to Bergen.

Alden and I had a wonderful time in Norway. We embarked at Bergen for a Hurtigruten cruise on a coastal ferry boat. Cruise passengers had comfortable cabins, our own dining room with lots of berries, cheeses, fish, and other typical delicious Norwegian fare. We also had excellent lectures on history, geography, fauna and flora, mythology, folklore, and every aspect of Norwegian life. Recent history was very tactfully handled by our guides for there were many German passengers. The Third Reich's treatment of Norway had been brutal, as Hitler built up defenses using forced local labor expecting invasion from Russia in the North. Many Norwegians lost their homes and their lives during World War II. Some survived by living under upturned boats during harsh winters. Their royal family had been given sanctuary in England along with their gold reserves.

We docked at Molde and Alesund, taking overland excursions and rejoining the ship at the next port. We visited Trondheim and Tromsø, where we attended a concert in the cathedral, emerging into sunshine well after midnight. We crossed the Arctic Circle with an entertaining ceremony as Neptune descended from the top deck and, with his cohorts, put ice cubes down passengers' necks. This reminded me of Neptune's arrival on the *Willem Ruys* as we crossed the equator. We visited the Lofoten Islands, where eider ducks famously nest and their down is harvested for exorbitantly expensive quilts. Sometimes the ferry made short stops, long enough to go ashore for a short walk, and for ferry passengers to do the same for their dogs and children traveling during the summer holidays. We were entertained by a blatantly touristic evening of Sámi culture in a large tent. The Sámi and the Inuit share a history of exploitation, with present-day politically correct governments (Norwegian, Finnish, and Canadian) trying to make up for past bad behavior. Tourists bring welcome revenues, but the Sámi people still own all the reindeer.

With my passion for dogs, not shared by Alden, I signed up for two sled dog expeditions. The first was to a large establishment where the female owner showed us a movie of herself and her team winning the Iditarod race in Alaska. Sled dogs are bored in summer, although they seemed happy enough, crouching above their kennels to which they were attached by chains, dozing the day away in the sun. The second trip was more exciting. I shared a minivan with five Germans who ignored me, but the young guides were very friendly. On arrival at the kennels, we were harnessed to six sled dogs, one each, and climbed up a hill from where we could see Russia. At the summit, the dogs were given water to drink and tethered to stakes while the humans enjoyed a barbecue of reindeer hot dogs. The descent was not so easy, and I sheepishly accepted a helping arm from a guide, making the feeble excuse that I wore the wrong footwear. Hiking boots would have been better than summer sneakers.

I was on the Shelter Island ferry on a cold day in February of that year when my cell phone rang, and it was my friend Irina

Ourosoff. She sought a companion for her October Viking River cruise from Moscow to St. Petersburg, and she characteristically needed to know now, immediately, if I would come with her. In childhood, I had always dreamed of visiting America and Russia. Surprised at myself agreeing to a third trip in one year, I did not hesitate to say yes.

We took the Hampton Jitney to JFK Airport and boarded Air France for Paris, then flew Aeroflot to Moscow. I had a similar reaction to my visit to the Taj Mahal—visiting iconic places in person does not disappoint. I metaphorically pinched myself as we rode the Metro, walked through Red Square past the Kremlin walls and Lenin's tomb, and admired St. Basil's Cathedral and the GUM Department Store by day and by night. Later we toured the Kremlin, which is actually a walled city, home to cathedrals, palaces, and museums, its origins dating back to the twelfth century.

We explored Sergiyev Posad, Russia's greatest monastery, founded in the fourteenth century, and its two cathedrals, one containing the tomb of the sixteenth-century tsar Boris Godunov. After visiting several other Russian Orthodox cathedrals and churches during our trip, I was impressed by the lavish restoration everywhere, no expense spared, especially the renovation of thousands of gilded icons.

Our riverboat sailed through the Moscow Canal (we must have been asleep when it navigated the locks) to the Volga River, disembarking at Uglich to visit the Transfiguration Cathedral and the Church of St. Dmitry of the Blood, where the body of Dmitry, son of Ivan the Terrible, was discovered, his murder ordered by Boris Godunov. We had tea with a Russian family who were gracious but no doubt carefully selected and paid to entertain foreign tourists. Our lecturers and tour guides were always upbeat about Russia's current nationalism and its history, and although they criticized past regimes from the tsars through Gorbachev, one sensed they would never say anything critical of Putin's government. Being with Irina was enlightening because Russian was her native language. She was cagey about her personal history, her family having emigrated before the Revolution to France, Belgium, and later the US, where she married Prince Ourusoff, who had an American mother.

In Mandrogi, a reconstructed traditional village of brightly painted log houses and museums dedicated to vodka and bread, artisans demonstrated their skills and sold pottery, weaving, and jewelry. We visited a stable where the owner proudly showed us a photograph of Putin—shirtless, of course—on one of his horses, and pointed out a log cabin belonging to him, which only differed from its neighbors because it had a helipad. Cruising down the Volga-Baltic Waterway across Lake Onega with fall colors, mostly aspens and birch at their best, we visited Khizi, famous for its wooden buildings, before docking in St. Petersburg.

This great city is a gilded and bold showcase reflecting the might of Peter the Great and the Empress Catherine. Grand boulevards, a lacework of canals (the Venice of the North), elegant baroque and classical buildings, and resplendent palaces grace the cityscape and its environs, while priceless art and world-class ballet have elevated Peter's city over the years more than he could have ever imagined.

Despite crowds and some closed galleries, the Hermitage was high on my bucket list, and I was not disappointed. We were less thrilled by a ballet that evening, no Bolshoi dancers present, but what the performance lacked, the surroundings made up for, as it had been Catherine's private theater inside one of her royal palaces. We visited the magnificent Catherine Palace in Tsarskoye

Selo, with its Amber Room; mahogany, rosewood, and amaranth floors; lush staterooms; the opulent Great Hall lined with mirrors and gold carvings, Chinese porcelain, and silk wallpaper. Our last visit was to the Peterhof Palace, Russia's Versailles, more glitter and opulence. There is much to be said for an autocratic government that can spend billions on restoration of its national heritage without hindrance from voters or partisan politics.

For my seventy-fifth birthday, the Thrupp cousins had given me a lavish lunch, repeated five years later in April 2018. The previous week, Wanda Rix and I took the train from London to Pairs for some intensive museum-going, staying in a charming hotel on the Left Bank and walking almost everywhere. We had the distinction of visiting the Louvre on the only day it had ever closed to the public because of Eastern European lowlife disrupting the peace, forcibly removing jackets from men to steal their wallets, so the museum security staff went on strike until more guards were provided. At that time, I was volunteering at the Metropolitan Museum of Art in the director's and president's offices two afternoons a week. They were sympathetic but critical in a sort of this-could-never-happen-here way, implying that their museum is better managed. Little did we all know then that seven years later, museums all over the world would close for months because of the coronavirus pandemic.

Lucky woman that I am, my eightieth birthday was celebrated in style on both sides of the Atlantic. Patti and Jack McGrath, my neighbors in New York City and East Hampton, gave a dinner in East Hampton. Other good friends, Ginny and Warren Schwerin with Alden Prouty, hosted a dinner at the Colony Club in New York.

My cousin, Lydia née Christie-Miller, whose wedding in 1969 to Ian McClure I mentioned earlier, joined the Worshipful

Company of Feltmakers, following in her father's footsteps (he would be so proud of her), and invited me as a birthday present to their Spring Livery dinner at the Vintners' Hall. The first known reference to Feltmakers as a distinct craft association was in London in 1180. They survived through the centuries and became synonymous with hatters, and they are now their livery company. Famous politicians, two First Lords of the Admiralty, two Presidents of the Board of Trade, two foreign secretaries, two lord mayors of London, several lesser mayors and ex-mayors, and nine knights belonged to the Feltmakers. They support several charities and are known for three particular hats: the Master's tricorn with white plumes, the Wardens' hats, and the hat that is presented to the incoming lord mayor each year, a tricorn with black plumes.

The banquet was lavish: the queen, Prince Philip, the Prince of Wales, the Duchess of Cornwall, and other members of the royal family were toasted, as were the guests and the Worshipful Company itself. The guests were distinguished, and many were titled or high-powered or both.

The following year, Lydia and Ian celebrated their golden wedding (fiftieth anniversary) with a lavish dinner on HMS *Drake*. Unfortunately I was unable to attend, having only just been released from a month in rehab, following three weeks in two hospitals after my cardiac arrest, resuscitation, and heart-valve replacement.

I flew to England for my actual birthday, staying first with Jacquie Drayton in London then going to Wodehouse to stay with Wanda and her family, who gave a celebration lunch. The house has not changed much since the sixties. It is comfortable in an understated way, full of good pictures and furniture. There were dining room meals for guests, a cozy, warm sitting room, and a more formal drawing room. When there were no guests, we hung out in the kitchen, warmed by the AGA cooker, and the room off it where family meals are eaten. There is always at least one Springer Spaniel in residence with beds in the kitchen and the sitting room. Most friends and family in England kindly turn up the heating when I come to stay, knowing that I have grown used to warm American dwellings after fifty years in this country. However, my East Hampton house, with so much glass and a twenty-foot ceiling in the living room, is hard to heat, and I turn up the thermostat when guests arrive.

My cousins, Peter and Caroline Cannon-Brookes, gave a magnificent birthday lunch for many family members, plus John and Wanda Rix, who drove me to Thrupp Farm, and two friends from East Hampton who were in England at the time, John and Alice Tepper Marlin. We ate at the huge table in their dining room surrounded by old master paintings and other art treasures. Caroline and Peter's daughter, Emma, made the most delicious, enormous chocolate cake. I was so happy to be with so many family members and friends on this milestone birthday.

When visiting the two Thrupp households, it is always a treat to have an outing with Emma and Andrew Coker. Andrew retired early from a career in public relations and is involved with worthwhile causes in their community. He enjoys taking friends to see places of local interest. A favorite tour is *Midsomer Murders* country because of the popular TV series. Their son, James, and daughter, Harriet, have both become engaged to their long-time partners and plan weddings post-pandemic.

In December, I gave myself an eightieth birthday present, completing my bucket list, for which I had waited fifty years, a nice round number. Fifty years ago, I was working for the Scott Polar Research Institute in Cambridge on the Antarctic ecology symposium. How fitting to head to Antarctica fifty years later, via a short stay in Buenos Aires where I spent a happy day with Alden Prouty's son, Brooks, eating, drinking, and sightseeing, touring Eva Peron's mausoleum and several important buildings.

While gathering early next morning in our Buenos Aires hotel for the flight to Ushuaia, three delightful, well-traveled ladies—Michele and Maureen, two sisters, and their sister-in-law, Pam Jackson, a retired US air force colonel—invited me to join them for meals and expeditions. After a day's shopping and walking around Ushuaia, Argentina's southernmost city, we boarded Hurtigruten's *Midnatsol*.

We had a calm crossing of the Drake Passage to Yankee Harbor in the South Shetland Islands.

We went ashore in cold rain to see our first gentoo penguins sitting on their eggs, which would soon hatch. Occasionally an ubiquitous skua would swoop down and steal an egg that had rolled out of an ill-made nest. We also observed leopard seals swimming or sliding on the ice on their tummies.

We sailed through Neptune's Bellows to Deception Island, Antarctica's Santorini in shape, but with an active volcano that last erupted in the seventies, spotting Weddell seals in the caldera and passing the remains of an old whaling station on the shore, before doing a steep climb up a hill to look at chinstrap penguins. Former stations belonging to Chile, Britain, and Argentina were destroyed in the earthquake, and only Argentina currently maintains one. Our foursome had grown to six with Steve and Jennifer Dobbs. Steve was introducing his wife to Antarctica, having been posted to the US Palmer Station some years earlier. Pam, Michele, Steve, and Jennifer did the Polar Plunge, while Maureen and I photographed their intrepidity. Back at the ship, we saw humpback whales and took many photos of them diving with a wave of their iconic tails. Our captain had a special affinity for whales and never missed an opportunity to slow the ship down or turn her around for the benefit of passengers rushing outside to chilly decks, cameras in hand. A storm the next day prevented us from landing on Anvers Island, so we missed a visit to a Chilean station.

While aboard ship, we attended superb lectures and movies by international scientists on every aspect of Antarctic wildlife, mammals, birds and fish, and geology, as well as history of early explorers, the whaling industry, and international "settlement" of the Seventh Continent. David Attenborough's films were very popular. We could also look at ongoing experiments through microscopes in a special area on deck eight where scientists were working, for example, on plankton, so important to the food chain, along with krill.

Besides whales and seals (Weddell and leopard, and sometimes crabeater seals were visible), we saw many wonderful birds, in addition to ubiquitous penguin colonies (chinstrap, gentoo, and the occasional Adélie), such as predatory skuas, Cape petrels, Antarctic petrels, Wilson's Storm petrels, kelp gulls, Antarctic terns, prions, and rarely black-browed and light-mantled sooty albatrosses. On December 16, we landed on Lorne Island, which is on the Antarctic mainland, and hiked up a ridge for more chin-strap penguin sightings and spectacular views. Hiking was actually quite tough, and Steve often gave us ladies a helping hand over rocks and steep ledges. One needed layers of warm clothing for the Zodiac ride from ship to shore, but when one started climbing with only boots and ski poles, one puffed and sweated.

Passing icebergs while we breakfasted, we cruised round Danco Island en route to Damoy Point near Port Lockroy. Unfortunately, there was too much ice to sail through the scenic

Lemaire Channel, but the Neumayer Channel was spectacular. We could not go ashore at Port Lockroy, where the British operate the southernmost post office in the world. A young woman who worked there came aboard and took our postcards back in her small boat for mailing with the requisite unique Antarctic post mark. Most of them reached their destinations via London some weeks later.

On our last day in Antarctica, we sailed to Wilhelmina Bay, named after Queen Wilhelmina of the Netherlands who died in 1945. We took shorter-than-planned trips by Zodiac through picturesque ice floes because the weather was deteriorating. We returned our borrowed boots to the tender pit and reluctantly surrendered our Leopard Seal Boat patches from our anorak sleeves to Hurtigruten staff. I discovered that Hector, who looked after my cabin so well during the cruise, had made me a little gray-and-white dog out of hand towels.

Some of us were fortunate enough to dine one evening with members of the expedition staff. The mayor of Beaverton, Washington, a retired National Park Service officer, and I sat at a table with young scientists from Finland and Norway, before watching the Ernest Shackleton movie following a lecture on seals. At 10 a.m. next morning, the captain announced that we had rounded Cape Horn. The first Europeans to do so were Le Maire and Schouten in 1616. On a small island off the coast of Chile, there is a lighthouse: the keeper, his wife, and three children are the only inhabitants.

We had a relatively calm voyage heading south, but the northbound trip was pretty rough before we disembarked again at Ushuaia. However, four of us, a German, a Norwegian, a Swede, and I managed a game of bridge one afternoon as the ship pitched and lurched, although equipped with excellent stabilizers.

# Thursday's Child

After flying for thirty-six hours, changing planes in Buenos Aires, I had happily completed the other half of my passion for polar places. I returned to East Hampton in time to spend Christmas Eve with my very hospitable friends Nancy and Paul Buscemi and their guests. I brought penguin-shaped chocolates from Ushuaia and received a fluffy toy penguin from our mutual friend Norman Abell, retired lawyer and superb bridge player.

# Chapter Twenty-One

The following year started off uneventfully with a March visit to friends in Palm Beach, but no travels were planned other than a family visit to the UK. During the summer, I was busy with tennis, beach days, social life, and canine clients. I woke up early on a Tuesday morning having some difficulty breathing but thought little of it and went back to sleep. However, when I was walking three or four dogs before breakfast, I felt so lousy that I called my neighbor Lynne Scanlon and asked if she could mind the dogs because I needed to go to the emergency room. She had the presence of mind to call an ambulance. I was given oxygen and taken to Southampton Hospital where they initially thought I had pneumonia. Thanks to Dr. John Reilly, who diagnosed heart trouble, specifically the need for a mitral valve replacement, I was transferred to Stony Brook University Cardiac Care by ambulance and scheduled for surgery the next day. During a pre-surgery catheterization to check if there were any other heart issues, I went into cardiac arrest. As mentioned in the Introduction, Dr. Henry Tannous, who claimed he never operated before going on vacation, happily made an exception in my case, and he and another surgeon, whom I never met while conscious, resuscitated me and operated successfully.

Later, I learned that Alden Prouty, who is my healthcare proxy, received a call on her way to the theater at Lincoln Center. Dr. Tannous told her they would not know the extent of possible brain damage or whether I would make it, for several hours. I owe so much to Alden, who visited me several times in hospital and rehab, taking charge, helping me to deal with doctors, social workers, and healthcare matters.

In spite of what doctors called an exceptional recovery, my restored life was temporarily complicated by a rare blood condition, endocarditis. In fact, they had to send samples to a special lab in Utah for diagnosis. This meant that I would need intravenous antibiotics for six weeks. I spent about ten days in St. Charles, a Catholic hospital in Port Jefferson. I had excellent physiotherapy while watching the Bridgeport ferry sail in and out of the harbor. I received special attention from one physiotherapist, Gary, who not only found me a great pair of sneakers (I was wearing Tevas, a t-shirt, and old dog-walking shorts when I was rushed to the emergency room at Southampton Hospital) but also gave me some of his girlfriend's runner t-shirts and some cotton pants. He wheeled me all over the place because I was not allowed to walk. St. Charles had treated victims of polio early in the twentieth century, and the lobby was full of photographs of children in antiquated wooden wheelchairs with primitive crutches. When I left, I gave Gary one of my get-well orchids for his girlfriend. The food was very good at St. Charles.

Because the intravenous antibiotics needed to be administered by nurses, I spent a month in the Hamptons Center for

Rehabilitation and Nursing in Southampton. I was overwhelmed by the generosity of family who sent flowers and called me from England and Ireland. Bridget Biggane, who had worked for the UN and *Women's Wear Daily*, a friend from my days of working in the New York fashion industry who retired to England, called for a long chat. From the day I went to hospital until weeks after I came home, friends were so generous with their gifts and their time. Some, besides Alden, came all the way to Stony Brook, including Patti and Jack McGrath and Virginia Schwerin. Three friends, fellow volunteers from ARF, collected my dogs from Lynne Scanlon the day I went to hospital and drove them to their regular Edge of Pond boarding kennel where they remained for a month. Susan Macy, Barbara Medlin, and Barbara Liberatore insisted on paying the bill when the dogs transferred to a dear friend's house for the final three weeks of my incarceration. Robin Foster, the kennel owner, who had boarded our dogs since 1995, also gave a compassionate discount. Jennifer Borg read in the St. Luke's church bulletin that I was very sick and offered through our mutual friend Patti McGrath to take the dogs to her house. They were supposed to be company for her elderly bulldog, who alas had to be put to sleep by his New Jersey vet, but Jennifer insisted on keeping Scott and Shawn, free of charge, until I went home, saying they cheered her up. Andrew Coker, my cousin, had asked Alice Tepper Marlin to inform St. Luke's Episcopal Church as well as my parish church, Most Holy Trinity, another "lucky-me" event.

Flowers, cards, emails, telephone calls, food, and visits meant so much to me. The center receptionists said I received more visitors than anyone in the facility, all of whom nobly braved the atrocious August Hamptons traffic to visit me. Our bridge director, Mark Shaiman, successful recipient of a heart transplant, visited me in Stony Brook and Southampton. He was treated like a conquering hero by the staff at Stony Brook, where he had spent time awaiting his transplant. Heart patients went home with a red heart-shaped pillow as well as diet instructions. Mark wrote on mine in black Sharpie "7NT." Benefiting from his advanced bridge lessons for the past few years, I should be a better player than I am.

Groups and individuals turned up, sometimes as many as six friends in one day. We sat in the small garden on uncomfortable chairs, in one of the reception rooms, or in my small room filled with flowers. Lilee Fell, a professional florist, sometimes accompanied by Jenny Berkeley, brought beautiful arrangements despite her busy life doing the floral arrangements for weddings and large social events all over Long Island. A night nurse took photos of Lilee's roses to send to her husband in India, who still had to wait a year to join his wife, an American citizen.

Among so many kind friends who visited me, Pat Hossenlopp from my book club always brought exotic edibles and drew artistic labels on the containers. Freddie Pellman also came from book club, as did Alice Tepper Marlin, who brought lunch with plates, glasses, and silver, a rare treat after daily plastic plates and mostly useless utensils—try cutting tough meat with a plastic knife. Irina Ourosoff from the Russia trip and book club helped me move rooms because first my roommate kept her TV on loudly all night. Joan Baum, my retired professor friend, writer and book reviewer, visited often, bringing books. Her thesis published as a book was on Ada Lovelace, daughter of Byron, inventor of the world's first computer. She lectures on many interesting literary subjects nowadays.

Beverly Kazickas and Rosemary Killen from Garden Club visited as did Anne-Marie Morton, my co-chair on the Members

Gardens Committee. Brian Stubelik showed up three times. I was happy to see my ARF volunteer friends already mentioned plus Nancy Buscemi, Mina Kahofer, and Susan Alborn, and Laura Aziz, my bridge partner. Marilyn and Wolfie Young, owners of Ollie, a Shih Tzu whom I boarded for years, now good friends, and Barbara Peltz brought delicious meals and stayed to eat them with me. Cathy Peacock brought lunch one day, enough for my supper too. All of their visits meant so much to me.

After so much physical therapy and extra time in rehab, coping on my own at home was easy, and I was able to drive and be sociable with friends again. After a busy but uneventful fall and winter, I spent eight days with Dotsy Letts in Palm Beach, visiting old friends and enjoying parties and warm weather.

When I flew back to New York, the pandemic was just starting. Marlene Schroeder's sweet English sheepdog, Willy, was booked for two weeks, but two days later they canceled their travel plans so I drove him home to Watermill. He was my last boarder until later in the summer. My little micro-entrepreneurial business died on the vine for a few months.

Essential businesses stayed open, such as food stores, banks, post offices, distributors, truckers, construction companies with some limitations, utilities, communications, and others, in addition to medical facilities, although many doctors resorted to telemedicine and nonessential operations were postponed. Liquor stores could sell curbside and make deliveries. They flourished in New York State but were closed in Pennsylvania, so Jimmy Warden in Philadelphia told me he had to drive to New Jersey to buy his Jack Daniels.

Second homeowners flocked out of New York City. Other New Yorkers came to the Hamptons and bought or rented houses. There has been a real estate and construction boom for the past year, with new houses being built and others renovated, causing a shortage of materials. However, some of the locals resented them, claiming that they were bringing the virus, stripping the store shelves bare, and "often behaving in an arrogant and entitled manner." Hundreds of freezers were ordered to stash food supplies, unnecessarily as it turned out.

It was gratifying to me that the influx of affluent New Yorkers was mostly helping our local small businesses. I have always supported the One Stop Pet Shop in Amagansett. Like many stores, they were taking orders over the phone. I told them that my rescue dog, Shawn, had almost severed my fingertip when I tried to pry a chicken bone out of his mouth, involving surgery to reattach it by Dr. John Anton at Southampton Hospital, so I was unable to drive for three weeks. Forty pounds of dog food was delivered to my doorstep by one of the workers on his way home in pouring rain. No charge for delivery, but of course I tipped him. Their small store had been cleaned out by pet-owning hoarders, but they were able to restock quickly and made up for a slow winter season in one weekend. Our independent bookstore, BookHampton, is doing well, and I buy most of my books there.

I wish my stepfather, Robert Niven, were still alive, but he died in 1976 as a retired brigadier general of the Royal Army Medical Corps, mentioned earlier on several occasions. His autocratic father insisted he follow in his footsteps and become a doctor, which he did not want to do. He compromised by joining the army and specialized in public health. During the 1950s, his team eliminated malarial mosquitoes in Singapore, and in the sixties suppressed a cholera epidemic in Hong Kong, though he was unpopular at the time for closing the beaches. With his dry sense of humor and innate good sense, I wonder what he would make of the current crisis. During the pandemic, I reread his letters from the seventies after my mother died. He was extremely well read and knew his history. His letters are witty and highly literate. He enjoyed visiting stately homes and those of lesser mortals, expressing his love of gardens, paintings, prints, and antique furniture.

An excellent article in the *New Yorker* by Geoff Dyer quoted Camus: "In times of pestilence there is more in me to admire than to despise." Dyer posited that with hoarding of toilet paper and other scarce items this may not prove to be the case. Referring to the admonishments not to touch our faces, he pointed out that Munch's screamer's hands are visible on both sides of his face.

An article mentioned a "murmuration of starlings," and that in 1890, a Shakespeare enthusiast reputedly released sixty of these birds into Central Park. There are now more than 200 million of them. We craved such non-coronavirus related news and tidbits. There was a plethora of quarantine memes, a paucity of masks, a cornucopia of dread, IV drips of information, and repeated exhortations to flatten the curve.

President Trump continued to confound the population with his pronouncements, the nadir being when he recommended ingesting household disinfectants, to the consternation of the medical profession. Lysol and Clorox jokes replaced toilet paper ones, but to foreign-born me, there has always been an American obsession with hygiene.

May was the third month of self-isolating and safe distancing. Spring came at last. I am forever grateful to Charles, who created our garden starting in 1973. Daffodils of many varieties, narcissi and jonquils, still flourish. During late March and April, I was able to give bunches to friends and neighbors and always kept a vase on my dining room table.

It was a strange Memorial Day weekend, with the usual summer season fundraisers canceled. Supporters were encouraged to buy virtual tickets and follow events online and on Zoom. Economically, the cancellation of events in a summer resort is disastrous, not only for the commercial enterprises, caterers, florists, and musicians, some of whom will not survive, but for the nonprofits who depend on summer fundraisers to bring in essential revenue.

Friends and acquaintances slowly returned from Florida, believing that chartering a small private plane was safer than flying commercial. My friend, Susie Cartier, considered it safer to buy four tickets on a regular flight, thus having a spare seat unoccupied for one tenth of the cost of flying private. Also, if one person should be infected, a private plane is a much more confined space and also there can be more turbulence.

On Pentecost, our Most Holy Trinity Church in East Hampton was recording the previous Sunday's Mass online, so I gave myself a dispensation and said my prayers while walking the dogs and chatting with neighbors at a safe distance. In the afternoon, I had wine and homemade apricot pie with friends, Katrina Vanderlip, a talented artist, and her husband, Ed Perlberg, an expert bridge player, in their beautiful Sagaponack garden. They keep the deer away from their flower beds with a concoction of rotten eggs.

We felt a bit guilty in our "bubble" here in East Hampton, surrounded by friends and friendly neighbors, enjoying wine and beautiful weather in each other's gardens, walking for hours every day, playing tennis and going to the beach during the summer months. We had access to well-stocked farmers' markets, supermarkets, and other essential businesses, while always practicing safe distancing.

Times have changed since my childhood at Coolavin when local vets treated the livestock that were cash crops and seldom had time for companion animals. Nowadays, our pets are at the mercy of our pocketbooks when they fall sick. People for whom stratospheric fees are no problem order treatments that formerly only human beings received, but vets will try to sell these to the rest of us, preying on our consciences and devotion to our cats or dogs. A friend reputedly spent $40,000 in one year on a rescued Labrador's teeth and hip replacement. Our pets are our children, so how can we deny them? For so many of us who live alone, they are our sole companions. However, they are still animals. I strongly believe that dogs will try to keep themselves going for our sakes, even when they are old or in pain or both and ready to let go. Some owners keep them going long after their time, but it is often hard to know the extent of their suffering.

My little black Shawn, who closely resembled a Patterdale terrier although his DNA showed other breeds, was rescued from ARF in Wainscott in 2015. He looked like a small Labrador. I adopted him soon after I had my beloved black Labrador Sophie euthanized at fifteen, suffering from old age and general infirmity. Our first Labrador, Thurber, had also lived to fifteen and died a few months before Charles. The funeral director did not demur when I asked for some of Thurber's ashes to be put in his urn before the Mass for the dead, though I never told the priest. Thurber's and Sophie's ashes are buried under the holly bushes with Adirondack stones noting their names and dates. Periodically, Scott digs a hole under the bushes to keep cool and covers the stones with earth.

Charles's ashes—except for a small amount buried in front of his beloved Bath and Tennis Club in Palm Beach—were scattered in the Atlantic in 2011, a memorable day when we took two boats out in Gardiners Bay, one belonging to Austin Salisbury and his wife, Pam, son and daughter-in-law of John and Susie Cartier, the other belonging to Alexander and Michele Heinrici. We had waited a year so that David Morrish and his wife, Kacey, could be with us. Rosalie Arkell brought white roses, which we scattered with his ashes. Then we celebrated with champagne and hors d'oeuvres and swam off the boats.

To continue Shawn's story, he had an exuberant personality, barked at and tried to chase anything that moved, from large trucks to small children on bikes or scooters and everything in between, especially cyclists and joggers. His name when he arrived at ARF from Dallas, Texas, was Daeshawn. At the age of seven, he became ill and he was tested for many ailments. In this area, there are many tick-borne diseases. He had been inoculated against Lyme disease, so when he responded briefly to antibiotics, we thought it might be ehrlichiosis. When he relapsed a week later, his regular vets recommended a specialist center, so on the hottest Saturday of the year I drove him to Veterinary Medical Center Long Island in West Islip. Because of the pandemic, we waited in our cars while our animals were examined and treated, periodically turning on our engines for the air conditioning. After a couple of hours, a young vet, Megan Davis, discussed Shawn's likely problems by telephone, and the prognosis was not good. I agreed to leave him overnight for more tests and a blood transfusion, handed over my credit card, signed a form stating that he should not be given CPR, and drove home.

At 5 a.m. my phone rang, and another vet, Dr. Gibbs, told me that Shawn was failing and asked me to authorize CPR and another blood transfusion, which I declined. I drove through early morning fog and unusually light traffic as fast as I safely could. Two missed calls told me that Shawn had died at about

6:20 a.m. of hemolytic anemia, a congenital malady. Even though I deplore the astronomical fees charged by these specialist animal hospitals, in addition to their specialized expertise and ability to cure many animals, they deserve credit for empathy with grieving owners. Shawn's still-warm body was brought out to a small tent (box of Kleenex provided) where I was invited to stay as long as I wanted. I was given a plaster cast of his paw print, arrangements were made for his cremation, his records were sent to his regular vet within the hour, and a sympathy card came in the mail two days later. The sympathy from friends and neighbors, especially dog lovers, was overwhelming. His "cremains" were delivered to my vet a week later in a beautiful ebony box, which sits on a corner-cupboard shelf. Thurber and Sophie were cremated in a less classy pet crematorium and were delivered in purple tin cans.

August 10 was the tenth anniversary of Charles's death. Attending Mass in the parish hall at Most Holy Trinity in East Hampton was my first time since the pandemic started. Patti and Jack McGrath came, which meant so much to me. When cases of coronavirus increased after Thanksgiving, I stopped attending Mass but planned to return in March 2021, two weeks after my second vaccination.

In mid-February, with the pandemic still raging worldwide, vaccinations are now being administered, somewhat chaotically and inconsistently, a sort of free-for-all. Those of us over sixty-five spend hours online trying to find appointments. Some of us get lucky, but others are still trying. Most of Europe is still in lockdown, and in this country we are urged to wear masks and observe social distance until most of the population has been vaccinated. Is it hard to live alone, or to be a parent and grandparent unable to visit with children and grandchildren. Walking most days with Patti and assorted dogs, I know how much she missed being able to visit with hers, other than via Zoom. It is particularly difficult for children going to school virtually and for their parents, and for students of all ages.

I consider myself fortunate to have good energy, good health, and plenty to do, especially writing this book. The dogs keep me busy and get me out for walks, and I keep in touch virtually with family and friends. I greatly enjoy playing bridge online with my Monday partner Sally Hill-Wood and on Wednesdays with Laura Aziz. On New Year's Day in Gorey, Ireland, my godson Rory got several of us together on WhatsApp, including his son Francis in Germany and the rest of the family in Ireland; his mother, Jan, whom he cares for; his former wife, Ester, who is Italian and still works at the Italian embassy in Dublin; his daughter Emilia; his sister Siobhan with her husband Dominic Ryan, and their children, Moira, Niall, Sally Felicity, and Hugh.

Personally, I like Zoom, which will probably continue to be part of our lives after the pandemic. Our book club has interesting monthly meetings, and it is stimulating to see familiar faces on the screen: Birgitta Fillipelli, our leader, Cathy Peacock, our host who keeps us in order, and other regulars—Ann Roberts, Mitten Wainwright, Toni Somerstein, Linda Blum, Freddie Pellman, Irina Ourosoff, and Alice Tepper Marlin.

About once a month I drive to New York and spend the night in my apartment. I pick up mail, which a kind friend and neighbor, Mary Tobin, a retired teacher of nursing, removes from my box in the lobby. She and her husband, David, live on the same floor, and she periodically waters my one remaining philodendron plant, which belonged to Charles before we were married, making it over sixty years old. I am sentimental about it because it refuses to give up the ghost. Sometimes there is a doctor's appointment and I visit friends, safe distancing. In

January, I cooked shepherd's pie in East Hampton and brought it to Anne (formerly Oliver) and Bob Schumacher. It had been a favorite dish of Anne and John Oliver's, but all men seem to love this old English comfort dish. The Olivers and Schumachers had known each other for many years. After the death of both spouses, Anne and Bob got married.

I am in close touch with my other godson, Fergus, in Hong Kong; his delightful Japanese wife, Maki; and their daughter, Marina, now twelve. They stayed with me in East Hampton after Charles died, and Marina, who was two at the time, loved to ride around the house on Scott's back. He was always a mellow dog, and Maki's video of it was all over YouTube in Japan. They lived briefly in San Francisco, where Fergus had an impressive IT job, and I stayed with them one December on Ashbury Street and enjoyed being back in that city after many years. At last, I told myself, I have family in this country, but he had an even better job offer and they moved to Hong Kong. Knowing my passion for dogs, they sent a particularly attractive doggy mask for Christmas this year.

Before we all get too much older, or worse, and while my memory is still holding up, it is time to draw a line under this chronicle of family and friends. I have finished inserting small memories scribbled illegibly on those old Tiffany cards, of which Charles ordered one thousand, when I wake up in the middle of the night and remember someone or some event. However inadequate or incomplete, my reminiscences must now stand as they are.

# Acknowledgments

I n chronological order, I am most grateful to Caroline Cannon-Brookes, my first cousin, for providing details of the Christie-Miller family history and to her husband, Peter, for information about their lives and careers. Caroline's sisters, Charlotte Beatson and Lydia McClure, also provided material about my father's family as well as their personal histories.

I thank my godson, Rory MacDermot, Prince of Coolavin, for supplying so much of my mother's family history, including our very own Romeo and Juliet story. Tragically, Rory died in May, 2021, in Wexford, Ireland. Other cousins were helpful on the MacDermot side, including Alan MacDermot and Jacquie Drayton.

A very special thank you to Isabel Carmichael of *The East Hampton Star*, who in March 2019 wrote "A Passion for Polar Places," which went viral locally. Many readers encouraged me to elaborate, so she was the catalyst for my writing this life story. She also provided editorial help. At that time, Julie Sakellariadis, who was President of the Garden Club of East Hampton, sent Isabel's article to the entire membership and has been a constant support.

I thank my dear friend Patricia McGrath, who on our almost daily walks during the pandemic put up with my writing-progress reports and made helpful suggestions.

Thanks to Joan Baum who talked to me about memoir writing and asked trenchant questions that helped to focus my efforts. She introduced me to Paul Pitcoff, author of *Cold War Secrets*, a much more in-depth memoir than mine, who constantly encouraged me.

My copyeditor, Lauren Jones, did a superb job. Author Stephanie Krikorian, to whom I owe the most gratitude, put me in touch with Lauren and then introduced me to Post Hill Press. Thanks to the team at Post Hill Press including Anthony Ziccardi, Michael Wilson, and Madeline Sturgeon; as well as Allison Griffith, Devon Brown, Allie Woodlee, Holly Pisarchuk, Alana Mills, and Christina Chun.

There are many references to dogs in my book. Were it not for Gail Murphy, the dog trainer who introduced Stephanie and her lively Cavachon, Skippy, to me, this book might not have seen the light of day.

There are many friends and family members who encouraged me to keep writing, too many to list by name, most of whom are mentioned in the book.

One small group of fellow volunteers at our local shelter, The Animal Rescue Fund of the Hamptons, were always supportive: Barbara Medlin, Barbara Liberatore, Susan Macy, Mina Kahofer, Nancy Buscemi, and Susan Ahlborn. Also, our Book Club never gave up on me.

# About the Author

Photo by Patricia McGrath

Maralyn Rittenour was born in Ireland. She has traveled extensively her entire life; worked in publishing, for MI6, and at the Scott Polar Institute in Cambridge, England. While in New York working for the governments of Ireland, UK, Hong Kong, and Canada for more than thirty years, she helped develop export business to the United States for many companies from these countries. She was also the executive director of the East Hampton Historical Society. Her volunteer efforts include the Metropolitan Museum of Art, Fashion Group International, the Junior League of New York, the American Cancer Society, the Animal Rescue Fund of the Hamptons, and the Garden Club of East Hampton. Rittenour plays tennis and is a great dog lover. She currently splits her time between East Hampton and New York City along with her elderly rescue dog, Scott.